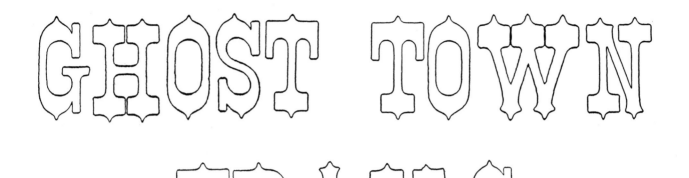

GHOST TOWN TRAILS

BY LAMBERT FLORIN

Maps and Drawings
by
David C. Mason, M.D.

Bonanza Books • New York

GHOST TOWN TRAILS

is dedicated to David C. Mason, M.D.,

whose help and encouragement

have made this book possible.

INTRODUCTION

In choosing the title for this book I have continued with the term "ghost town" as used for the two previous volumes. It is used in the broad sense, too broad, say a few critics in their reviews. They point out such towns as Jamestown, California; Leadville, Colorado; Virginia City, Nevada; Deadwood, South Dakota and Tombstone, Arizona as not being ghosts in any sense. I like to think a certain hue and cry would have been raised had I passed over these historic communities and left unmentioned the colorful and romantic events in their lusty lives.

It is true enough these places and others are not dead to the point of being completely abandoned but in calling them ghost towns I take the literal meaning of the word—"a shadowy semblance of its former self." To me this seems to apply to towns in a state of suspended animation or lately resuscitated as well as those in a complete demise.

It may be of some significance to mention the towns referred to above have not objected to my including them in the ghost town category. They depend largely on the trade of tourists absorbing some of the history and atmosphere of the old days and the citizens in showing a town off proudly are quick to admit "she ain't what she used to be."

Another fact is, a town may be as dead as last Christmas—and still be alive. Any of them are subject to sudden change. Mountain-perched Mammoth, Montana, once completely deserted, has been repopulated of late by summer residents, happy to camp in the old houses while heat plagues the flatlands. Molybdenum is discovered near decaying Kokomo, Colorado and presto! . . . shining new buildings spring up almost overnight as the old town sits up and rubs its eyes. Some of these transfusions often prove to be temporary, the alerted village settling back for another siesta.

Until the summer of 1955 my two weeks' vacation had been devoted rewardingly to climbing jaunts in the mountains of the West—the Canadian Rockies, Cascades and High Sierra. It was not always possible to find companions with like interests. In 1955 I persuaded Dr. David Mason to accompany me on a trip into Crabtree Meadows in the Sierra. I held out the alluring prospect of getting there by horseback, packing out, climbing Mt. Whitney from the west, camping overnight on the summit and descending the eastern side. Along the way we would botanize, fish for the famous Golden Trout native to the lofty rivers of the region. If there were time, we would visit Bodie, casually heard of some time previously.

There must have been a few times during the trip David wished he was back in Oregon ease and comfort. He had done no mountaineering. We almost missed the pack train at Whitney Portals because of a dead battery back on the road. The day in the saddle riding over Muir Pass must have seemed at least three. His freshly caught trout curled up like wood shavings in the pan and we couldn't separate bones from flesh. We endured a terrific electric storm on the Mt. Whitney summit, complete with deluges of rain, hail and snow, a great show of lightning and thunder. We crouched on our respective rocks under plastic tarps and just hoped it wouldn't get worse. We suffered through a bitter cold night in the stone shelter on the summit to be greeted by a windy, cheerless dawn with sheets of rain which precluded either making breakfast or taking pictures. Slogging down the mountain on trails filled by rivers of storm waters, we reached our little tent to find it blown down, water can tipped over and a small lake soaking up the equipment. It was no time to ask David how he was enjoying things and he volunteered no sentiment, although he was more cheerful than I was.

The pure cussedness of weather and circumstances must have affected our reactions next day when we drove into Bodie. The morning was bright and sunny, the white granite spire of the mountain standing sharply against a deep blue sky. The tumbling waters of Lone Pine Creek cascaded past our camp under pleasant control. After a good breakfast, a short drive took us through fantastic, inconceivably ancient granite formations called the Alabama Hills and into the town of Lone Pine. Then on to Bridgeport and the dirt road to Bodie.

Here was a deserted main street, lined by rows of frame and brick buildings with gaps where a fire had taken toll, filled with sagebrush or crumbling freight wagons. Not a living soul was visible in the city that once harbored twelve thousand.

Lonely now were the scarred hills where once swarms of miners were extracting millions in gold. We walked along board sidewalks on which booted feet had stomped and high button shoes pattered. We peered through boarded-up windows into rooms where people had lived, loved, fought and died.

Up on the hill overlooking the town there was a pitiful collection of wooden headboards, some enclosed by tottering picket fences. Here lay many of those who had roistered in the saloons, labored in the mines or made a living the soft way of parasites—the gamblers and frail sisters. Where epidemics had swept through the camp in the whispered hush of death and dynamite had blasted out graves, there was only peace and quiet.

A second look at the buildings showed plainly they were but one stage away from eternal dust. I wanted to get to work with my camera to record the fading remains while they were still there. When I looked around to see where David had gone, I saw he already had his camera on a tripod and was carefully focusing on the old firehouse which still held equipment in some wistful bravado.

I went to work in another direction and didn't see my friend for hours. A band of sheep drifted along, their bleatings as forlorn as the surroundings. Toward evening, after several trips back to the car for additional film, filters or lenses, we piled our gear into the back of the car and drove off in silence. Suddenly it was broken by a sound sweet to my ears. David was asking: "How would it be if we spend our next vacation searching out and photographing more places like Bodie?" There was my reward.

And so began a search that hasn't stopped yet, the quest for dulled remnants of a lustier day. As the pile of pictures grew, so did the wish to share them with others. Public exhibitions in several large cities produced suggestions that the effort should be extended even farther. The book, *Western Ghost Towns*, was the natural result. It brought some of the fast-fading Western Americana into the view of the whole country, Canada and even many countries in Europe. Work was immediately started on another volume to be called *Ghost Town Album* and as it became obvious that the numbers of old mining, cattle and fishing towns would easily justify another book, *Ghost Town Trails*, began to form.

Gathering material for these has been a lot of fun with enough hard work and anxiety in it to make the effort a challenge. Until last summer all traveling had to be done during vacation periods, at first two weeks, then three, each year. As more time became available, I covered more country and made return trips to areas I had missed earlier. There was more organization to the jaunts now, camping simplified with a camper mounted on a pickup truck which has four speeds to get up more narrow, steep dirt roads and making it possible to stop overnight almost anywhere without the labor of packing and repacking. Yet even this rig would not go into some isolated places and I took eqiupment for footwork. I now carry mountain boots with heavy rubber lug soles and a packsack loaded with first-aid kit, flashlight and a few old candle stubs for starting fires with wet wood. With camera, telephoto lenses, filters, tripod and the like, I can get to the most secluded, hard-of-access spots.

A surprisingly large amount of equipment is necessary for gathering book material. This includes a portable recorder to tape interviews with local characters and the "oldest inhabitants." Also I read onto tape much material prepared by libraries and historical societies and take also reference books and maps. Photographic gear embraces a battery of optical instruments, two long lenses of 450 mm. and 600 mm. (seldom used) and a Quester with a focal length of 1070 mm., actually a compact telescope capable of taking a close-up picture of the moon, stars, a bird or flower hundreds of feet away.

David Mason still accompanies me on his vacations, gathering ideas and making sketches and photographs for later use in doing the chapter heading illustrations, end sheet drawings and maps which contribute the fine touches to the books. If his vacation ends when we are in Rapid City, South Dakota, or Santa Fe, New Mexico, he flies home to his medical practice. Then I have to rely for companionship on my little black cocker, Toody. She is a veteran ghost town prowler and, being a ham at heart, tries to get into every picture.

There are many pleasures connected with these trips besides seeing the towns. There are countless flowers and plants to be admired at close range. Deer may walk through camp in the evening, coyotes howl startlingly close at night. Morning brings a medley of bird calls and if pinon nuts are ripe, there will be a great chattering of squirrels as they gather them. Often seen in various ghost town areas are elk, buffalo, antelope, marmots and other animals.

The desert at certain times offers a profusion of wild flowers in clumps and great blankets, the foothills often covered with lupines, poppies and penstemon. Higher up are acres of avalanche lilies and dodecatheons, those rosy shooting stars, alpine versions of the "bird's bills" of our childhood.

The many types of trees in the western states and Canada offer variety, from the spruces of Colorado to the native fan palms of the California desert regions. It is interesting to note the availability of timber, as this was of vital importance to the first prospectors and miners attempting to erect some sort of shelter. The camp might be in the highest mountains near or above timberline as at lofty Animas Forks, Colorado, where a city was built in eternal snowdrifts at 11,000 feet elevation or often as not in some situation like Ballarat, California. The old camp, which was named for Ballarat, Australia, in supersitious hope of matching the fantastic discoveries there, was built on the edge of a dry lake bed where salts lay dazzling in the hot sun. No tree grows here. The nearby barren Panamints offer nothing more than sparse greasewood, so shelters and business structures had to be made of the earth itself, mixed with hard-to-get water and shaped into blocks.

There were certainly no timber trees in Pine Grove, Nevada, and not even clay, so rocks were used for the building of the first town. A collection of buildings was later erected nearer the mines, for by that time lumber could be hauled in. In Loomis, Washington, in the midst of heavy stands of Ponderosa pine, the first structures were of logs, then whipsawn lumber, handplaned and fastened with hand-forged, square-headed nails. These are often found on the ground in old camps, dropped from disintegrating frame buildings. They are logical and legitimate souvenirs to carry home. So are the sun-purpled bottles and other remnants scattered in the bushes or dumps around the towns.

Not so are parts of buildings themselves, bricks, boards or furnishings. To take such, in my mind, is vandalism, destructive and contributing strongly to the disappearance of the towns. Many a fascinating settlement that should have stood as a monument to the resourcefulness of the early settlers has been carried off bit by bit. Repeated from the last volume is the wail of a rancher's wife near Kelly, New Mexico: "The souvenir hunters are carrying everything off, even the headboards from the cemetery. Next they'll be digging up the bodies themselves." I thought it unwise to tell her I once knew a photographer who used to carry a gunnysack full of human bones to add atmosphere to his desert photos.

The old headboards in the early cemeteries are full of history. Many offer testimonials to the value of paint in preserving the surface. Often inscriptions painted in black, while weathered for many years, stand in high relief against a background sandblasted as much as a quarter of an inch. Sometimes the paint has faded out, but sidelighting will still reveal the names and dates. As long as these boards stand in place, they should remain untouched. I once turned a rock marker, with its pitifully scratched inscription to a long-dead infant, just enough to allow the sun to cross-light it for a picture record, then carefully replaced it. In the case of a board imbedded in the ground however precariously, one can only make the picture and hope for the best or possibly wait while the sun wheels around far enough to light the edges of the message.

After the camera, I think the tripod most essential. Handheld shots are adequate for news pictures or snapshots for casual viewing but for professional use which calls for careful consideration of light angles and precise light reading, the camera must be steady. Photos in these books are printed from finescreen copper plates but engravers can reproduce only what is in the picture—texture, details, contrasts.

Even the simplest camera, under the most favorable light conditions, will make an acceptable picture. It always holds true it is the man behind the camera that is important. But ideal conditions for easy attainment of a good negative are not often present. The better the camera, the more it will offer in meeting difficult situations. For me the Rolleiflex fills these needs. I do not hold an ultra fast lens to be essential as the tripod eliminates speed as a necessary factor.

The idea there is one place better than any other from which to make the picture seems elementary. Yet it is wise to take time exploring various positions. Try lying prone or getting up on something higher. The camera can record only what enters the lens. It cannot interpret what the operator sees or would like to see.

I think filters are an absolute necessity. Most delicate color nuances are lost when translated to black and white unless the filter first separates blue from white so clouds can be recorded or light colored areas of buildings will stand out against a deeper toned sky. Most useful is the red "A" or, if the consequent slow exposures are not practical because of waving grass, sagebrush or trees, then the yellow "K2" or orange "G". This points out the value of having a camera offering a wide range of shutter speeds including one as slow as a full second. With an "A" filter, using film with speed of around 100 A.S.A. in full sunlight, I find most exposures made at 1/5th second, using an aperture of f.22. The small stop brings almost everything at various distances into focus. If a certain object is to be accented, the background can be rendered inconspicuous by use of a wider aperture and consequent reduction of exposure time.

These remarks apply generally to making black and white photographs. They are most important to the ghost town books and to me the most satisfying, having a large potential in the darkroom. Color transparencies also have several uses, one of them at public showings to illustrate talks on the subject. I carry two Exactas for the color work, making a color duplicate of each black and white shot. For these I usually hold the camera in the hand. Modern color film is quite fast, speed is not reduced by filters and slides made at 1/100th second rarely show any blurring due to camera movement. Color made for reproduction is exposed in a second Rollieflex, making $2\frac{1}{4}$ x $2\frac{1}{4}$ transparencies. The second Exacta is for emergencies and is kept loaded just for peace of mind in case of loss or break down of the first and to save reloading when haste is necessary. When David is traveling with me, he duplicates all this equipment, admittedly a large assortment. I would name as essential one 35 mm. camera for color, one of larger negative size, say $2\frac{1}{4}$ x $2\frac{1}{4}$, for black and white, a steady tripod, "A" filter and a good light meter.

In tracking down ghost towns, it is well to check on dubious roads by local direction. The schematic diagrams in the books are intended to give an idea of the position of the towns (often not on current maps) in relation to known points. Follow these in accordance with the current oil company maps. The last spur road may not be shown on these and certainly the condition of it should be checked. Do not place too much credence on local information as to what remains "up there." You may get some idea but the value or beauty of what is left of the old town appears in the eye of the beholder. Inquire if there are any other disappearing towns in the neighborhood for they often come in groups. It is not pleasant to get all the way home and hear about another ghost you left just over the hill.

Good hunting!

Lambert Florin

TABLE OF CONTENTS

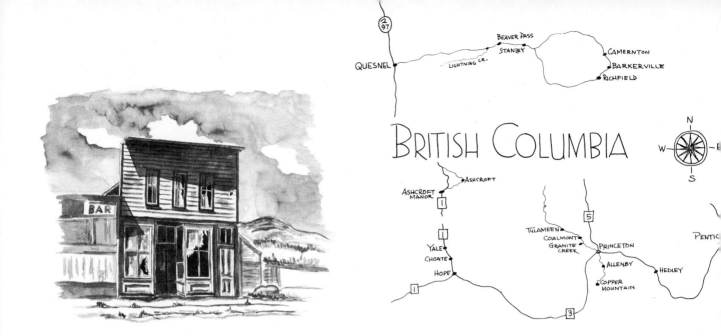

BEAVER PASS, B.C.

You were on your way to Barkerville gold but right now what you wanted most of all was a drink, strong and heady. In the middle 1800s the stage ride to the Cariboo country was pure punishment and by the time a man got to Beaver Pass the jolts of the hard road and jaws of winter had flayed his nerves raw. With utmost compassion, the bartender in the town's famous hostelry set a bottle before each man to nurse as long as he wished at four bits a long swallow.

The last stretch of the old Cariboo Road to Barkerville started from Quesnel where the Quesnel River joins the mighty Fraser — named in 1909 by Simon Fraser for his French Canadian lieutenant Jules Maurice Quesnel. The town which grew up at the junction was for a time called Quesnelmouth and was so referred to in early issues in the renowned newspaper of the area, the *Cariboo Sentinel*. Original pronunciation was near "canal" but has become more like "quinel," accented on the last syllable.

Since the Fraser was navigable at Soda Springs north, more or less so as far as Prince George (although impassable above Yale, then the head of navigation from New Westminster), Quesnel enjoyed a position as port. It was an important place as the source of the supply in the later days of the Cariboo gold rush and never became a ghost town, flourishing today as a modern city on a main highway.

It was a stage trip from here to Barkerville, an ordeal in summer, nightmare in winter. Temperatures sometimes dropped to 60 below, 30 below being common enough. Some of the decrepit vehicles on the road used burlap flaps instead of doors. Passengers bundled up as best they could but came so near being frozen it took a long time to get their hands unlocked from the whiskey bottles.

At Murderer's Gulch, where a man named Charles Morgan Blessing was slain and his body buried, cliffs closed in so tightly the stages literally had to squeeze through. Holdups frequently took place here, bandits dropping to the driver's seat from above. To counter this menace, an especially strong coach was equipped to carry a box without handles, one weighing as much as 500 pounds when filled with gold, an awkward prize for the most adroit highwayman.

Earlier stages often met their predecessors, the packers, along the way. And since pack animals had the right of the road, coaches would lay back and let the strings of mules or bulls file by. Most famous of these early packers was one John Jacques Caux

13

who hailed from the kingdom of Bearn in the Pyrenees near the Spanish border. Better known as Cataline, Caux was a character in a day when almost everyone could have fitted the calling. He was tall and well built with wide shoulders and narrow hips, wearing luxuriant black hair so long it fell down on his shoulders, and tucked into heavy woolen pants, was a "boiled shirt" sans collar. A heavy drinker of cognac, he considered it equally good externally and after each libation poured some of it on his head,

massaging the fiery liquid into his scalp. To this practice he attributed his fine head of hair.

Cataline was famous for more than his eccentricities. He was completely dependable and could be trusted to pack the most valuable load of gold. Friendly with the Indians who gave everyone else so much trouble, he never lost a load to them. In fact, on one fateful trip when his animals were lost, he delivered the cargo on the backs of Indian women. Cataline served the camps for many years but along with

RUINS OF OLD BEAVER PASS HOUSE near "home stretch" of Cariboo Road, first stop reached among the gold towns, last stop before the diggings at Stanley. Hostelry offered substantial food, heavy on bacon and beans. Beds were primitive. Hides stretched across wooden frames held piles of straw on which were spread blankets and furs. When business was good and beds full, guests could select softest planks in floor.

other packers was displaced when the road was made good enough for regular coach and freight wagon travel.

Of all the intriguing stories of early day travelers to Barkerville, that of one Lauderdale takes bizarre flight. Young Lauderdale, of Scotch-Canadian ancestry, was unusually handsome with a fine physique, both endowments saving his life, if the story is to be believed. He was one of a party of thirteen which had started for the gold fields from Portland, Ore. They traveled up the Columbia, turned north, and during the winter of 1859-60, were caught by a band of Chilcotin Indians, all massacred but Lauderdale. A lovely young princess was so taken by his physical charms she pleaded with her father to save his life. The chief, with a sense of humor of his own, had the man stripped of his clothes and turned loose in the snow. Lauderdale ran for his life without a backward glance for the girl who had saved it. When he was winded and half frozen, a horse caught up with him, on its back the princess and his clothes. The early movies never did it better.

COTTONWOOD HOUSE might well have looked like this when built in 1864, two years after discovery of gold in Barkerville. Now a private home not open for visiting, it was established as a first stop after leaving Quesnel on way to gold fields. All buildings of small town have vanished except for this structure and several large barns.

RICHFIELD, B.C.

"Dutch William, restless and enterprising, left the others basking before the burning logs and traveled up the creek until he found the bare bedrock cropping up in the stream. He tried one panful of gravel but obtained none of the precious metal. He tried another from the side where there was a high ledge and to his great delight found himself rewarded with a dollar to the pan. The gravel was hard frozen to the rock and when detached with difficulty was thawed in the cold stream. Time passed quickly and he was soon forced by darkness to return to the campfire. He showed his companions the prize he had obtained but possibly they discredited his statement for they determined to return to the Forks. Having no pick, Dutch William was obliged, unwillingly, to return with them though he had provisions for some days more."

So were the events on Williams Creek in February of 1861 chronicled in the *Victoria Colonist* of Nov. 5, 1863. It then appeared Dutch William Dietz scoured the camp of Antler for a few tools of his own, confided in three other men more willing to believe in his find than his erstwhile companions and returned to the area with them. They found plenty to confirm the story but the three new men returned to Red-Headed Davis' store for supplies, taking precautions to leave a man on guard just in case the secret leaked out. It was a useless gesture. Although the supply trip was made on snowshoes in record time, "the whole creek was staked off into claims over ground covered by eight feet of snow." Leaving his partners hacking at the frozen gravel, Dutch returned to Antler for a rocker which he carried to the diggings

RICHFIELD COURTHOUSE is only building of camp remaining. When hanging was ordered, temporary scaffold was erected in front of it. On one occasion double gallowses were set up, one victim of justice being James Berry who had shot James Morgan Blessing on road to diggings. Loot was roll of $20 notes and stickpin of unique design, later noticed in Berry's tie by Barkerville's colored barber, Wellington Delaney Moses, a friend of Blessing. At trial, evidence of stickpin (with tiny human head accidentally mounted upside down) was sufficient to convict. Other man on double gibbet was Indian convicted of murdering white man at Soda Creek, way station on road to mines.

on his back. Open-heartedly he stopped frequently to chop out brush so others, though uninvited, might follow more easily.

The first straggling assemblage of tents and shacks began to take form on one side of the stream now called Williams Creek and when the need for a gold commissioner was filled by Thomas Elwyn, the growing camp was referred to as Elwyntown. The name seemed inappropriate to miners proud of the golden wealth pouring out of the riverbed and they came up with the more satisfying one of Richfield.

The raw camp spawned troubles in the form of murder and violence. Trials had to be held for the miscreants and a substantial log cabin was commandeered for courthouse until it became inadequate and a new one was built. The judiciary was even responsible for expediting travel into the town, judging from an item in the *Cariboo Sentinel* of June 11, 1866: "We understand Judge Cox had to pay $250 for shoveling snow from between Van Winkle and Richfield so as to enable trains to get in"... the trains being strings of pack animals.

Another new structure in Richfield was heralded in the July 13 issue, two years later, headed: "St. Patrick's Catholic Church. His Lordship the Right Rev. Bishop De Heromes, D.D., will perform the ceremony of the Benediction of the above church and bell on Sunday next, 19th, services to commence at 10 o'clock A.M."

Gold commissioner Elwyn was replaced by Chartres Brew who died May 31, 1870. The June 14 *Cariboo Sentinel* displayed on its front page a black-bordered obituary: "On Tuesday last Mr. Chartres Brew died at Richfield. In the early part of last winter Mr. Brew had been taken ill. He was born, we believe, in Limerick, Ireland, and was about 59 years old. He was buried in the Cameronton cemetery on Williams Creek on Thursday last. A large procession followed the remains to the grave."

Immediately below the notice was an advertisement making the most of the lugubrious details. "Memory presides over the past—Fell's Coffee over the present. It has but one shrine and that is every breakfast table. Its aroma walks the earth like a spirit and can be found at respectable dealers in British Columbia. BEWARE OF SPURIOUS IMITATIONS!"

Richfield had a short life and a merry one, its gaiety being stimulated by potations in numerous saloons along the creek banks, the sudden demise taking place when the golden wealth was suddenly pinched off. The rest of the nuggets were securely buried farther down, and deeper in the gravels, in one side of the stream in what had been in the bed in prehistoric days. But before these were discovered, Richfield as a city died, its inhabitants going to other strikes and other saloons.

Dutch William, the man who sparked the brief and fiery history of Richfield as well as the whole pageant of other and larger gold strikes in the Cariboo never shared in the wealth resulting from his discovery. Poor food and the deprivations of the raw frontier took early toll. While the story of his find was being hailed and discussed in Victoria, he was lying there in a sickbed. He died a pauper in 1877.

STOUT'S GULCH, just below Richfield and just above confluence with slightly broader canyon of Williams Creek seen at right angles in middle distance. Edward Stout was Indian fighter in youth, one of party attacked in Fraser River canyon in wars of 1858. Indians had used up arrows poisoned with rattlesnake venom and Stout was hit with regular one, lived to become one of prospecting party discovering Williams Creek. After active life in gold fields, he retired to live in Yale, dying at 99. Stout always maintained he owed his long life to never having touched liquor. He did not mention scarcity of snake venom.

BARKERVILLE, B.C.

Canada was great green banks of timber ripe for the cutting. It was rivers teeming with salmon. It was mountains and creek beds glittering with golden gravel. And all of it was accepted as food and cover and for building canoes by a few Indians—a limitless supply for themselves and future generations.

To the browbeaten, half-starved English sailors whose ships ventured into West Coast coves, the wonderland was something else. It was freedom. Billy Barker was one of them. He was hungry for a new life and jumped ship when he heard the news about gold along the Fraser and its tributaries. Billy was tough. He got to the diggings on Williams Creek and set to work in his own unorthodox way to make a fortune. No geologist, he sank a shaft some distance from the stream itself, prompted by some inner light to explore the possibilities of a prehistoric stream bed or because it was the only spot available.

Billy and six partners, all Englishmen and most of them ex-seamen, began to dig August 13, 1862. When the hole reached 35 feet, a few superstitious ones wanted to quit. It was the 13th, a bad day. Their funds had run out, but lucky for them and the future of Barkerville, an "angel" who was reputed to be Judge Begbie of Richfield, staked them for a few more days.

At 50 feet down the men struck an old river channel. A shovel full of gravel was sent up and panned in the creek. It yielded $5. Struggling to control their elation, the men at the bottom filled the hoist bucket to the brim. This panned out $1,000. In the panic that followed everything came to a stop, except the men's feet which, after dancing, were headed for neighboring Richfield and its saloon.

The lack of one of these in the new camp was soon remedied. In less than a year there were half a dozen drink emporiums for the population of some 10,000. Since winter began to set in soon after the big discovery, and winter in the Cariboo was 40 below with deep snow, the first buildings were of logs, later of whipsawn lumber. Except for Chinatown on a short side street, all of Barkerville was strung along one single street. Buildings were elevated a few feet,

DENTIST'S OFFICE showing lifelike display — exhibit created with help of B. C. Dental Association and Dr. Lloyd Day of Quesnel.

EXHIBIT IN ORIGINAL DOCTOR'S OFFICE brings to life scene enacted many times when injuries were frequent. Figures were created by artist Mrs. Herbert T. Cowan of North Vancouver after detailed study of old days.

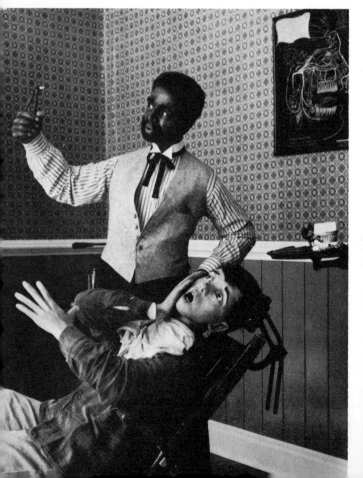

as were sidewalks, because miners would frequently dam the creek for a time in their hasty searchings of the gravel and Williams Creek would head for its former channel and tend to inundate Barkerville. And there were other hazards in the street. Oxen and other beasts of burden were not too sanitary, garbage was left anywhere and, except for August, the mud was kneedeep.

Billy Barker could take no real pride in all this growth. He was a worried man. The January after his strike he decided he could afford to be married since gold was pouring from the shaft in a blinding flood. On another 13th he married a widow in Victoria and brought her to camp. It is presumed the new Mrs. Barker had heard more than rumors of her husband's wealth, that his looks had not attracted her. At 42 he was wide and stubby, bowlegged and bearded. Most of the other miners were younger, better looking and Billy found it increasingly necessary to spend huge sums on his bride to bring back her attentions.

Although his company soon took some $600,000 from the hole in the creek bed, Billy went through his share quickly, dividing it between his wife and the saloons. As soon as it became evident his resources had struck bottom, his mate left the camp for greener pastures in company with a younger man. Abandoned and lonely, Billy soon spent what little was left and when the mine failed, he made a living cooking for road crews. Drinking and a persistent sore on his lip cost him one job after another and he wound up in the Old Men's Home in Victoria, dying of cancer July 11, 1894.

Meanwhile, Barkerville was mushrooming with new discoveries. The nearby Grizzly mine had a weekly payroll of $10,000. One "clean up" at the Raby claim yielded twenty pounds of gold and this was not unusual. The Caledonian at the edge of town brought in more than $5,000 a day for a time, the Ericson turning out nearly ninety pounds of gold every week. In 1865 this working paid a dividend of $14,000 a share.

Since the area not actually occupied by the town was packed solid with claims of this kind, Barkerville flourished and in the heedless rush burned to the ground in September, 1868. Flimsy stovepipes projected shakily through the tinder-dry roofs of late summer and showered sparks on the shingles. When rebuilt, the town resembled its earlier self except that spaces were left for side streets and walks in front of business establishments were connected at a level.

Some time before the fire, Barkerville had acquired a newspaper which was to exert a strong influence on the life of the camp—the *Cariboo Sentinel*. Items gleaned from its files reflect the feelings of the day. Reports were coming in constantly of new strikes, the issue of May 10, 1866 carrying this item:

"We have been permitted to peruse a letter received by a gentleman on the creek from a friend, an old Cariboo miner who has been to the Blackfoot country. Writing from Walla Walla he says—'I have been to the Blackfoot mines. They are better in my opinion than Cariboo ever was and much more extensive the gold being of a much finer quality and all of it of a course (sic) nature, bringing readily $18 per ounce. The country is very accessible to the miner, he can pack his tools and grub on a horse, get astride of another and go just where he pleases. He can kill all the game he wants; I think the deer are in greater abundance than they are around Victoria. Bear, elk and mountain sheep are plentiful; the winter has been severe for this part of the country, the snow has been two feet deep.'" The writer of this letter was probably as much bemused by the ease of transportation as anything else for getting around in the Cariboo was notoriously difficult. However, the Blackfoot diggings were apparently something less than expected. An item from Cache Creek dated May 18 stated: "A good number of miners are on the way back from Big Bend and they give a horrid account of it."

Hard rock mining was attempted from time to time with discouraging results. Said the *Sentinel*: "Last fall some little noise was created by the discovery of a lode on the ridge that divides Williams

REMAINS OF ANCIENT SLEIGH, essential to long, hard winter life. Mining came to halt when wet gravel froze hard and water was not available for washing and panning. *Cariboo Sentinel* of May 14, 1866 reported: "Symptoms of a change in the weather — rained heavily whole afternoon. Apprehension felt for sudden rising of creek." Next issue said: "The creek is beginning to resume its appearance of summer activities and in another week, when the time of layover expires, we expect to see every old claim at work in a fair way of taking out pay . . . The banks are not yet thawed out to allow hydraulic washing to commence." Next week paper warned: "Miners would do well to bear in mind the period to which the claims were laid over by the Gold Commissioner expires on Sunday next, 20th inst. and that all ground must be represented by that date."

OLD BARKERVILLE welcomes arrival of fresh beef. Cattle are being driven up main street in old picture from Provincial Archives taken nearly 100 years ago. Water was not piped to individual houses but conveyed in wooden troughs to barrels in street (foreground). Some buildings are identifiable today, notably Anglican Church at end of street.

Creek from Grouse Creek . . . A shaft was sunk on the ledge to some depth and a ton of rock was got out and transmitted to San Francisco for assay; up to the present moment however nothing further is known respecting it; it is even asserted that the rock still lies on the wharf where it was landed in San Francisco untouched." The item ends on a querulous note: "Shall we ever get satisfactory results at that rate?" Apparently not, a later paragraph states. "A return has been received to the assay of the portion of the quartz sent to San Francisco last fall. The results have not been learned."

Although there was plenty of gold in Barkerville, the terrible road conditions in winter often kept food out and the *Sentinel* tells of near-famine: "There is not a pound of beef or mutton to be procured at any of the butchering establishments on the creek. At Richfield, we believe, there is a small quantity of fresh pork which sells readily at 62 cents a pound, Mr. Toomey and Mr. Clark are both out after cattle and are expected back in a few days; until then we will have to betake ourselves to the old fare of earlier times, beans and bacon, for a change." But even

beans and bacon were not always available and sometimes neither were such staple articles as candles. Again the *Sentinel*: "In consequence of the scarcity of candles, we notice several persons are availing themselves of a large quantity of beef tallow accumulated by them during the winter and are now busy converting it into candles which they readily sell at $1 per pound."

The advent of the first pack trains in spring was also news. The issue of June 4, 1866, joyously proclaimed: "A train of 20 pack animals being the first arrival for the season got in yesterday morning . . . brought in a load of potatoes which are being sold for 15 cents a pound." This cost must have been prohibitive for a later report had it: "The trail is in a very bad state but the expected arrivals of several later trains is expected to bring prices down considerably." A late storm delayed the trains and the next issue's column "From the Outside" carried the illuminating statement: "Due to wires being down we have no news."

The *Sentinel's* advertising columns also show an image of life as it was. Restaurants, saloons and

MAIN STREET OF TOWN is deserted in early morning. Town enjoyed main prosperity in 1860s and early '70s, was genuine ghost town for many years, reviving temporarily during excitement of dredge operations on neighboring Antler Creek in 1920s and on Pine Creek 1948-50. Other spurts came when Cariboo Quartz Mine opened for short life in '33 and gold mining in neighboring new town of Wells when Barkerville was home for workers. When restoration began some four years ago, about 20 people lived in once teeming city.

cafes were regular advertisers and not given to undue modesty. One stated: "Occidental Hotel and Restaurant—Thurbers and Lawlors, Props. This house has been fitted up on the restaurant principle with a view to the comfort of the public and will be conducted in a manner to ensure the satisfaction of those who are disposed to favor the proprietors with their patronage. Meals at all hours. Good beds. The bar is furnished with the best selection of Liquors and Segars."

The Oppenheimer Co. had a clearance sale and told the public: "Provisions, Liquors, Segars, Clothing, Boots, Shoes, Mining Tools, etc., at COST PRICE! to make room for new stock to arrive as soon as the roads are open." Saloons were also regular advertisers. Said one: "Great attraction! Every night at the Fashion Saloon. All lovers of the Terpsichorean Art are invited to call and enjoy themselves, when a hearty welcome to all will be extended. Good order observed."

Saloons and dancehalls maintained an attraction known as "Hurdy Gurdy Girls." The *Sentinel* describes them with something of a sniff: "They are unsophisticated maidens of Dutch extraction, from 'poor but honest' parents, and morally speaking they are not what they are generally put down for. They are generally brought to America by some speculating, conscienceless scoundrel of a being commonly called a 'Boss Hurdy.' This man binds them in his service until he has received about a thousand percent for his outlay. The girls receive a few lessons in the terpsichorean art and are put into some kind of uniform with a headdress resembling in shape the top-knot of a male turkey. The Hurdy Gurdy style of dancing differs from all other schools . . . the more muscular the partner, the nearer the approximation of the ladies' pedal extremities to the ceiling, and the gent who can hoist the 'gal' the highest is considered the best dancer." It was generally known that these girls, besides cavorting publicly with the miners also indulged in some remunerative extracurricular activities in the backroom. It was said that during one such session an over-eager lover upset the heating stove and thus started the fire that devastated the town in 1868.

Remarkable and somewhat unique in a mining camp was the almost total absence of violence, shoot-

21

BILLY BARKER AND HIS TREASURED WATCH, a display in museum now maintained in Barkerville. Billy rests in Ross Bay cemetery at Victoria where he died. On evening of July 11, 1962 simple ceremony was held there honoring his memory in connection with dedication of Barkerville as Provincial Historic Park. Native of Barkerville, Miss Lottie Bowron pulled cord to unveil plaque. Service extolled Billy's generosity to out-of-luck miners, omitted his prodigality in saloons which resulted in dissipation of fortune taken from Williams Creek.

M.D.'S EQUIPMENT as found in old buildings of camp searched by restorers.

ings and lynchings in Barkerville, and this in spite of a population made up of youngish, mostly single miners from every walk of life and several countries. This was probably not due to more brotherly love than usual but because getting in and out of town was so hard. It was a task in summer and a quick get-away in winter was next to impossible. A man might think twice before pulling a gun.

There was some friction between the numerous Americans and the big segment from the British Isles. When nationalities conflicted, it was usually due to the inherent desire of the Americans to have the biggest and best of everything—but a sense of humor on both sides usually saved the day.

In point, was the flagpole incident. Martin's American-owned saloon boasted the tallest flagpole in town. From it waved the Stars and Stripes which the Canadians did not mind until the holiday celebrating the admission of British Columbia as a province into the Dominion drew near—the First of July. The day before, a few young Canadians went into the woods and found a tree that would make a taller flagpole than Martin's. They cut and dressed it, waited

for darkness and dug a ten-foot hole, erected the pole and rigging it with pulley and rope. Daylight revealed the new Canadian flag flying several feet higher than the American one. When the amazed Americans saw it, Martin was the first to break into a hearty laugh. He opened his saloon, invited everybody in and set up free drinks with Canadians as guests of honor. An international incident was averted.

It was a time when people favored every new nostrum and patent medicine and a profitable section in the *Sentinel* advertised these cure-alls. Wellington Delaney Moses, Barkerville's colored barber, was a steady contributor. His notice in the issue June 21, 1866, read:

"Moses Hair Invigorator—to prevent baldness, restore hair that has fallen out or become thin and to cure effectively Scurf or Dandruff. It will also relieve headaches and give the hair a darker and glossy color and the free use of it will keep both hair and skin in healthy state. Ladies will find the Invigorator a great addition to the toilet, both in consideration of the agreeable and delicate perfume and the great facility it affords in dressing the hair which when moistened with it can be dressed in any desired form, so as to preserve its place whether plain or in curls. When used on children's heads, it lays the foundations for a good head of hair."

Though Mr. Moses promised much he publicized evidence of miracles performed to back him up. "Sir," one letter he had received read, "in the years 1860 and '61, from long and severe illness my hair became very weak and was falling out in a most fearful manner. I was in dread of becoming entirely bald. After a few applications by you, and after using three bottles of the Invigorator my hair was restored and is becoming thick and strong as it ever was before."

Mr. Moses, emboldened by his success, ventured to install Barkerville's first bathtub. It was placed in the back room of his Shaving Salon and although everyone in town was aware of the novelty, its owner celebrated the great occasion by publicly inviting all to the "opening of the new Bathroom," adding discreetly—"Private entrance for ladies."

Prosperity could be read into the *Sentinel's* columns but the day came when it was painfully evident gold in Williams Creek was not going to last forever and the hopes for some fantastic lode in quartz outcroppings grew more and more remote. In June of 1868 L. A. Blanc had confidently held up his business as: "Photographer Artist. Cartes de Visita. Timbre de Poste, Portraits, Ambrotypes, Leather Pictures, Milanotypes, Views of Houses, Claims, etc. Single or Stereoscopic Portraits taken on White Silk, Linen or Cotton Cloth." In the '70s his newspaper insertions had fallen to "Great reduction in prices. L. A. Blanc wishes to inform his friends and the public that he has for a few months only Greatly Reduced His Prices to suit the times. Miners leaving for the new mines on the Peace River will do well to take advantage of this opportunity," and in the same issue appeared another notice: "All parties desirous of obtaining copies of their prescriptions for having them refilled will please call soon as I intend leaving for the Peace River mines." A line in smaller type followed hopefully: "Parties owing small accounts

EXTERIOR OF ST. SAVIOUR'S. Building was started in 1869 with long period of sacrifice of personal health and finances of Rev. James M. Reynard. Arriving from Yorkshire about 1865, Reynard was aghast at lack of morals and worship, set to work with zeal that sapped his strength. With meagre funds, saloon was purchased, used as church Sundays, school weekdays. Fire of '68 destroyed it. Reynard wrote: "All my efforts and expenditures have been in vain." For a time he came close to giving up struggle for new church, then tried personal solicitation of merchants to no avail. Suddenly Barkerville had a change of heart, people and merchants rallying around pastor with funds. On Sunday, Sept. 24, 1870 first services were held in now venerable structure. Later near starvation and rigors of Cariboo winters without proper heat and clothing broke Reynard's health to point he was forced to leave pastorate, dying in '75. Church is almost same as he left it. Though it was not part of official restoration, the committee carefully added few boards and panes of glass. Plans under way for new foundation.

INTERIOR OF ST. SAVIOUR'S ANGLICAN CHURCH. Beautiful vaulting of natural wood ceiling in Gothic design over apsidal recess was patterned after that in some English cathedrals. Bishop's chair is accurately fitted together without nails. Sacred structure is not exempt from vandalism, brass cross surmounting edifice for many years having been stolen in 1961. Cigarette butts are frequently thrown on floor.

will please call and settle same. James P. Taylor Drug Store."

In '66 a claim in the area could not be purchased at any price but the time came when they were hard to dispose of and such advertisements as this were common: "For Sale—one full interest in the MacLaren Claim." The MacLaren had been one of the best producers. During the Barkerville heyday, this news had appeared: "Above 160,000 taken out in two weeks. 1132 ounces washed up July 30. 2,620 ounces taken out in one week. The prestige of Cariboo is well sustained." Now, struggling to maintain optimism, the news ran: "The Mucho Oro Co. in Stout Gulch made expenses this week. The Good Hope Co. made wages for the week." Then the *Sentinel* became frankly despairing: "The Hope Co. have abandoned their ground."

A dwelling was not to be purchased for any money in '66 but as decay set in advertisements like these were placed in the paper. "For Sale—well built house pleasantly situated at the head of Stout's Gulch. Two rooms, woodshed and carriage house." And: "For Sale, a first class cabin near Barkerville, suitable for winter as it has a double roof."

More claims petered out, businesses failed as the population moved to the more promising Peace River diggings. Just as the camp had been filled with miners abandoning the California gold fields, Barkerville was now losing its people to a more glittering prospect. Before long even the loyal *Sentinel* was discontinued and that marked the end. Barkerville stood empty, forlorn.

In late years the Province of British Columbia became aware of the historical importance of the old camp and began a program of restoration. This has been carried on with attention to the minutest detail, hulks of buildings bolstered up without obvious changes, stairways long dangerous have been replaced with weathered and unpainted but stout boards to resemble the originals, countless other unobtrusive repairs and replacements made.

In August, 1962, just 100 years from the day Billy Barker made his big strike on Williams Creek, the Centennial Celebration was held in the old town, a fine museum dedicated by Premier A. C. Bennett marking the official opening of Barkerville Historic Park, after which the crowd pressed into the newly restored Theatre Royal to watch a special performance of "The Rough Diamond."

DEBRIS OF BUSY TIMES in Barkerville is piled in rear of firehouse and Theatre Royal. Fire protection was not thought vital in early days, town leveled in '68. Shortly before fire, Theatre Royal advertised "The Cariboo Amateurs will perform Blackstone's laughable farce 'A Kiss in the Dark' — interlude — Glees, Duets and Songs to conclude with Joseph Lynn's farce 'Fish Out of Water.' Adm. $1." Restoration started search through attics and storehouses of old camp, brought to light most furnishings of old theater. First play presented after refurbishing was "A Diamond in the Rough," produced from script in possession of Mrs. Joseph Wendle, longtime resident of town. Yellowed sheets bore lead pencilled note — "No good." Modern producers disagree. Play first staged in New York in 1841 brought howls of laughter for quaintness.

CAMERONTON, B.C.

It was a strange procession that moved down the ruggedly primitive trail. First came a man leading a horse hitched to a sleigh and on it, a wooden coffin. Inside this was a slightly smaller tin one holding the frozen remains of the woman who had married John Cameron and came with him to the Cariboo to find gold. The last member of the group struggling through the snow was John himself, both hands busy trying to keep the coffin from tipping over every time the sleigh careened over rocks or logs and steadying the bags of food and fifty-pound sack of gold on top of the coffin.

John and Sophia Cameron had been married in Cornwall, Ontario. They had set out for the new world, the West that was very far west, arriving in Victoria in March, 1862. They took the Cariboo Trail, reaching the site of what would be the boom town of Cameron in August.

Also heading for the gold fields along Williams Creek was Robert Stevenson. Along the way he had bought a bunch of horses in the Okanogan country, sold them in Lillooet for $10,000 and arrived on the creek as the only person likely to be endowed with money. He had prospected without settling on a claim for a month when the Camerons arrived. They became acquainted and were shortly partners. The association was a stormy one, marked by many quarrels and fallings out, but when the test came Stevenson was the only one to come to the aid of John Cameron.

There were other members of the company formed to pool resources and labor—Sophia and five more. When the time came to stake out the claim, its location was decided upon only after heated arguments and Cameron was all for backing out. It was Friday and he said he would start no venture on such an unlucky day. Persuaded to go ahead, he insisted on a location on the left side of the creek, Stevenson holding out for the right. Later this man wrote: "If he (Cameron) had followed my advice the claim would have paid double the million dollars it did." The

LEGENDS ON MANY HEADBOARDS in old Cameronton cemetery are indistinct, others speaking clearly of tragedies of long ago. Cameron himself chose site. Someone wrote of first burial — for Peter Gibson, July 24, 1863: "One of Cariboo Cameron's men died and they hauled him up on the side of the hill and buried him there." Marker at left in photo reads: "In memory of Chartres Brew, born at Corsefin, County Clare, Ireland, 31 Dec. 1815. Died at Richfield 31 May 1870. Gold Commissioner and County Court Judge. A man imperturbable in courage and temper endowed with a great and varied administration capacity. A most ready wit, a most pure integrity." Burial ground is only evidence of Cameronton. Decayed remnants of once roaring camp persisted on banks of creek, were finally engulfed in maw of dredge.

location was at last agreed upon and named The Cameron August 22, 1862. On the same date in December, Stevenson said: "We struck it very rich at 22 feet. It was thirty below. Dick Rivers was in the shaft and Halfpenny and I were at the windlass. Rivers called up from the shaft: 'The place is yellow with gold. Look here, boys. He held up a piece of rock the size of a dinner pail. I laid down on the platform and peered into the shaft. I could see gold standing out on the rock as he held it." Chunks of frozen rock and gravel came up in the bucket with frenzied speed to be thrown into the meagre flow of the stream to get it thawed out for panning. What little water they had froze in the intense cold of the Cariboo winter and though the wealth of the claim had been established, operations had to be suspended.

But Sophia never learned of the gold pouring into her husband's pockets. After only a few months which seemed like years to her "in this God-forsaken wilderness" she had died and was buried inside a small cabin, the first of a series of her tombs. Over her grave her husband swore she would not have to rest in this "womanless land" any longer than necessary and set to work feverishly to harvest as much gold as he could.

In the middle of winter he decided the time had come, removed the body of his wife from the grave and tried to find someone to help him get it to Victoria, offering $12 a day and a prize of $2,000 to anyone who would aid him. There were no takers. It was then his partnership with Robert Stevenson panned out. "Bob" offered to go along on the dangerous trip "but not for gold." Cameron collected all the gold he could, the supply augmented by a sizable amount

WATER SEEPAGE FROM HIGHER Williams Creek was constant hazard in mine shafts, removed by pumps operated by Davis or Cornish water wheels like this one on Morning Star claim. Flume, at top, carried water to buckets. Central shaft worked pump as with windmill.

Billy Barker raised by public subscription in Barkerville, just above Cameronton. Only Cameron knew how much he was taking along for expenses but the bag was supposed to weigh fifty pounds. This, with supplies, was placed on top of the coffin and the partners set out. In many places the trail angled so sharply stakes had to be driven in a row on the bank to keep the sleigh with its precious burden from overturning. When it did slide off the trail, both men struggled mightily to get the four-hundred-pound vehicle and load back on track and headed in the right direction. At one bad spot the men met a miner who volunteered his services in getting the load the rest of the way. With only a few upsets, the party finally arrived at Fort Douglas where they boarded a steamer. But even the boat had trouble. Unable to buck a squall, it had to lay to in a cove to wait for better weather.

In all, the trip to Victoria required 36 days, the arrival being at the end of April. Another funeral and burial was held for Sophia, with Cameron and Stevenson as the only mourners. The latter returned to the diggings but Cameron waited for the November arrival of a ship to take him and the body to Panama. Once again his wife's remains were exhumed and from Panama taken to Cornwall.

Upon arrival at Christmastime, there was another funeral service at which most of Sophia's relatives were present but she was not yet to rest undisturbed. A vicious rumor was circulated purporting Cameron had killed his wife, disposed of her body and smuggled a cache of gold back home in the coffin. So again the casket was opened to the light of day showing Sophia well preserved by the combination of freezing weather and liquid spirits in the tin liner. The fourth burial was the final one.

While Cameron was establishing a farm near the grave, spending much of the gold dust which had come on the long trail with his wife's body, events were happening fast in the British Columbia town that bore his name. In the boom, Cameronton had extended itself to the edge of Barkerville which had likewise grown to fuse with Richfield. These three towns along Williams Creek made a continuous street some three miles long with no appreciable indication of the beginning or end of any one. Barkerville had the newspaper, the *Cariboo Sentinel* and carried news and advertising from Cameronton as freely as those more local. One paid notice dated May 10, 1866 read: "Cameronton Reading Room and Circulating Library—$2 per month. Parties are solicited to subscribe. John Bowron, Librarian." Another in the same issue stated: "Billiard and Bowling Saloon. C. Fulton, Prop. There is no distillery in this establishment. Strychnine and rotgut find no place here."

Sporting events were duly chronicled. A display appeared May 10: "Grand Entertainment—Best Layout of the Season! No Humbug! No Bilk! A grand exhibition of the noble art of self-defense will be given at Loring's Saloon, Cameronton, May 12, 1866, on which occasion the following gentlemen will appear—Mr. George Wilson in glove fight with any man in Cariboo for the sum of $500. Harry Shannon will be matched with George Fairbrother to be followed by four other fights. The entertainment will be interspersed with Songs and Music suitable for the occasion. Big Time. Everybody Come. Admission— Front Seats $2 Back Seats $1. Doors open 7 ½ o'clock Commence at 8 o'clock." Shortly after this a "Society Item" was seen in the columns of the *Sentinel*, headed: "Sparring Exhibition. We understand the entertainment came off on Saturday evening last, at Cameronton, and was well patronized by lovers of the manly art. The affair passed off very satisfactorily and was the source of some little profit to the manager."

On May 17, 1866 this notice appeared: "Miners' Ball and Concert on the Queen's Birthday, May 24th. Mrs. Clunes begs to inform the miners of Williams Creek, Lowhee Creek, Grouse Creek and Van Winkle that she intends giving a Benefit Ball and Concert on the 24th of May, the best ever given on Williams Creek when she respectfully solicits the patronage of the public." The report on this festive affair appeared May 28. "Mrs. Clunes Ball and Concert came off at Cameronton on the Queen's Birthday and was well attended. The music was first class and the dancing was kept up to a late hour in the morning, everything passed off pleasantly."

Meanwhile in the Old Country, Cameron was not doing at all well with his farm. He had spent almost all the fifty pounds of gold but while there was still some left, he gave up and returned to the diggings to recoup his fortune. But things were different on Williams Creek now. The old days of scooping up gravel laden with nuggets were long gone. The ones of mechanized mining had arrived and Cameron did not have the cash for a new start. The good claims were taken up and there was no place for the stranger he had now become.

Unexplained is what happened to his interests in Cameronton. There seems to be no record of money being sent to him while in Cornwall or any waiting for him on his return to the claim. It is supposed he sold everything before he left the creek. But it is recorded he became a broken wreck of a man and died exactly fifteen years from the day he left Victoria with Sophia's body. He was buried in the cemetery overlooking the scene of his sudden rise to wealth and of his heartbreak.

JOHN AND SOPHIA CAMERON shown just after their wedding, surrounded by members of the party in picture from Archives in Victoria. Date was about 1859. First home in raw, new country called the Cariboo on Williams Creek was in small house at Richfield. When claim was established farther down creek, little cabin was erected there, served as home for couple during short period of happiness, ended by Sophia's death in 1862.

CHINESE MASONIC HALL occupied central position in once extensive Chinatown. Chinese Freemasonry originated in ancient history, had no connection with A.F. and A.M. rites. Chinese had difficulty maintaining position in Barkerville because of "outlandish ways." *The Cariboo Sentinel* in 1869 complained editorially that "Chinatown is universally voted a nuisance in every way, shape or manner. Pigs are fed in the streets in front of buildings; there is no regular sidewalk, drainage corrupted with animal and every kind of filth. Pig feeding in the streets should be stopped forthwith." The Orientals grew some vegetables and in periods of food scarcity raised price of tomatoes from 10 to 20 cents a pound. News item of '72 told of a "Sale of Celestial treasure. We understand that a Celestial lady from the Flowery Kingdom changed hands during the week at the handsome figure of $700. It is said the lady, who is a votary of the Cyprean Goddess, feels highly elated that her entrancing charm and wonderful fascination should realize such a satisfactory price."

STANLEY, B.C.

Fantastic tales of enormous amounts of gold taken out of Williams Creek and other streams of the Cariboo pop up out of the dust and rock. The claim of Bill Dillar and his partners produced in one working day 102 pounds of the yellow metal. Even at the going price of $20 an ounce, Dillar piled up a fortune, dutifully paying off his stockholders at $10,000 a share every Sunday.

Many other claims produced in like fashion, creating the impression every prospector who clawed his way over the infamous Cariboo Trail struck it rich. The facts are far from this. It is said the actual average "take" of the eager gold-seeking thousands during the palmiest days along the upper Fraser and its tributaries was little more than $600 a year.

One of these who fell into the average category was Samuel Montgomery. His headboard, still standing in the Cameronton cemetery, states he was born in Enniskillen Fermanagh, Ireland, on Oct. 28, 1814. A sailor for some fifteen years, he became involved in the rush to the Sierra gold fields, drifting on to the Cariboo when the California gold supply began to fail.

The ex-argonaut settled on the banks of Lightning Creek and never went "outside" for forty-two years. Sam found a little gold, enough to keep him from starvation. At 82 he made what he said would be his last effort, took hold of a claim on Van Winkle Creek, a tributary of Lightning, and on it sank a seventy-eight foot shaft. At the bottom, he dug horizontally as far as he was able, hoisting every bucket of dirt himself. The result of all this effort was almost complete failure and Sam was a broken old man.

During the years he had been grubbing away, other miners around him had been more successful, some spectacularly so. Two cities had sprung up around Montgomery, almost without his noticing them—Stanley at the Lightning's confluence with Chisholm Creek and Van Winkle having its short, happy life two miles farther on where Van Winkle Creek came in. Over the years the Stanley area yielded more than $10 million but old Sam got none of it.

About the turn of the century, a group of more successful gold diggers—Harry Jones (who told the story) with George Rankin, Fred Tregillis and Joe Spratt—formed a company to explore an old claim, once a part of the South Wales workings but declared worthless. More out of pity than any other reason, and almost too late, the partners decided to "include in" old Sam Montgomery. The outfit was formally

called the Little Van Winkle but in deference to the well-loved senior partner was familiarly referred to as the Montgomery.

Now came the climax of Sam's long, hard years of labor. In 1902 the Montgomery drift penetrated a piece of ground so rich the usual "clean up" had to be held every day, wages paid out of the resulting pile of dust and nuggets, the remainder divided between the partners. This method of paying off eliminated detailed bookkeeping and satisfied everybody. But poor old Sam could not take the sudden prosperity. He soon died from an excess of regular eating, wearing decent clothes and keeping himself comfortably warm. He was buried on the hillside with many of his cronies. A picture taken in 1862 shows Van Winkle as a huddle of some dozen log buildings. These constituted the "downtown core" and included tin shops, bakeries, blacksmiths and the usual assortment of saloons and gambling houses.

In those early Cariboo days it was the custom for a poker player, disgusted with a run of bad hands, to blame the deck and throw the whole deck over his shoulder, cards strewn all over the floor. It was said the practice was carried on to such an extent the floor would be "ankle deep in cards" when the players

THOMPSON ROAD STEAMERS as advertised in Victoria *Colonist*, were utter failures on the Cariboo's rugged roads.

LY BRITISH COLONI
d Victoria Chronicle.

BRITISH COLUMBIA, THURSDAY MORNING, MARCH 23, 1871.

New Advertisements.

STEAM TO CARIBOO!

The British Columbia
GENERAL TRANSPORTATION COMPANY

Will place Four of THOMSON'S PATENT ROAD STEAMERS on the route between Yale and Barkerville in the First Week in April, and will be prepared to enter into Contracts for the conveyance of Freight from Yale to Soda Creek in EIGHT DAYS. Through Contracts will be made as soon as the condition of the road above Quesnelmouth permits.

Rates of Passage will be advertised in due time.

BARNARD & BEEDY, anagers.

quit. Since no freight of any kind could get to town during the long winter, miners eventually ran out of cards. At this point, the discarded decks would reappear, thriftily salvaged and sorted by the saloon swamper who sold them once again.

Since most Lightning gold was found near Stanley, Van Winkle clung to life for a while as a supply depot for the bigger centers, including Barkerville farther on, eventually dwindling away. Hardly a trace of the town remains today.

Its neighbor had been named for Edward Henry Stanley, brother of the Frederick Arthur for whom Vancouver's Stanley Park was named. The town was more solid and wealthy than Van Winkle—and wilder. A man visiting in one of its brothels had to take every precaution against being rolled, making real relaxation impossible. Most of the hotels and all the dance-halls were either illicit houses or meeting places for them. The old Lightning Hotel was the last to close its doors, having lasted long beyond the life of the town.

One enterprising individual, not cut out for a miner, more fitted for promoting and merchandising, and who ended his days in Van Winkle, was Josiah Crosby Beedy. Beedy's most spectacular venture was his fleet of fantastic vehicles to take over the onerous task of transporting freight from Yale, the head of navigation. In 1871, Beedy with partner Francis Jones Barnard of Barnard's Express, applied to the legislature for a charter to run a train of "Thompson's Patent Road Steamers" over the Cariboo road. In the petition he stated optimistically: "There seems to be little doubt of the road steamer carriage being far safer than the stages drawn by horses. The drivers are to be sent from England and are to be men picked for the service."

Six of the outlandish contraptions, crosses between steam rollers and tractors with treads, arrived from England and two were actually started on the road. Difficulties beset the rigs from the start. For the sharp turns on the switchbacks, they did not have the flexibility of horse-drawn vehicles and narrow turns had to be widened. But the obstacle that stopped them for good was the steep grade up Jackass Mountain. The rigs could possibly have made it without loads and with the aid of horses but no extra animals were available. The costly experiment was a failure. At least one of the steamers was kept in British Columbia to replace oxen in logging operations.

Beedy returned to the Stanley area after that fiasco for a retail venture with a man named Townsend. It was called the Van Winkle Store, and according to its advertisement in the Cariboo *Sentinel*, carried "everything required in a mining camp."

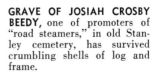

GRAVE OF JOSIAH CROSBY BEEDY, one of promoters of "road steamers," in old Stanley cemetery, has survived crumbling shells of log and frame.

YALE, B.C.

The violent river was called the Fraser. Fifty years before, the first white man to make an attempt to navigate it was the explorer Simon Fraser and about it he wrote: "The water which rolls down this extraordinary passage in tumultuous waves and with great velocity had a frightful appearance." Draining a vast area of snow-packed mountains the river is dangerous, even at lowest levels when little snow is melting. With spring freshets extending over a long time because of the varied terrain, it can rise a hundred feet and carry everything loose before it.

The Fraser canyon above New Westminster is somewhat deeper and broader, the waters roll with less violence and, in the early days, ships were able to make headway as far as the raw frontier town of Yale nestled on a narrow shelf on the north bank. Vancouver, as such, did not then exist, the small community being referred to as "Gastown." From Yale all traffic for the gold fields took whatever means was available for the even rougher land journey, the means including all manner of strange conveyances.

One primitive method of transporting the prospector's worldly goods was by the trundle barrow. A four-foot wheel was equipped with a rack on each side, wheelbarrow handles front and rear, the load evenly divided on the racks. One man got between each set of handle grips and away they went. Several hundred miles of this took heavy toll of the prospectors but some made it to Barkerville.

Other methods of trail transport were the fire-breathing behemoths, Thompson Patent Road Steamers which never got over Jackass Mountain and the even more exotic camels which frightened other animals to the point of jumping over cliffs into the river far below. More stable and dependable were the oxen or bulls, mules and horses.

At first these pack trains did not have far to go as the early strikes of gold were on the Fraser itself. The gravel bars extending into the rapids were loaded with it but the panning could only be done when the water was low. One method of locating the richer deposits was to dump a quantity of leaves into the stream and follow them. Where they tended to bunch up in eddies, circles were staked off as likely spots where gold particles might have landed.

A man standing exposed on one of these bars was a prime target for the arrows or bullets of ever-present Indians who resented the white man's invasion. One gold seeker was working the gravels with a rocker on a bar near Yale when he was startled by a shot. There was a hole through his rocker and it seemed the next one would be through him. Having no place to hide, all he could do was watch the Indian raise his rifle for another shot. There was a shot, not from the Indian but from a prospector on the shore. The Indian toppled into the river and the miner went on with his panning.

Before long the placer gold in the Fraser's banks was exhausted but then came reports of fabulous amounts of the yellow metal being taken out of Williams Creek and the streams at Quesnel Forks and Horsefly. The real rush out of Yale now set in and the town saw its heyday as a shipping point.

The prospector going north found Yale the last place to get liquor, women and gambling and those coming "outside" found freedom and license after long months of enforced abstinence. With no restraints, Yale became another Barbary Coast. It was considered the most wicked spot on the Coast, San Francisco having tamed down some with the end of the Sierra gold rush. In fact, it was the wilder element from the California town that came to Yale and gave it an impetus to lawlessness.

OLD ANGLICAN CHURCH OF ST. JOHN THE DIVINE, only remaining relic of roistering old Yale. Religious services were first held in old store by W. Burton Crickmer, June 10, 1860. New church was built one block away in 1863. Age and long periods of disuse caused such deterioration that in 1952 structure was condemned, causing such a furor campaign extended across Dominion to raise funds for restoration. Original logs now covered by boards, new foundation placed and even pulpit provided, convenience lacking in all years of history. Original wooden cross, rotted at base, was sent to Provincial Archives at Victoria for preservation. Verdure so conceals edifice visitor must look twice to find it.

One unholy pair, Ned McGowan and John Bagley, refugees from the California Vigilantes, teamed up with one Hicks, the Yale Gold Commissioner. Through his position the latter got hold of a fifty-year lease on the best placering grounds near Yale, then gouged the miners for short-term rentals. With the strong-arm help of his cohorts, he then extorted these miners with a "protection" racket. Miners who couldn't afford or refused to go along were brutally tortured or murdered. Killings in the saloons and brothels were common, bodies dumped into the turbulent Fraser. If they showed up downstream, they were considered victims of Indian outrage.

Shipments of gold from Williams Creek usually came down the Fraser canyon on muleback, later by horse-drawn stages. The bags and boxes of treasure were reloaded on boats and barges at Yale and this shift was more hazardous than the whole trip south with all the road agents it engendered. Once this hurdle was surmounted, the gold was considered safe in New Westminster. It was melted into bars here and as much as $100,000 might be piled on a table in a bank awaiting shipment to San Francisco.

Yale suffered a slump between the periods of Fraser wealth and the Williams Creek boom but that was nothing compared to the doldrums the town endured in the late 1870s when the main Cariboo rush ended. The once wild stopping place became a virtual ghost town. New life was breathed into it when the Canadian Pacific Railway began construction of its western end in the early '80s. With the arrival of 2,500 white rail construction workers and 6,500 Chinese laborers came a bigger boom than before and once again vice was rampant. A huge red-light district was organized. There were no restrictions to prevent rollings and murders, miners patronizing the girls at the risk of their lives. This seemed to be accepted, however, for Yale supported at least twenty "madames" each of whom managed many "frail sisters," not to mention the many girls in business for themselves. Faro, chuck-a-luck and keno in the gambling dens offered easy ways to spend railroad wages. No one gambling dared protest if he felt cheated. He was always aware of the raging Fraser a few feet from the door.

With the completion of rail laying, peace descended. Modern laws were less tolerant of gambling and violence with the result of greater prosperity. Yale dozes now, as deeply as it can, being only a stone's throw from a fine new highway up the Fraser Canyon.

YALE OF GOLD RUSH DAYS on narrow shelf beside boiling Fraser River pictured in old photo from Archives in Victoria. Main street was on waterfront where violence centered, a continuous row of false fronts. Up to Yale Fraser was navigable, above it canyon narrowed to funnel river into roaring rapids. To go overland, trails and "roads" were hacked out of canyon sides, traffic continuing to gold fields at risk of life and limb.

PROVINCIAL ARCHIVES

ASHCROFT MANOR, B.C.

The Cornwall brothers, Henry Alan and Clement Francis, established Ashcroft Manor, the very successful stopping place on the road to Barkerville. Being good Englishmen, they brought familiar customs with them and wanted to start a few old country sports. To this end, they imported some English hunting horses, fine Arab stallions and bought from the Duke of Beaufort twenty foxhounds.

Earlier, in 1862, the brothers had imported some cattle from Oregon. This meant cowboys, and there being none locally, they got these also from the States. And for a proper fox hunt who would ride the English hunters? Who else but the cowboys? Since there were no foxes in the country, coyotes would have to do. But on one point the Cornwalls insisted there would be no deviation. The proper terms for all phases of the hunt must be used.

The Americans sat in a row on a rail fence while instructed in all these proper terms. The first man sighting the quarry was to call out - "Where away!" When the direction taken by the "fox" was determined, the spotter was to cry - "Yoicks!" as a signal to get ready. Then all riders would take off at the shout— "Tally Ho!" But the Cornwall brothers were to suffer deep chagrin. The actual hunt went according to the best tradition up to the time the first coyote was sighted by a leathery cowhand from Wyoming. All the training in hunt vernacular went skittering over the sagebrush when he yelled out—"There goes the so-and-so—Now!"

Another story about these "fox hunts" is told by Mr. J. Alan Parker, the present occupant of the hundred-year-old hostelry — Ashcroft Manor. The hunting party was on its way to the huge Roper ranch on Cherry Creek in the direction of Kamloops, making an overnight stop at Christian's Hotel. There was no place to put the twenty foxhounds except in the pig pen, occupied by two immense sows. When the dogs were let out the next morning, they were so stuffed that even with whippings they would not pursue the quarry. There was no hunting that day and the stopover cost the party an extra twenty dollars for the sows.

The Cornwall brothers each kept diaries. "Their versions didn't always agree as to details," says Mr. Parker, "but the books do tell a lot of history written in faded old ink with quill pens." These documents are treasured in the Provincial Archives at Victoria but Mr. Parker is familar with their content.

"The Cornwall brothers came to the Crown Territories from Panama in 1858. Landing at Victoria they took another steamer up the Fraser River to New Westminster where they hired horses and rode north through Pemberton Meadows via Lillooet, over the Pavilion Mountains and came down into this beautiful valley."

The brothers liked what they saw—a paradise for horses. The bunch grass stood knee-high and water in the stream, later called Cornwall Creek, was so abundant the horses had to swim across it. The creek is now dry, being diverted for irrigation.

Henry and Clement returned to New Westminster and purchased a thousand acres of the valley land, presumably with some influence as the Surveyor General of the Crown Territories, Sir William Trutch, was induced to lay out the boundaries of the new domain and start proceedings to get a road built over a new route to avoid the dangerous mountains the Cornwalls had been forced to cross.

The road was all-important, the Cornwall plan being to build a comfortable inn for travelers on their way to the Barkerville gold fields. All went well and the Manor was built, at first called 103 Miles House in the

ST. JOHN'S CATHOLIC CHURCH stands on the Lillooet Indian Reservation near Cache Creek and Ashcroft. Complete isolation makes it most conspicuous sight for miles. First church built by whites in early 1860s was Protestant Anglican, one erected originally at Ashcroft Manor, later moved to edge of cliff above town of Ashcroft. Until 1955 Catholics of Ashcroft traveled to church below, then temporary Catholic house of worship was set up in old building at Ashcroft, served until 1961 when new church was built in town. Bonapart River flows past old edifice shown here, joins Thompson River near Ashcroft which enters Fraser in canyon below.

prevailing fashion indicating distance from Yale, head of navigation on the Fraser.

The hostelry was stoutly built and it is as sound today, constructed of the only material available—logs. The roof was covered with hand-split shakes, the floors made of one-and-a-half-inch planks. Additional buildings were put up close by for accommodation of the help and to corral the horses and bull teams of travelers and pack trains. Ashcroft Manor became a busy little community soon requiring a post office and church.

In cases of transgressions against the law, justice was meted out in a room of the Manor, designated as a Court of Law, with Clement Cornwall as Justice. There being no jail, prisoners were shackled to leg irons and allowed their freedom. None tried to get away as there was no place to go. One case mentioned in Clement's diary concerned a Pierre Philendreen accused of selling liquor to an Indian who subsequently fell from his horse and was killed. The accused was convicted, fined $200 and costs.

About this time a sawmill was built, powered by a waterwheel operating in Cornwall Creek. From then on, buildings of whipsawn lumber were rapidly added to the community. Farmers and ranchers were settling in the valley and a flour mill also powered by the stream was erected for their convenience. For every two sacks of wheat they received one sack of flour, the diary states. The grinding stone, oldest in British Columbia, still stands near where it was used.

In 1886 the Canadian Pacific extended its rails to a spot in the river valley below the Manor, the terminal called Ashcroft Station. Two men, Harvey and Bailey, formed a partnership and started a store across the street from the new depot. It was around this nucleus the town of Ashcroft sprang up, a flourishing place today.

The original community at the old hotel has all but vanished, only the Manor and outbuildings remaining. The little Anglican Church has been moved away, though still in sight, corrals and barns gone, post office moved down the steep hill to town. Sturdy old Ashcroft Manor conceals its ancient logs behind a facelift of boards, even these dating back to 1902. The shakes were replaced by shingles which lasted 40 years. The composition roof is new and surmounted by a T.V. aerial. But the rooms retain the original atmosphere, though kept immaculate for visitors.

ONE OF ORIGINAL LOG CABINS put up 100 years ago as auxiliary quarters for help at Ashcroft Manor, built before Cornwall sawmill, powered by now dry Cornwall Creek. Original domestics were Indians. Later, when Canadian Pacific Railway came as far as Ashcroft, construction crews brought many Chinese which were stranded at end of rail laying. Some found employment at bustling Ashcroft Manor, among them Wing Wo Ling, affectionately known as "Old Loy." Arriving at Manor about 1882, he soon showed skill as cook, presided over huge wood range many years. Buildings are surrounded by miles of sagebrush, not indigenous to area, brought in on hooves of cattle driven from Oregon, according to Mr. Parker, owner of Manor.

COPPER MOUNTAIN AND ALLENBY, B.C.

"It was the middle of the night. Flames lit the sky and people were screaming so that in no time everyone in camp was awake and saw the big three-story bunkhouse was afire. There was a balcony on the third floor, a man on it begging for someone to catch him when he jumped but he was so large and heavy no one was willing. He just went back into the flames to die. Several others were trapped and burned to death. These and the men killed fighting the flames made eight lives lost. And in the morning when the ashes were cool enough to investigate it was found a ninth man had been dead before the fire started. He lay on his cot, a knife in his back."

Those are Etta Ferguson's words describing her experiences in the devastation at Copper Mountain on March 18, 1928. She was born in the mining camp and spent all her early life in the rough-and tumble before the huge Granby Mining Company expanded the "hole in the ground" operation. And the stirring events that occurred before her father came to work in the mine were told and retold as she walked her dolls over the ore tailings. Etta is Mrs. William Ferguson now living with her husband and three teen-age children on a farm at the base of the last steep grade up Copper Mountain.

"Thirty-five years ago," she continues, "mining there was very much different from the big Granby operation. All the copper was taken out of a deep shaft, the opening just a hole in the ground. When I was a little girl, my mother would let me walk to work with my father, whose name was Alexander Corci. And how I shuddered and cried with fright when I saw him crawl down into that black hole on a flimsy rope ladder. After that mother discouraged my going and I'm glad she did because one day father stumbled and fell a long way down. He was badly hurt and suffered for years before he died."

The area along the river called Similkameen is rich in Indian legend and the stream links the many mining towns from near Hedley on the south to Tulameen on the north. Before the river existed cataclysmic upheavals formed the mineral deposits and then came violent volcanic outburst which lifted the very rugged ridges including Copper Mountain. Then deep valleys were gouged out in an icy glacial period, one of the long troughs occupied by the rushing Similkameen.

The first white men in the Similkameen, Okanogan and Tulameen Valleys were fur traders, including those of the Hudson's Bay Co., organized in 1670. The period when fur was king extended well into the 1800s. One of the trappers was James Joseph Jameson, born in Kentucky in 1828, who had ten children, James, Jr., being born in the Kamloops, B.C., area August 26, 1864. The father and family settled in the Similkameen Valley in '82. Out of his life came the discovery of copper in the area.

OPEN-PIT OPERATION introduced dangers to aboveground population, not existing in days of deep shaft mining when hazards were confined to miners in underground passages.

The elder and junior Jamesons were hunting on the mountain and although they had plenty of meat for their first winter both had new rifles and wanted to try them out. After some hours without success on the rough and heavily timbered peak both saw a deer and both fired at the same moment. The deer went down and lay still until James, Jr., walked almost up to it, when it scrambled up and disappeared into the timber. Chagrined, the hunters stared at the spot where the deer had lain and the father continued to stare after the son had turned away. Plain to be seen in the rock was the bright greenish tinge of copper.

The Jameson family seems to have "sat on" their find for ten years until their friend, R. A. Brown, interested in trapping, visited at the home and learned of the discovery. The claim was recorded by Brown and Jameson in October, 1892, and the first mine worked was the Sunset, followed in rapid succession by the Oriol, Jennie Silkman, King Solomon and others.

All these were ordinarily successful but because the ore was refractory, treatment difficulties prevented any big success. But by 1914, when Pardoe Wilson surveyed for a railway line to Copper Mountain and Princeton at the junction of the Similkameen and Tulameen, things began to look up. Labor troubles, which were to harass operations at intervals to the very end, delayed actual shipping of the ore until October, 1920. The war then forced closure by dropping prices to an unprofitable thirteen cents.

The nearby town of Princeton (so named because the Prince of Wales stopped there) was suffering ups and downs with the fortunes of the copper mines and had become a virtual ghost town with the low ebb suffered by the Canada Copper Corporation which had acquired the controlling interest in the mines.

In 1923, the giant in Canadian mining operations, Granby Smelting and Power Company, Ltd., was running out of raw material in its massive holdings at various locations and sent men to look into the possibilities of exploiting the undeniably rich deposits on Copper Mountain. When this news leaked out, Princeton began to breathe again. Actual activity began when Canada Copper Corporation was absorbed

HEADQUARTERS AND RESIDENCE for mine superintendents overlooks densely forested hills around Copper Mountain. Copy of picture was currently sent to former resident, Mrs. Etta Ferguson who replied: "You can imagine how I will treasure my picture since the beautiful bungalow burned to the ground after you were here."

COPPER MOUNTAIN STREET SCENE. Enough old residences remained at time of photographer's visit in August of 1962 to give town form, have since been leveled by fire along with predecessors.

MESS HALL AND COOKHOUSE, latter with enormous ranges, stand among wreckage of other buildings. Tree is *Pseudotsuga douglasi,* commonly Douglas "fir," distinguished from true fir by cones hanging beneath branches instead of growing erect.

by the Granby interests and one of its subsidiaries, Allenby Copper Co., developed huge smelting plants at Allenby near Princeton at the bottom of the steep grade from the mines. Raw ores were now loaded directly into railway cars at the lower level opening of the mine and run by gravity to the refinery.

Mines and smelters were brought to full capacity in 1926 and the following years were golden ones for all concerned. Temporarily there were no labor disputes and prices were satisfactory. Little shaft mining was done, during the summer months half the ore taken out of the Mountain coming from three open pits or "glory holes." In 1926, 665,000 tons of ore went down the steep grade to the Allenby mills.

There were 44 individual houses for families of miners on the peak as well as bunkhouses, mess halls and showers, etc., for 218 single men. A huge company store stood on an eminence, rented to a Princeton man, W. A. Wagenhauser. Large office buildings and machinery houses were built and the mountaintop camp took on the aspect of a good-sized city. Then on March 18, 1928 came the tragedy of fire which Etta Ferguson experienced.

All the victims were buried in Princeton cemetery on March 23 except one which was sent to Penticton. An investigation was launched into the murder without conclusive results yet a few facts were turned up. The victim, Ralph P. Bassett, had won a lot of money in a poker game the previous evening and a man known to have quarreled with him was seen to remove his belongings from the bunkhouse before the fire and leave town in a hurry the morning after. This man was never tracked down. Confusing was the sidelight that, a few days later, the body of a Chinese worker was found hanging from a beam. It was apparently a suicide, nothing definite linking him to the murder.

Etta Ferguson relates another incident of the raw life. "It was gruesome but no more so than many other accidents in the mines. Wally Beckman, a man independent and intolerant of company rules, refused to wear his safety belt while shoveling ore down the last chute at the top of the vertical shaft leading to the ore cars below. One day the man guiding the downcoming ore so it would be spread evenly, noticed the shoveler's hat coming down. Then came his head and other parts until the whole body arrived."

MINERS PASSED THROUGH this building on way to shaft opening. In spite of some serious accidents, overall safety factor in mines was high. When shaft was abandoned in favor of open pit, it was blasted shut but continues to sink. Town is now posted as being extremely dangerous.

ONE OF "GLORY HOLES" resulting from open-pit operation. As vein was opened up, operation became increasingly expensive as ground on top, "overburden," had to be removed in ever-increasing amounts. Nevertheless, with modern machinery, this type of mining is still more economical than deep shaft.

ALLENBY, some 10 miles below Copper Mountain mines, in middle distance of photo, may seem like thriving city but is entirely abandoned except for skeleton crew maintaining and guarding expensive machinery. About one-fourth of workers in heyday resided in company-built section complete with movie house and stores, now all moved or destroyed. One-fourth of workers lived in nearby Princeton.

And a brighter note. A big celebration was held on the Mountain Friday, April 11, 1930, when the long-planned-for community hall was dedicated. In the beautiful dance area, 72' x 42', speeches were made, a bountiful repast served and the big dance lasted all night. This happy spirit of fiesta held over for several weeks but in May, Lt.-Gov. R. R. Bruce, at a reception given for him on the Mountain, announced a fact already whispered, that the mines would soon be closing. Again labor troubles, falling copper prices and depression had won out. He voiced the hope that "the trade winds will soon blow again."

The years following were ones of desperate effort for miners and smelter men just to stay alive. Work of any kind was almost impossible to get. Yet on June 12, 1937, the work whistle blew once more. Amid general rejoicing a trainload of ore left the mountaintop and was sent to Allenby where the smelters were fired up and ready. The activity was marred by a bad accident in August, at four in the afternoon, when a man cage crashed to the bottom of a shaft due to failure of the hoist apparatus. Drs. R. J. Wride and Paul Phillips are given credit for saving the lives of all but one of the seriously injured men. But the mines were operating again, the people making livings and almost everyone was happy.

The exception was the company itself. Granby was having a hard time in the fall of 1939 to defend the fact it was shipping copper concentrates to Japan. There was little consolation in the fact that the Canadian and British governments were giving full approval to the deal.

Criticism was not too blatant for Granby meant too much to the community. Since it had reactivated the mines and smelters in 1937, wages alone amounted to $4 million and millions more had been spent for equipment, in income taxes, etc. However, when Japan attacked Pearl Harbor, Canada was soon at war and shipments came to an end.

During 1952 the crew working on the mountaintop

totaled 560 with 431 underground. Together with the men working in the Allenby smelters, the grand total on the Granby payroll was 853. Yet the rosy picture was not to last. In April of '53, General Manager J. A. C. Ross announced that due to poor prices, the entire operation would cease forthwith. This meant complete abandonment of Copper Mountain and Allenby, a crushing blow to Princeton as well. All buildings on the Mountain have since been destroyed, all residences at Allenby removed, the permanent buildings at the smelter remaining.

The one-time big town on Copper Mountain with its schools, stores and other buildings now presents a "scorched earth" aspect. Etta Ferguson presumes the company, if it ever does resume operations, will scoop up the whole place in open pit ore removal. "But," she adds, "it is beginning to look as though that will never happen. For a while we were looking forward to seeing the cars going up the mountain grade again. Now we feel it would be too bad if they did. Things are very peaceful here as it is."

CORE SAMPLINGS by the hundreds of thousands filled two buildings, made at frequent intervals over many years to determine direction of vein. Cylindrical cores were split in two, carefully laid in grooves in drawers and numbered to be compared with records.

SETTLING LAKE created by retaining dike, when tailings began to foul sparkling waters of Similkameen River. Solids have appearance of fine sand, are ground residue when copper concentrates removed from finely crushed ore.

GRANITE CREEK, B.C.

John Chance was out to make some money. He figured that taking a bunch of horses from Washington state to the raw frontier town of New Westminster, B.C., was maybe a little easier than driving a swarm of bees, but he had a hankering to do it.

He had the iron nerve, too. And by veering from the regular route, he set off a gold rush that made the wild spot along Granite Creek boom into the third largest city in the Province of British Columbia.

Local historian John Goodfellow pins it down in his *The Story of Similkameen*. . . . "For some unaccountable reason, after he (Chance) reached Princeton, he did not follow the Dewdney Trail but went up the Tulameen past Aspen Grove and followed the old Coquihalla Trail."

The memories of Henry Younger Lowe of Tulameen go back to the turn of the century when he arrived from Wales to set up a log cabin on the lower level area near Otter Lake, called Otter Flat and later to be known as Tulameen. Henry was a friend to all the Chinook Indians thereabout. Since his arrival was only a few years after that of John Chance, he gives his reason for the horse wrangler going the way he did.

"Some of those poor devils hadn't seen a woman for months. They were well aware the Chinooks spent the summer berry season in this valley along the Tulameen and Granite Creek. They also knew the squaws were left more or less alone to do the picking while the braves hunted in the mountains. Also that their chief was willing to allow the girls to extend hospitality to the roving young white men, assuming there would be a consideration of some beans, tea and flour. John Chance was after klootchman and that's how come he went so far out of his way."

Even after such dalliance Chance was not quite ready to get back to the business of pushing his horses on toward the Coast. Like every other wanderer of the day, he was part prospector and could not resist dipping his pan into the little creek that flows into the Tulameen at this point.

What he found made him "whoop and holler." The sounds scared the horses but Chance couldn't care less. He washed pan after pan until he had a goodly pinch of gold dust, then hurried on to New Westminster with his animals and disposed of them for funds to purchase supplies. He registered his claim, making every effort to keep it secret, but the word was out that John Chance had discovered gold and he was followed by an eager band of hopefuls. They staked out claims along the creek and as the time was July, slept on the ground, too busy to build cabins.

Chance and his new-found friends panned plenty of the "maddening stuff" and the little group expanded into a horde that needed shelter when the nights grew cold. Logs were the only building material available

PLAQUE ON MONUMENT beside waters of creek where Chance found gold. The *Similkameen Star* of Sept. 10, 1915 wrote of Granite Creek in prosperous times: "E. P. Cook, the pioneer merchant of Granite Creek, was to Princetown last Friday. In 1885 when he walked into Granite Creek carrying his blankets it was with difficulty that he made his way along the crowded main street. Twelve saloons did a flourishing business and closing hours were unknown. The town was the third largest in B. C., being only exceeded by Victoria and New Westminster. Kamloops would probably come next in size. Placer miners in 1885-6 took probably $800,000 in gold and platinum out of Granite Creek." John Goodfellow thinks this is exaggerated, the actual amount somewhere between this and the sum officially reported.

FRONT DOOR DETAIL of "house of pleasure." Structure extended back to shed and attached outhouse, had basement as well. Method of notching ends of logs is varied, chinks first filled with chips and scraps, then clay.

GRANITE CREEK

GOLD WAS DISCOVERED HERE
ON JULY 5 1885 BY
JOHN CHANCE
TWO THOUSAND PEOPLE
PARTICIPATED IN THE RUSH THAT YEAR
AND IN 1886 GRANITE CREEK
WAS THE THIRD LARGEST CENTRE OF
POPULATION IN THE PROVINCE

"FANCY HOUSE" in Granite Creek had second floor where girls cooperated. Woodshed at rear is covered by hop vines, persisting from early days. Addition is of whipsawn lumber but no entire building so constructed remains on Creek. All structures, some 15, are of logs, some retaining roofs, one occupied. Beyond is Douglas fir forest.

and cabins sprang up along three "streets" parallel with the creek on one bank only where the walls were not too steep.

Rev. George Murray was the first preacher to hold a church service in Granite Creek. Since the scene is described as having "tents aplenty but really no houses," the event took place about August that first year, 1885. One log building was being built for a saloon. At three logs in height, the Rev. Murray appropriated it and after services the hat was passed for gold dust. When a real church was built, the log cabin reverted to its original mundane status, a saloon called the Adelph.

Walton Hugh Holmes, born in England in 1853, made a visit to Granite Creek in '85 and wrote: "On leaving Tulameen we began to meet people and six miles farther on when we came in sight of Granite Creek, it looked like an anthill. Several hundred men of all sorts, saddle horses and pack animals, tents on both sides of the river. What a sight! All available space taken up for tents. Camp fires everywhere. There was one small cabin built by Mr. Alison for a store but there were no supplies in it. Only some tin plates and iron knives and forks: no provisions procurable and they were badly needed. We found our pack

trains would be welcome when they arrived. The most of Granite Creek was staked off for claims. They were only 100 feet long from high water mark across the creek. There was no government office to record them, so it was not long before we had to appoint a recorder, a Mr. H. Nicholson, pro tem, until a government agent was sent in 1886. . . . By that time Granite Creek was quite a town, all log houses."

Through July, September and October the workers received $90,000 in gold. There were 62 claims of 300 feet each, and the population totaled almost a thousand, one-third Chinese. In January of the next year, the gold commissioner, G. C. Tunstal, said there were 40 houses, six saloons, hotels and seven stores. The year 1886 was the year of peak production of gold and platinum, officially reported to the Commissioner as being $193,000. Humans being what they are, it is safe to assume the actual figure was much larger.

When the easily garnered wealth began to thin out and no lodes were found, people began to move away, some to dig for the much less glamorous coal then being mined in the area. Fifteen years after John Chance had found his gold, Granite Creek was a ghost town.

41

COALMONT, B.C.

Just previous to November 19, 1858, when the British Columbia mainland across the straits from Vancouver Island was proclaimed a Crown Colony, an exploration by John Alison turned up an open outcropping of coal in the banks of the Similkameen River. "The vein was fully exposed," he reported. "It was very thick with interlaced seams of resin all through it. You could set it afire with a match. It seems strange that nature had not done it with a bolt of lightning long ago." Trappers and homesteaders hastened to load toboggans and sleighs to transport the new and free fuel home.

This was in an untouched wilderness, teeming with wild animals. Walter Moberly in his *Rocks and Rivers of British Columbia* gives a vivid picture of an encounter with one of them. In the spring of 1860 he "had entered into ̦a contract in partnership with Mr. Edgar Dewdney to build a trail from Fort Hope on the Fraser River to the Similkameen River on the east side of the Cascade Range, in order to reach the diggings on the latter river where gold of fine quality had been discovered.

"Meeting with a very severe accident, I was laid up for some days in a miserable swamp, with only an Indian boy for my companion. When I felt a little better, I rode a mule down to a small log storehouse which we had at a little lake.

"I arrived in the evening and soon lay down to rest in the lower of two bunks in one corner of the house. As I lay there watching the moon shine through a large square opening in the roof that served the purpose of a chimney, I heard something walking on the mudcovered roof and quietly got up with my revolver. I thought it might be an Indian intent on stealing some of our supplies or rum, of which we kept a good supply in the house. I saw what I took to be a hand coming down through the opening, evidently feeling what was below. This was repeated several times, when I managed to get into such a position as to leave the moonbeam between myself and the invader. Instead of an Indian I made it out to be a panther, this making me very uncomfortable. As soon as the moonlight came between us I fired, and as I found in the morning some blood on the roof, I must have hit the brute."

One cougar shot in the area by Charlie Shuttleworth measured 9 feet, 2 inches in length. It weighed 240 pounds and "was rolling in fat." The hunter said the animal would kill an average of two deer a week. Encounters with bears were frequent. Trapper Frank Le Farge was walking toward Hope one evening as darkness was settling. He vaulted over a large log on the trail, landing squarely on a bear's back. He backed off and although the bear was as startled as he was, it charged. La Farge was forced away from his gun but somehow managed to get at his knife as he tried to scrape loose from the slavering jaws and sharp claws. He stabbed frantically and finally struck a vital spot, both he and the bear collasping. Only the bear died. Another trapper, George Aldous, happened along shortly to help La Farge to the little hospital at Chiliwack where he recovered in a few weeks.

Before the turn of the century, Henry Younger Lowe was freighting on the old Cariboo road to the north and not having much work as the gold mines were just about depleted. When he left home in Wales he had told the folks: "I won't be back until I have made my fortune," and since he had not, he drifted south to the scenic valleys of the Similkameen and Tulameen.

Acquiring some land near Otter Lake about 1905, he built a log house in which he lives today. Others stopped at the site on a level piece of ground at first called Otter Flat, then Tulameen. Most of the Lillooet Indians picking berries and hunting in the area were friendly and remained for a time, slowly drifting away as more settlers came in. Hank Lowe built houses, among them the first board house in the growing town, selling them to the new people.

He spent much time hunting, ranging the hills and valleys, and when the Great Northern Railway needed coal to fire the locomotives of trains for the projected route to a point 26 miles north at Blakemere, the line sought out the man who knew the country best— Henry Lowe. The young Welshman soon convinced the man he refers to affectionately as "Sam Hill" there was plenty of coal available, sufficient to fuel the locomotives at this point for many years to come.

Henry is vague about details of what happened in the ensuing struggle for power between the Great Northern and Canadian Pacific, saying only: "The C.P.R. won out and that was the end of Sam Hill." The new line continued to take most of the coal.

During the early days of railroad construction, Tulameen and Coalmont boomed. Young Lowe took on other jobs such as laying the foundations for the pretentious new Dominion Hotel in 1912. It was built by a man named McRea, usually called "Mac." He had espoused a wealthy English widow for his second wife and it was she who financed the enterprise.

After several years of successful operation, the hotel began to lose patronage, because Mac was "acting queerly," it seemed. Then for several days the proprietor was not seen around the hotel. Hank and several others broke into the now shabby and empty Dominion and found Mrs. McRea lying on a bed, blind from cataracts. She had no idea where her husband was.

Hank took to the mountains and finally came upon McRea. "The man had no gun and no haversack," he relates, "and he stared at me like a wild man. I said to him, 'Mac, what's the matter with you? Why don't you come down to the hotel with me?' He stared some more without a word and turned away. I said to him, 'The hell with you then,' and left him. He was never seen again."

A large coal mining operation was started on the mountain directly above nearby Coalmont and Granite Creek. The latter had been a fabulous gold camp and now on the decline, offered a ready-made bunch of miners who had only to change their trade skills for coal. Perry Wilson and Blake Burns were friends and partners, holding the most shares in the new venture, and gave parts of their names to the town developing on the mountain—Blakeburn.

COALMONT IS SLEEPIER today than in 1912 when *Coalmont Courier* was distributed on streets. Paper carried banner head on front page —"Circulates in every home in Princeton, East Princeton, Tulameen, Aspen Grove, Merrit, Nicola, Hedley and Keremeos and around the Terrestrial Globe." Editor Ed Clark confidently predicted Coalmont "is the city of destiny, the coming coal metropolis of Southern British Columbia, with a population of 10,000 in the near future." One advertisement urged hesitant buyers of Coalmont real estate: "Take time by the forelook — she has no back hair." Although several streams ran close to community they were usually contaminated by mining operation so water supply came from wells like this one in center of town. (Little black dog, Toody, author's constant —and hammy — companion, managed to sneak into picture as signature.)

Hank Lowe was in on that town's beginnings. "I hauled the first frame bunkhouse up there," he said, "before there was any road. I'd haul up supplies, too. If there was heavy fall of snow when I was up there, I'd fill about eight sacks full of coal, pile them on a toboggan made of a twelve-inch piece of lumber, let out a whoop and a holler and the horses would tear down the hill, making a trail for the rest of them." The bakery had remained in Granite Creek and owner F. M. Cook continued to bake bread, carrying it up the Blakeburn miners.

Lowe had located four veins at Blakeburn, each known by a numeral in order of their operation. As the vein was penetrated the "hanging wall" or roof was supported by pillars of coal, two or more feet thick. When the end of the vein was reached, further exploration was made to determine whether the vein was only "faulted," continuing in another direction a few feet away, or whether there was no more coal. If the latter, equipment and men were withdrawn from the workings, the pillars mined out as the men retreated. This naturally caused collapse of the hanging wall.

The quality of Similkameen coal which made it unsafe to stockpile at the mills because of spontaneous combustion, now worked to cause the province's worse disaster. Veins 1, 2, and 3 had been finished without incident but 4 lay smouldering, and on August 13, 1930, all hell broke loose. Hank Lowe tells the story.

"I was up on the mountain when I heard the noise but at first I didn't know what it was. I hurried down to Tulameen and met Mrs. McIntosh on the street. I asked her what was the matter. She threw her apron over her head and burst into sobs, saying: 'They're all dead.' I knew then because we had disasters like that in the mines in Wales, my uncle killed in one. I hurried to the store and found a list posted with the names of all the young fellows that had been in the mine at the time, 48 of them. Next day we knew they were all dead for sure, suffocated by deadly carbon monoxide fumes."

The men were buried in the Princeton cemetery with services by Catholic and United Churches, the sad series of funerals beginning with Albert Cole, 19, and ending with John Smith, 36. For their families a relief fund of $33,000 was raised in Princeton. It helped greatly but now the "Hungry Thirties" had begun. Blakeburn mines were closed after the disaster, never to reopen. The collieries at Coalmont at the bottom of the "mountain of coal" ceased to work when the coal supply was shut off. Tulameen, with its beautiful Otter Lake which area had served as a residential section for the men and families also died when they went elsewhere to work. Granite Creek was already long dead, the ring of ghost towns now in full circle.

OLD DOMINION HOTEL rears its bulk in lonely isolation at Tulameen which was close enough to serve Coalmont as residential section. Was built by "Mac" McRae in wildly turbulent, prosperous period of railroad construction. Smaller hotel nearby was put up by Lars Anderson. Until railroad tracks were completed, bars in both were three deep with thirsty workers. Depression came with end of railroad building, smaller hotel burning to ground, perhaps man-fired. Asked if he thought Dominion's owner was responsible, oldest inhabitant Hank Lowe said in lowered voice: "Son, as sure as you're born, he did it. Maybe not himself but in those rough days it was easy enough to get a couple of transients drunk and they'd do anything." Tulameen, dead as coal mining town, lives meagerly as resort. Beautiful Otter Lake is close by, cottages lining shore whose occupants fish in summer, hunt in fall.

HEDLEY, B.C.

The Indians along the Similkameen and its creeks had no use for gold and no incentive to work for it. In the '60's they watched the white man sloshing gravel around in big pans, picking out flakes of something yellow and went back to their tipis, giving thanks to the Great Mystery that they were not that hungry.

Yet the white men, they saw, needed Indian furs and in a spirit of barter instead of fight some awkward trading was done, neither faction being able to understand the other's words. When the trade language known as Chinook jargon infiltrated from the lower Columbia River where sailors were fraternizing briskly with the local tribes, the B.C. miners were able to say "Hyas kloshe" and settle down to some plain and fancy horse trading.

The *British Columbia Quarterly* of April, 1948, describes the location of Hedley as "lying at a point where Twenty Mile Creek, after swinging around the western base of Nickel Plate Mountain, emerges from its canyon to cut a boulder-strewn channel through the river benches to flow into the Similkameen River a short distance below the town."

The name Hedley is very common in Britain and Canada and several men of that name were connected with the early history of the mining camp. Rev. J. W. Hedley served the Keremeos area as minister and moved to Hedley Camp in 1902 which was probably named for R. Robert Hedley, manager of the Hall Mines Smelter at Nelson, B.C. This Hedley had grubstaked Peter Scott, the first man to get things going in the lode mines along the Similkameen in 1896. Earlier efforts to work claims had failed for lack of finances, notably those of George Alison, James Riordan, Edgar Dewdney and J. Coultard.

Peter Scott had a vast ambition to make his newly located Rolle the biggest thing in mining history and, with Robert Hedley's money, set about to do it. Other claims were taken up in rapid succession, among them the Mound, Copper Cleft, Horsefly, Bulldog, Nickel Plate and Copperfield. And it was the Nickel Plate, not the Rolle, which turned out to be the most successful—the first producing lode mine in the Similkameen.

This one was started by a combination of circumstances. One was the staging of a fair at New Westminster, at that time the metropolis on the Coast, later swallowed up by a faster-growing Vancouver. Another was the fact that New Westminster was hosting a distinguished visitor, M. K. Rodgers, moving force of the vast Marcus Daly outfit in Butte, Montana. All that remained for a catalyst was for Wollaston and Arundel, owners of the struggling Nickel Plate, to bring a few chunks of its ore to the fair and let events take their course.

Rodgers was actually on his way to Cassiar, due to sail the next day from Victoria, but he had a few hours to spend and "took in" the New Westminster Fair. When he saw the Nickel Plate ore samples, his eyes bugged out. Cagily, however, he examined the samples carefully, concluding they must be "salted," referring to the artificial enriching of ore to give a false impression of value. After locating the mine's owners who were standing by, he was willing to believe the samples were genuine, cancelled his sailing arrangements and was on his way next morning to the mines on the Similkameen.

Rodgers took a look at the mine, accepted a few pieces of ore and took them to be assayed. The results were so high he felt Wollaston and Arundel had handed him something special, went back to make a few choices of his own. What happened after his private assay made history for Hedley.

Wollaston and Arundel were "fit to be tied" while Rodgers was "fooling around," so cagily had he concealed his intense interest. The owners' funds were running low and they began to fear a collapse of their hopes. Then one day as Arundel was walking dejectedly along the board sidewalk in front of the bank, a hand reached out and touched his shoulder, then a familiar voice: "I'd like to complete the deal we mentioned the other day." Arundel was stunned at the sight and sound of the Butte man. He went inside the bank in a daze and was handed a check for $79,000.

In January money began to flow into the camp and the first large expenditure was for a tramway. The mine openings were located in "impossible" places, clinging like flies to vertical faces of cliffs hundreds of feet above the town. With the tramway completed in October, 1902, the "muck" could fly down on a spider web of cable. At the landing place a large stamp mill for crushing and a cyanide plant for refining were built and milling began in May, 1904.

The camp had always been inaccessible. The first sizable shipment of supplies came in 1898 from Fairview, when George Cahill, one of the first owners of a Hedley claim, brought in a 35-horse pack train. As the camp grew larger, ways of getting supplies in had to be worked out. A 15-mile cut-off was built from Keremeos road, shortening the distance from the coast to Princeton and Hedley.

The camp was now in the throes of a boom and enjoying it. In 1904 the big Similkameen Hotel was

MINE BUILDINGS of Hedley Mascot cling precariously to steep cliffs (upper left). Hedley rose in importance as mining camp when Granite Creek placers declined, was for many years most important gold center in entire Similkameen area. Lode mines like this resulted from discoveries in rich veins after depletion of deposits in gravels of Similkameen River at mouth of tributary, Twenty Mile Creek, now called Hedley Creek. Elevation of town at base of cliffs is 1,700 feet, mines on overhanging mountain sides 3,000 feet higher.

built, the first good stopping place and an elegant one. The New Zealand Hotel went up in 1905; both hotels were destroyed by fire, the latter in 1911, former in 1916. The town had general stores, butcher shops and all kinds of mercantile establishments. One structure had no need for advertising—the three-story one down on the point where Twenty Mile Creek enters the Similkameen, where the workers could spend their money on all pleasures of the flesh.

More respectable were the Bank of British North America, first in the Similkameen, telephone office and imposing school on the hill replacing the original, a room at the rear of the Methodist Church. The school also suffered disaster, demolished by a massive earth slide.

There were many golden years for the community but in 1930 ore became so poor operations were suspended. Hedley, like many other one-industry towns, suffered severe depression pangs. In 1932 the mine was sold to John Mercer Exploration Company

which found a new paying lead, extending Hedley's lease on life. A modern village was built around the mine on the 5,000-foot perch, connected with east-west highway by a mountain road.

But, had everyone read the production report of the Hedley Mascot, the other big mine, they would have known the town was doomed. The report started out bravely but carried a stinger: "During the thirteen years ending April, 1949, the Hedley Mascot fractional claim yielded over $8,500,000 in gold. Exhaustive explorations elsewhere on the property yielded interesting indications but sufficient ore was not found to warrant continuation of milling."

The next year saw the closure of the Hedley Mascot and 1955 was the end of the fabulous Nickel Plate and the little town of the same name in the clouds. Hedley was on its way to becoming a ghostly spectre. Flood and fire had always beset the town and in 1956 a searing blast took down several hotels and other structures. The ones remaining are largely empty and faded.

RIVERSIDE, WASHINGTON

Gun-toting, cattle-rustling Frank Watkins rode at the head of a string of stolen horses. He had run away from the rope in Oregon, chased by a mob and now, in 1903, was arriving in fresh territory and headed for Williams' Saloon in Riverside.

What Watkins liked was hot toddies such as Tom and Jerrys and he had heard how good Jack Williams could make them. He stomped in, pounded on the plank bar and demanded one of Williams' specials.

Watkins' reputation, not for consuming hot drinks but for confiscating hot horses and cattle, had preceded him. The tea kettle was steaming away but the bartender thought it was out of the cowboy's line of vision. He was not about to indulge cattle thieves' whims. "Ain't no more hot water," he sang out. But Watkins had heard the simmering kettle even though he couldn't see it. "Well," he drawled, "no more use for that thing then." And he moved out to sight the kettle and shoot the spout off.

The rustler hung around Riverside all winter. He seemed to think he rated the protection of the law, unaware that the townspeople were wary of him. Twice he went to the sheriff with complaints he had been shot at, once exhibiting a hole in his hat to prove it. "Too high," the sheriff may have said.

One evening the next spring he rode into Riverside, bedded his horse in Kendall's Livery Stable and after supper climbed into the loft to sleep in the hay. As other sleepers in this early day flophouse were waking and shaking the grass seeds and nits out of their ears, they noticed Frank Watkins was not stirring in his nest. He was dead with a bullet in his head.

At first it was called suicide but Watkins' gun was found beside him unfired and there were no powder burns on his skin. Nobody cared much how the cowboy had died and the questions asked of the other sleepers and witnesses at the inquest were desultory. No one appeared to press further inquiry and the business was settled. Watkins was buried without ceremony beside the road entering town. The grave can still be seen and may even have the little fence around it.

Richard Sutton tells this story, especially if you call him "Dick." His father, Robert W., brought the family to Riverside from Genesee, Idaho, in a covered wagon in 1890 and Dick grew up here, marrying in 1908 and rearing a family of five boys and five girls.

The early prosperity of Riverside was due entirely to its road position, freight teams and boats using it as a convenient stopover for loading or unloading. The actual year-around head of navigation was Brewster, where the Okanogan River meets the Columbia. Most of the year the former, which flowed past Riverside, was too shallow for steamboats, even the shallow draft paddle-wheel vessels, but in spring it swelled with melting snow from the mountains. That was a period of feverish activity and a fleet of loaded steamers brought a steady stream of supplies to Riverside, the center for a vast area of mining and farming communities. Merchants stocked up for the whole year and mine owners replaced equipment parts. As soon as flood waters subsided, river traffic was finished for another year and shipping activities began. Goods were moved to outlying points and Riverside was the headquarters.

At the turn of the century, the town decided it deserved the honor of being the county seat. Growing pains were about over and things were booming. A large store operated by C. E. Blackwell and Co. stood proudly on the waterfront near a big hotel, the Occidental. A bank was doing a flourishing business and the interest was 12 percent on loaned money. For a while it was squeezed in one corner of Pat Carney's saloon but the enterprising banker, Arthur Lund, quickly expanded into a separate building and even established branches of the bank in neighboring towns. With all this the populace thought Conconully had been on the top of the Okanogan heap long enough.

Heading the ensuing county seat fight, one-sided with Conconully sitting smugly on its prestige, was the fiery editor of the Riverside *Argus*. Outspoken, vituperative, Wallace Struble spared no dirty words in supporting the proposed shift. This was the same period county elections for officials were scheduled and although most candidates were vigorously for or against the change, all kept their opinions buttoned up for fear of losing votes. When the election was over, Riverside was right where it started. Conconully held the county seat until 1914 when it went to Okanogan.

Struble put up another good fight but another losing one over the matter of a bridge over the Okanogan River—at Riverside or Okanogan? Final disposition was made in secret and editor Struble sounded a bitter blast in the *Argus* of Dec. 8, 1908. "On Monday last the retiring board of county commissioners awarded a contract to the Puget Sound Bridge Co. for the sum of $10,500 for the erection of a 'steal' bridge across the Okanogan at the village of Okanogan. The contract price does not include approaches which will probably swell the total $500 or more making the cost of the structure at least $11,000." The next paragraph was set in capital letters. "The awarding of this contract was done, the *Argus* is informed, with extreme secrecy. In a star chamber session at which only the commissioners and one Harry J. Kerr, 'Mayor' of Okanogan village, were present. Even the people of Conconully, except those in on the deal, were not aware of the proceedings and expressed surprise that

LIVELY SCENE ON WATERFRONT about the turn of the century — photo copied from calendar of Dick Sutton, pioneer resident of Riverside, showing large shipment of wool arriving from ranch of Clay Fruit to be loaded on sternwheelers tied up on Okanogan River bank.

Driver of wagon at left is Bert Winnick, his lead team Baldy and Jake; on next wagon is driver William G. Reeder, owner of freight line with headquarters at Brewster. Reeder had small terrier which nipped at heels of out-of-line or laggard horses. On driver's seat of third wagon is "Six-Shooter Andy" Southworth who habitually carried gun and bowie knife. Standing on ground at Andy's right, sporting boiled shirt, is ship's captain of Griggs Steamship Line. Loose horse in foreground is Nespelum, privileged race animal which didn't have to work and turned rump to photographer.

such a high-handed course should have been taken by a retiring board of commissioners."

The Okanogan *Independent* of Oct. 10, in a resumé of the historic battle said it had remained independent but did point out the advantages of the Okanogan site, prophesying that "the pendulum of development will swing in favor of Okanogan, that the bridge will have marked convenience in the transportation of trade to the growing communities of the Tunk Creek and Omak Creek areas," further pointing out that the railroad would be coming along in a few years and would likely bypass Riverside.

Riverside and the *Argus* editor must have sensed the truth of the prediction but to see it in the public prints was a punch below the belt. And Struble must have felt a certain satisfaction when the bridge was finished and proved to be eleven feet higher than needed to clear the tallest stack on any sternwheeler, which made the cost excessive and the approaches too steep to use in icy weather.

Riverside settled down to enjoy what it did have, its famous week-end dances in the big hall at the south end of town. These were held on Friday nights instead of Saturday because of the Sunday races at a fine track near the river. And also due to the Sunday racing, Authur Lund reaped a harvest by keeping his bank open.

True to the ominous prediction, the railroad did bypass Riverside when it came through in 1914, a blow to the town depending on road and river traffic. It was left sitting on the banks of the Okanogan to grumble and nurse the stray wagon freight. And the final stroke of destiny came when a modern highway was built to the north of the town.

In 1958 Stanley Hixon, a rancher in Tunk Valley, with "a small fortune tied up" in a museum on his ranch, decided something must be done about Riverside's retrogression, pointing out the 1896 population had dwindled to 186. He put over the plan of selling the town as a ghost town, building on its heritage to attract tourists the way the two famous Virginia Cities had. He enlisted the aid of the two grocers, tavern, dairy and roofing companies, about the only merchants remaining, and formed the Riverside Historical Association. Memberships were sold for $5, ground broken and plans made for a fine museum town utilizing the large collection of Hixon's ranch.

Mrs. De Tro, of H. De Tro and Co., general merchandise, said, when interviewed in 1963; "Oh, that all fell through. The thing was too optimistic. They planned too big. They spent all their money but couldn't do enough and no tourists came. Mr. Hixon and his wife separated and he moved to Arizona. The ghost town venture is a thing of the past."

OLD RIVER SCENE is often attributed to Riverside but structure showing in right background is Bureau Hotel in Okanogan. Owner Capt. Charles Bureau, more efficient as shipbuilder, constructed steamer *Enterprise* shown at right, piloted by Jack Brown. Other boat is *Chelan*; pilot—Capt. Grey. This picture, as most other old ones in this group, was taken about 1907 by Frank Matsura. He was pathetic little Japanese, arriving in Conconully in 1905. Developing a knack for photography, he gathered simple equipment, recorded hundreds of happenings. He moved to Okanogan in 1907, expanded interest into livelihood, was a lonely figure under racial prejudice. Early one cold Sunday morning about 1913, he was walking down street when he saw open window at back of store and was suspicious. Alerting sheriff, was told to fetch owner living some distance away. Storeman, responding to knock at front door, found Matsura dying on step. Suffering from tuberculosis, he had run all the way and had hemorrhage. Little photographer left behind invaluable heritage of historic pictures.

NIGHTHAWK, WASHINGTON

Hiram Smith, called "Okanogan Smith" by friendly Indians of the Similkameen Valley, was elected to the territorial legislature of Washington in 1860. After serving one term he settled on his ranch near Chesaw, tended his orchard for 40 years and died peacefully, surrounded by his many white and Indian friends. He left a considerable estate with no will in evidence and his affairs were in such a confused state a lawyer was engaged to untangle them.

He did and made a good thing of it—attorney James M. Haggerty of Portland, Oregon. He completed the legal work, established headquarters at Loomis and started a systematic search for mineral prospects.

Not a man to work with his bare hands, Haggerty planned to become a wealthy miner by his wits and he was right. Newspapers of the day stated: "Haggerty appropriated three mining claims which turned out to be good producers." These mines were strung along the Similkameen in an area where nighthawks, sometimes called "bull bats," were very prevalent and the supply center that sprang up here was named for the birds.

The Ruby, Kaaba and the more famous Six Eagle mines were among those developed by Haggerty. Had he confined his activities to them and not let his tongue wag so much when he was drinking, he would have been spared some grief. He had moved from Loomis but liked to visit his former haunts and brag about his success as a mine operator. And if he had only stopped there, accepted some scorn and let it go at that, he would have gained some stature. But he made a fatal mistake one evening in his cups at a Loomis saloon, an ill-timed comment about a mine on the hill above Loomis.

The Palmer Mountain Tunnel mine was of more than doubtful merit and all the local gentry were aware of it. In spite of this, the owners had sent a John Wentworth to Portland to cajole innocent investors into sinking money into the property. The population of Loomis and the mine owners rationalized that selling this stock was not really dishonest, that further development so financed would certainly turn up a rich vein that might be the making of everybody in the town. Gilbert Alder was one of the residents who, while waiting for this to happen, had put in his time farming and raised a crop of sugar cane. The long hot summer matured it enough for Alder to make some molasses and he proudly brought a jug of it to the saloon to show it off.

OLD BARN, says Leo W. Andrus of Nighthawk, was built by father known in community as "Daddy" Andrus. Dating from 1900, venerable structure still serves purpose. International road runs past barn, crosses Similkameen on bridge close by.

RUINS OF OLD NIGHTHAWK MILL are composed, in general, of rusting machinery. Town itself lay in valley in middle distance beside Similkameen River. Surrounding hills are typical of Okanogan Highlands, those near town are sparsely timbered, with heavier stands farther away.

This night he stepped up to the bar, ordered a drink and displayed his jug of black molasses as an example of what the area could produce. Haggerty felt a great urge to push his importance into the conversation and pompously declared:

"Well, it's a good thing Loomis can produce molasses. It'll never turn out any gold from that damn mine."

It would have been better for Haggerty if he had tried to shoot somebody. At his words several men jumped up, threw him to the floor while Alder poured the contents of his jug over the spread-eagled form. Another man rushed upstairs to the business quarters of one of the girls and grabbed her pillow. The cotton slip was quickly split and the feathers shaken in snowy humiliation over the sticky coating of blackstrap.

OLD PICTURE reproduced in Okanogan *Independent* shows group dressed in Sunday best gathered outside Log Cabin Saloon in Chesaw, few miles from Nighthawk. Sign on Chop House at right advertises meals at all hours, 25¢.

Chesaw was mining and farming center, never very large. Main feature was hostelry Bungalow run by hospitable Chinese who gave town name. Bungalow was open to all travelers, owners respected in a day when Orientals were generally despised.

Log Cabin Saloon in Chesaw

NIGHTHAWK HOTEL was built by Ed McNull for drummers in boom days. Later when Nighthawk Mill was running "full blast" Ewing family took it over as boardinghouse for mill workers. It stood vacant for many years near the little grocery store operated for 25 years by Mr. and Mrs. Lynn Sullivan who now live on Palmer Lake a few miles south.

Haggerty was allowed to slither to his feet but was jerked off them and put astride a hitching rail that had been yanked loose and given a rough ride out of town. His face was never seen again in Loomis. Whenever he had business in Spokane, he avoided the town and went by way of Oroville. When he died years later, he asked that he be buried at Nighthawk— "But don't take me through Loomis."

Nighthawk had been built where the ground was level but the main producing mine was across the Similkameen. A footbridge was good enough for the early traffic but when it became inadequate, a ferry was put into operation by William Berry, an observing and enterprising man. After several passengers had asked him: "Where can a fellow get a drink in this town?" he started a saloon with financial help from his brother Joe. It was a success in summer when the dry and dusty wind blew, a success in winter when at forty below a man needed warming.

About the turn of the century the Vancouver, Victoria and Eastern ran its line through Nighthawk and the town looked forward to a rosy future. For a time it seemed to be coming true as all heavy equipment for the mines including that for twelve-mile-distant Loomis, was rail shipped to Nighthawk. This meant freighting lines were based here, large livery stables maintained, as well as hotel, store and several more saloons.

When business of transporting mine equipment and passengers was flourishing, the rail line, a branch of the Wenatchee, Oroville and Great Northern, ran from its connection at Spokane through Danville, Molson, Chesaw, Nighthawk and Hedley, B. C., terminating at Princeton where it connected with the Canadian Pacific. By 1950, the line had been cut to a spur fifty-odd miles long from Oroville to Hedley. Freight was limited to a small amount of farm equipment and produce with a passenger or two now and then, the train coming to Nighthawk twice a week, the engineer always on the lookout for a flag signal that someone wanted to get on. A tiny one-room customs office stood beside the single track.

Now even the Tuesday and Friday arrivals of the train have ceased. The tracks are gone, so is the customs house. There is only one business in Nighthawk now—the little general store.

LOOMIS, WASHINGTON

The first question the judge asked the mammoth lady was: "Did you intend to kill these men?" Her answer put an end to the proceedings. "Hell, no! If I had wanted to kill them, they'd be dead."

It all came about because sheepherders were anxious to get their woolies to summer pasture. Just above Loomis was a regular route by which the animals were moved but obstructing it were several ranches from which permit of access had to be obtained. One of these ranchers was a lady reputed to weigh some four hundred pounds, with a temper to match. One band of sheep moved too slowly across her property and she told the herders to hurry them along. When they still didn't go fast enough to suit her, she got her .30-.30 and sent several shots over the men's heads. They filed a complaint of attempted murder and the sheriff, unaware of the lady's bulk, went after her in his little buggy only to return to town for a dray wagon. After she was released, it was used again to take her home.

The first settlers in the Loomis area operated a large cattle station owned by Phelps Wadleigh and Co. in the early 1870s. In the bitter cold winter of '79-'80 their entire herd of 3,000 head perished, wiping the enterprise out of existence.

While the cattle station operated, helpers had started small farms on the side and when the station was gone, some of them stayed on. One was Alvin Thorpe, a man of experimental nature, a unique type in a day when harsh realities forced pioneers to take the accepted course. He got his supplies the hard way like everybody else, freighting them in, and one bad spot on the route was the crossing of the Columbia River. At this point a "ferry service" was operated by one "Wild Goose Bill," a fleet of three canoes conveying passengers and mail, cattle and horses swimming. On one of his trips Thorpe bought some peanuts to put in a crop. He planted them carefully but none ever came up and he later discovered the nuts had been roasted. He tried it again with green ones, grew several crops at a profit.

A rancher who made a more lasting imprint on history and gave the town its name, was J. H. Loomis who started what became a trading post and then a large general store in a somewhat accidental way. Seeing that many of the ranchers ran out of supplies before fresh shipments came in, he thought he would help them out by laying in extra goods for himself. When his shortsighted neighbors ran out, he would let them have what they needed at cost. Later, when joined by a partner Gus Waring, he was induced to

raise the selling price a little and buy larger amounts next time. The system proved the beginning of a long and profitable business.

Waring was a man of many talents. Educated at Harvard, friend and contemporary of Theodore Roosevelt and Owen Wister, author of *The Virginian*, he tried making a success at architecture in his father's office, gave it up and left for Portland, Oregon, with wife and three children. He worked on a railroad there for a short time and then headed for the Okanogan country, working first as a cowman, then barber, cook and carpenter before settling down as successful partner of Loomis. Their trading post became the largest business in town. Many "characters" of the Okanogan range were customers, two of the most famous being friends of Waring—"Okanogan" Smith and a missionary, called saintly by many, Father de Rouge.

Between Loomis and Oroville are the remains of a home, built in 1860, and orchard of Hiram F. Smith. He was prominent in local affairs, friendly with the Indians who gave him the name, "Okanogan." Elected to the legislature in 1865, he had to go through British Columbia, down the Fraser River by steamboat and cross Puget Sound to reach Olympia, the territorial capital. Returning to the Okanogan, he brought apple and other small fruit trees and peach seeds. These trees still grow at the site, are over forty feet tall, were the first orchard trees in an area now world famous for apple production.

During the early period of ranching in the area, various mines were discovered which gradually pre-empted farming in importance. A variety of metals was found in the hills around Riverside, the Solomon group working on a "huge body of ore" yielding as high as 50 percent lead with silver 25 to 70 ounces per ton along with some copper and gold. Tungsten was also found but ignored until the first World War when that metal came into demand. Other mines included Black Diamond, Whiskey Hill, Bull Frog, Golden Zone, Kit Carson, Six Eagles and Why Not?

Among the more famous was the Pinnacle which had a strange beginning. Original discoveries were made at the site in 1880. The first men to work it got out a lot of gold, took the metal outside to have it melted so it could be sold and never came back, leaving foreman James O'Connel to wonder about them. He waited a decent interval, then relocated the mine. When it was legally his, he named it the Pinnacle and he was soon called Pinnacle Jim. He was a strange, stubborn man. Where others carried six-shooters,

DETAIL OF EARLY TYPE LOG BOOM used for hauling in winter. Mountains around Loomis were once more heavily timbered, most trees of two pine types — Ponderosa and lodge pole. Former are most useful for lumber, latter once used by Indians for lodges, later by whites for cabins and as poles and posts. One of largest early frame structures in Loomis was trading post of Waring and Loomis. As store moved into other quarters, building was remodeled into church, addition of steeple being biggest change. It changed hands under several denominations, was razed in 1958, found to be sealed with 8-inch pine boards, hand-planed.

he carried a bowie knife and occasionally brandished a heavy gold-headed cane.

John O'Hearne was a close friend who became Pinnacle Jim's partner and they got along well except when drinking. One of their bitter arguments started in the saloon of the Wentworth Hotel and Jim rashly asked John outside to settle it. The latter carried a gun and it proved superior to the knife, Pinnacle Jim lying dead at the end of the battle. O'Hearne was tried for murder but freed as having shot in self-defense. Shortly after this came inquiry from a lawyer as to James O'Connel's whereabouts, an uncle having died and left him a large sum.

Such affrays were not uncommon in Loomis. Children sent to the grocery store had strict instructions to walk down the center of the street, not on sidewalks where they would encounter drunks weaving out of saloons and "those terrible painted ladies." They were to continue in a straight line until opposite the grocery and then to make an abrupt turn and go straight in.

Walter Allen who still lives in Loomis tells a story of those early days. "When I was a young man there was a district at the foot of the hill where there were several 'houses.' One of them, the best known, was called 'Big Edith's'. I had a friend who dared me to ride my cayuse right into the parlor and in those days I never backed down from a dare. We went down there on our horses and I rode up the front steps and

through the front door with no trouble. Then I rode through the hall and came to a sort of screen of strings of beads hanging in front of the parlor and started to ride through. When my cayuse felt those beads swishing across her shoulders, she bolted. We went on through the parlor and through the back door that wasn't even open. There was a porch in back, quite high from the ground. My horse turned a somersault and I landed partly under her. Didn't break any bones, but was pretty shaken up."

Mail service encountered some difficulties getting started. The last distribution point was Marcus and when anyone left there for the Loomis area he was given what mail there was and was expected to carry it to town and dump it where it would be claimed by addressees. One young man made the trip rather often and went to the trouble of personally delivering letters, collecting 25 cents for each. It was soon noticed a large amount of the letters were worthless advertisements and inquiry revealed the enterprising youth was furnishing a mailing list to advertisers in Marcus.

Loomis had an official post office after 1888. Judge H. Noyes, who had come out from Springfield, Massachusetts, and bought an interest in the trading post of Waring and Loomis, was first postmaster. A branch office was established for ranchers on a farm owned by Jess Huntley. He was a busy man, abrupt and irascible, and although holding a mail franchise he was unwilling to take the time to wait on people

GAUNT CONCRETE SHELL identified as early power generator for mines, sawmills and crushers, incongruous in now unpopulated area near Loomis. Water provided ample power, was carried down to plant from mountains above by flume, remains showing above structure. After passing through generators inside building, water was carried away through now yawning hole in floor. Small settlement grew up around plant, even a jewelry store operated by Bill Kepp. A laundry was established by Henry Decent so close to the stream it was washed out in the first heavy spring freshet.

or deliver letters. When a bag of mail came in, he would dump it in a large box on the counter and let everyone dig through it. One day he was getting ready to plow and a man asked him to look for a letter he was expecting. Jess retorted sharply—couldn't any damn fool see he was busy and couldn't he look for it himself? The man took offense, reported the incident and the postal authorities wrote a caustic letter to Huntley, ordering him to deliver all letters to patrons and give no back talk. Gathering all mail and equipment into a bag, he drove to the office at Loomis and angrily dumped the contents in the middle of the floor. "There's your damned post office!" he fumed.

There was social life of an elevating sort in Loomis and one cultural influence was a fine band. It was made up to a large extent of men employed in the Palmer Mountain mines. The Company provided tailored uniforms, the band practiced in the Eagles' Hall and performed at affairs in neighboring towns as well, being paid $100 per performance.

While all the mining excitement was going on, there was a steady amount of ranching in the surrounding hills. This did not provide the same sort of thrills that mining did but it had its compensations. There was young Joseph Rice in Spokane who yearned to be a rancher and had ideas of homesteading on Palmer Mountain. He hesitated to ask his sweetheart Helen Fitch to marry him and go to such a wild country but she was willing. They were married in 1903 and homesteaded on Palmer Mountain four and a half miles from Loomis.

At first Joe had to work in Tillman's Sawmill to get started but this was a stroke of fortune as he fell heir to a lot of cull lumber and with it built their first home. Later the couple got enough money for a more pretentious place and the first home became a chickenhouse. Funds for improvement came slowly but Helen and Joe were hard workers, determined to make a success. They planted wheat and in the fall a thresher crew would arrive at the farm on its rounds, the threshers' wives in at the big dinner and carrying

DECAYING RUINS OF CABINS built in 1890s high on Gold Hill above Loomis. Great excitement prevailed when first discoveries were made but cooled somewhat when difficulty of moving ore to mills became evident. John Reed and "Irish" Dan McCauley found gold in a piece of quartz on the steep mountainside about 1890. They had no capital for hard rock mining and sold out to a company naming itself Gold Hill Mining Co. It started operations, had great difficulty getting ore down mountain to mills at Loomis. Road was constructed but washed out at every rain or when snow melted. First enthusiasm generated building of small settlement just prior to turn of century. Gold return was finally judged too small to justify better road or building of mill at site, entire project abandoned around 1910. At present, steep winding road to ruins is badly washed, long hike required to reach remnant of short-lived gold rush. Almost all trees are second growth; virgin stand cut when mining was carried on, was spruce, larch, pines with scattering of Douglas fir.

LOADED FREIGHT WAGONS pulling into Loomis from Oroville — photo in collection of Walter Allen of Loomis. On driver's seat are Mr. and Mrs. Frank Schull. Dick Sutton says: "Frank did a lot of freighting, mostly of ore to Spokane. On the return trips he carried lots of whiskey and wine for the saloons. Some of the saloonkeepers were Jack Long, Jimmie Kenchlow, Johnnie Woodard and George Judd." Man on ground holding dog is identified as Al Carroll. Perambulator is mounted on rear wagon.

away tales of the Rices' baked beans. Helen had her own recipe and grew her own beans from a "start" brought along from Spokane. The variety name for these succulent beans, a little larger than ordinary, was never known. They were just "Helen's Beans."

After wheat was threshed, Helen and Joe made frequent trips south to Tonasket with loads of grain, starting about four in the morning to get to market early. And Helen made thirty loaves of bread at a time, selling them around the area. She kept a large flock of chickens, a six-foot fence protecting them from marauding coyotes. The eggs and churned butter also helped out in income.

The water supply was a spring at the bottom of a very steep slope from the house. After staggering up the bank a few times, Joe rigged up a contraption to ease the situation. He equipped a large wheel from a broken washing machine with a cable to which a bucket was attached. When the wheel was turned, the cable took the bucket down hill and overturned it in the spring. Continued turning of the wheel brought the full bucket back.

The distance to Loomis was usually covered by buggy in summer, sleigh in winter. If the snow was frozen hard, the latter with no brakes could not be used on one steep hill. So Joe would have to walk for the mail. He carried a shovel to open the trail below and to put it to good advantage on the steepest pitch, he sat on the scoop and slid down.

There were other breaks from drudgery. In winter, a little lake higher up Palmer Mountain froze practically solid. The couple cut ice and stored the harvest in an icehouse they built. In summer, ice cream parties were often held, either at the Rice home or neighbors.

Sometimes Helen took horseback rides around the country when she felt the need to get away for a change. Her favorite mount was a mare named Tootsie, brown with three white stockings, and no one else could ride her. The two would have a wonderful time, leaping over logs and low fences.

And the dances at Loomis were the best of all. They danced the favorites like "Black Hawk Waltz" and "Three Step" but there were enough Swede loggers wanting some Hambos and Schottisches. Helen says when one of these Norsemen with a few drinks in him would whirl her around in a Hambo, she could hardly stand for dizziness at the finish.

Once there was a masquerade and she wanted Joe to dress as an Indian. There being no costume rental in those days, she cut a picture of an Indian suit from a mail order catalog and copied it as best she could. She insisted he have long black hair and she achieved this by cutting off the luxurious tail of a white horse, dyeing it black and sewing it to a skull cap. Joe won first prize.

But the homestead was increasingly a burden and after both Joe and Helen had long spells of sickness, they abandoned the old place in 1914. Long years later they realized $120 by selling the property to a sheepman. By then the buildings had fallen into decay and Loomis was declining to the point where all property values were next to nothing.

The last ores were taken from the Palmer Mountain Tunnel mine in 1927 and this marked the finish of Loomis as a going town. It is quietly peaceful today with only a handful of people. Helen Rice, now a widow, lives in Portland and furnished the author with much of the information about the Okanogan area.

RUBY, WASHINGTON

At the height of Ruby's success as a boom town, the Ruby *Miner*, on June 2, 1892, editorialized: "As Virginia City is to Nevada so is Ruby to the State of Washington. Ruby is the only incorporated town in Okanogan County. It is out of debt and has money in the treasury. Public schools are open nine months of the year and are under the management of competent instructors, these furnishing unsurpassed advantages. LET US MAKE SOME MONEY FOR YOU IN RUBY. THIS DISTRICT IS APPROPRIATELY TERMED THE COMSTOCK OF WASHINGTON."

Ruby's first butcher, W. A. Newcomb, was a jolly, friendly man who was popular with the citizens, a fact that served him well later. He was known to have an ample supply of fresh meat and one day somebody found out why. The butcher was a rustler on the side and when cattlemen came into his shop with a rope, he was put under protection of the sheriff and hustled off to Conconully for trial. The guards were friends and being friendly, all got drunk as lords and on the trip Newcomb made an easy escape.

County commissioners held a special meeting, the second in Ruby's history, to vote a reward of $500— and hoped the townspeople would match it—for the capture of the butcher-rustler. Notice of the reward was posted in Ruby, advertised in the Portland *Oregonian*, Seattle *Post-Intelligencer*, Walla Walla *Statesman* and Victoria (B.C.) *Colonist*.

Whether or not the reward was responsible, Newcomb was apprehended and brought back to Ruby. Tempers of cattlemen had now cooled enough to try him in a local court, where he was judged not guilty and freed, jurors being friends of the affable Mr. Newcomb. His experience apparently chastened him and he afterward bought his beef.

As a silver town Ruby had a series of booms and relapses as new discoveries were made and old ones faded out. It was a raw-edged town with little regard for law and order. On one occasion a few town toughs were idling on a bench outside Billie Dawson's hotel when the stage pulled in with a stranger on top. He was wearing a white plug hat, the like of which had never been seen in these parts. Lounger Len Armstrong bet Al Thorpe, considered a crack shot, that he couldn't put a bullet through the trick top piece without hitting the head under it. Without hesitation Thorpe drew his gun and fired, putting a neat hole in the upper crown. When the visitor protested at the violent reception to Ruby, Thorpe apologized and set up the drinks.

The same hotel was the setting for another shooting incident when Jonathan Bourne, who had spent half a million in his silver mine which was currently in low production, found he couldn't meet the payroll. A crowd of irate miners assembled outside the hotel and, not knowing which room Bourne lived in, shot out all the windows.

Bert Comstock ran a saloon in Ruby; John Bartlett, a store. The former had eyes for Bartlett's wife and she responded. The pair left town together; in a few days Bartlett's body was found in his store, dead apparently by suicide. The fleeing couple had take the Bartletts' baby daughter with them and when she reached fifteen, Comstock deserted the mother and married the child.

Ruby shared Indian troubles with Conconully. Walter Brown had a dairy between the towns, delivering milk to both. He attended a Fourth of July celebration in Ruby, arriving just in time to witness an atrocity. An Indian brave name Pokamiakin, as handsome as he was bold and brash, came into the crowd with a fast horse he had stolen, well-known race horse, Nespilim. Sheriff Bill Tiffany ordered the Indian to dismount and submit to arrest but the brave refused and spurred the animal into a spurt. Tiffany galloped alongside him, grabbed Pokamiakin by his long, black hair and dragged him along the ground. Dairyman Brown, in telling the story, said the crowd was sure every bone in the Indian's body was broken but he got to his feet running. In the hail of bullets, both he and the horse were killed.

Winter snows were cruel to towns in the area, avalanches frequent and crippling the mining camps situated at the bottom of steep slopes. One such slide in Ruby crashed down on an engineer named Magee and his two helpers who were pinned under a flume, which fortunately allowed them to breathe and saved their lives. Not so lucky was a young Ruby man who taught school in Conconully. He was buried in a slide on his way to the school, found dead in the big snow pile.

Richard Price, later scheduled to preside over the never-held trial of lynched Indian Steve, was sent into the area by the Indian service to make a survey on all white men who had Indian wives. He was to determine nationality, tribal connections of women, number of children, wealth and social standing of couples. It was never revealed what purpose the survey was to serve, but it gained good results for Price. He was justice of peace in Ruby and a well-versed counsellor on Indian affairs.

HOTEL BUREAU in nearby, hated rival city, Okanogan, was long time in building since builder, Charles Bureau, described as "handsome Frenchman," was too busy with many girl friends in Portland. Started about 1900, hotel was still unfinished in '20s when Bureau died. Four-horse stage regularly covered route from Oroville to the north, calling at Riverside as last stop before Okanogan.

BANK ROBBER LEROY, alias Charles Ray or Andrew Morgan, shown in newspaper photograph with Sheriff "Baldy" Charles McLean after capture by Sheriff Fred Thorp. Prisoner shows desperate gleam in eyes even in poorly reproduced photo, also wounded finger. Likely LeRoy was even then planning escape which took place soon after.

LOG CABIN ON JOHNSON CREEK, where in 1888 first Okanogan county commissioners held meetings under confusion due to fact county seat was undetermined. Delegations from Ruby and Conconully gathered in separate camps outside cabin to carry on campaigns, Ruby delegation promising office space free from taxes, Conconully five acres of land for county buildings. Stimulating refreshment caused boisterous demonstrations, Ruby people forming circle around cabin, dancing and shouting —"Ruby for County Seat!" Decision went to Ruby, lasted for 11 months, then to Conconully until 1914.

OLD RUBY pictured in only known photo, has been completely ravaged by time, fire and vandalism. No building remains in lusty, boisterous town called "Babylon of the West." Ruby was early county seat, had no office buildings or safe. County treasurer found himself in tough town with county funds of $1,800, placed money in can, buried it at his ranch. Although some gold and considerable copper were mined here, Ruby depended on silver and silver crash of 1893 sent camp rapidly downhill. Remaining residents moved to one-time rival, Conconully.

CONCONULLY, WASHINGTON

It was high drama even for the raw West. Sheriff's deputy, Pete Barker did not like the looks of the stranger watching the L. L. Work Bank in Conconully. He told Sheriff Fred Thorp the fellow was far too interested in the bank's workings. Thorp took a good look at the man but could not get worked up over the idea of arresting him for doing nothing. By chance a man-wanted poster came in the next day depicting Frank LeRoy, wanted in the east for burglary. The face was that of the stranger.

Thorp found him in the Morris Saloon playing pool with his back to the door. With his .45 at the man's back, he said quietly: "I'd like to search you, if you don't mind." LeRoy swung around and said: "Sure." Then starting to open his jacket, he jerked a pistol from a shoulder holster and fired. The bullet went wild and LeRoy went into a fast dance, making himself such a difficult target Thorp's first shot also missed, his second taking off a finger, making LeRoy drop the pistol.

He broke for the door, drawing another gun from a second holster with his left hand. Another shot from Thorp caught the fugitive in the right shoulder. He spun around and dropped. While the sheriff was grabbing another gun, LeRoy gained his feet and ran staggering up Salmon Creek. He quickly collapsed, blood running from his mouth. He was carried to the jail on an old barn door.

While waiting for Dr. Polk, a search of the man and his belongings revealed two more guns, a set of burglar tools and some loot from a recent robbery in Brewster nearby. The doctor reported the patient would live but recommended he be locked up. The "maximum security" cell was without heat and as a bed patient, LeRoy was put in an outer room and given watchful care for about nine days. His guard was then lightened but in reality the burglar was feigning extreme weakness. Aware of tools in a closet, he got into the sleeping jailer's room one night, stole shoes, overalls and a blanket which he wrapped around himself Indian fashion and faded into the night. This was November 7, 1909.

LeRoy got safely to the nearby mining camp of Ruby, got a long-bladed butcher knife and at the home of Casper Miller demanded an outfit of clothes and probably some food. During the next three days Sheriff Thorp tracked him to a clump of sagebrush near the little community of Malott, leveled his rifle at the fugitive and gave him a choice: "Come out with your hands up or be blown to Kingdom Come." LeRoy stood with his hands high cursing: "If I had anything but this knife, I'd kill you right now!" Tried for burglary, he was adjudged a habitual criminal and sent to the state penitentiary at Walla Walla for 99 years. He was later paroled.

Although the Conconully jail later developed many weak spots, it was planned for strength. At one of the first county commissioner meetings careful details were specified for the detention of future prisoners. The jail was to be built of "two by six scantlings, spiked together—spikes to be not more than six inches apart." Orders were placed for 24 pairs of hand-

JURY PANEL at trial in 1906 on front steps of courthouse, photo owned by Helen Rice. Her brother George, top row, third from left, worked for freighting outfit, hauling logs on sled through town when load overturned on bridge over Salmon Creek, was tapped for jury duty while ruefully surveying wreckage. Standing at extreme left, top row, is Judge Hartew. Next, Mr. Gibson, then young Fitch, next to him, Bill Sproul. Next is unidentified, then Ham Pinkerton. Man leaning against post is unknown, next and final two are Ed Sayles and Bill Gamble. Of the front row only two are identified — at left, standing with hand on rail is Mr. Jay. At right, man with interlaced fingers is Joe Pinkerton.

"STREET SCENE ON SUNDAY," another of Frank Matsura's vivid pictures of Conconully in bygone era. Note raised sidewalk giving pedestrians some protection from mud and snow. No protection was possible when Salmon Creek flooded down main street. Wave more than 50 feet high was known to come down canyon after mountain cloudburst.

In May of 1892 one such disaster swept many buildings down street ending up as wreckage on huge delta of sand also carried by waters. Safe was washed out of one building, never found. One woman, safely out of home, missed her glasses, rushed back to get them, was swept away with house, body later found in wreckage, hand still clutching precious spectacles.

cuffs and three pairs of shackles complete with chains and 24-pound balls.

Nevertheless, from its building about 1891 to the time the courthouse was wrecked about 1915, the pokey suffered ridicule and abuse because of frequent escapes. Early one spring when snow was beginning to melt and the ditch under the lockup was filled with icy water, two thieves were incarcerated and told they could build themselves a fire in the stove. Instead, they built it on the floor and when the flames had eaten into the boards enough to weaken them, the men took a plank and poked out an opening over the ditch. The first man got down with no difficulty but the second was so fat he stuck midway. His friend came back to poke the hole bigger and pull the fat man down through.

One Sam Albright heard two of his friends were lodged in the famous calaboose and came to Conconully with another friend, Clint Williams, to have a chat with the prisoners. The visitors found the jailer absent, unlatched a window and climbed in. The reunited foursome had a friendly game of stud, after which the callers gave the inmates some books and candy and departed the way they had come, relatching the window.

Proprietor Gibson of the store of that name in Conconully tells of a jail break with a different twist, when Ben Snowden was jailer. "Old Ben had three fellows in there, one named Kallentyne. When Ben took their food in, one of the men was doubled up on the floor like he was sick and Ben set the food down to go and see what was the matter with him." It seems the jailer always kept a rifle hanging on the corridor side of the door and the prisoners knew it. When Ben bent over, the two on their feet ran for their gun while the one on the floor held Ben. The rifle came cracking down on his skull, almost killing him, and the three took off, hiding in the brush at the edge of the lake. Sheriff Thorp quickly organized a posse and surrounded the patch of willows and aspen trees.

When he demanded the fugitives' surrender, the man with the gun threatened to shoot anyone who moved closer. Thorp was a man of courage and strode forward, but there was no shot—the gun had jammed in the beating of old Ben. The three walked out meekly and were returned to jail.

Then there was the day in January, 1891, when Indian Steve was jerked from the same jail by a howling mob of drunken miners. They tied his hands behind his back, blindfolded him and forced him down the road to a large tree. A heavy limb stuck out horizontally about fifteen feet up and a rope was thrown over it, the other made into a noose which was

PICTURE MADE IN 1962 shows town in opposite direction of early-day photo. Historic courthouse stood in grove of pines at bottom center. Comparatively new church is at right on site of earlier one destroyed by fire. Indian name of Conconully meant "clouds" or anything threatening, in this case monster supposed to live in lake of same name. Sparsely pine-clad hills are typical of Okanogan Highlands, large section of north-central Washington, extending into British Columbia. Modern camp ground and State Park are at right of picture. Lake teems with regularly planted trout, mostly rainbows averaging 8 to 11 inches.

looped around Steve's neck. The lynchers hauled him into the air, jerking him up and down. The body swayed there a day or two and then the rope was cut off, the tied end remaining until the tree was cut down in 1938.

This lynching and other incidents were part of the "Conconully Indian Scare." The government restricting of the Indian population to the nearby Colville Reservation was difficult or impossible to enforce, the natives making sporadic forays into Conconully and neighboring Ruby, Tonasket and Loomis.

They were suspected at once when the dead body of C. S. Cole, driver for the freight line between Okanogan and Conconully, was found near the road near the close of 1890, wagon rolled over the cliff and horses gone. There were no clues until a squaw who loitered around Conconully began spreading rumors that Indian Johnny and his friend Indian Steve had done the deed. Asked why she would inform on Johnny, her "fella," she said she had tried to get him to marry her but he would not. She said one reason he had picked Cole, aside from stealing the horses, was that the freighter had poked fun at the Indian about his feeble attempts to raise a mustache.

Deputy Ives took off after the pair of braves who he heard were at an encampment near Chilliwhist. Johnny saw him first, drew a gun and fired, the bullet grazing Ives' cheek. The deputy's shot was more deadly, hitting the Indian in the head and killing him.

During the gunfires a squaw was wounded, which further angered the sullen tribesmen. Bad feeling was so strong Ives decided not to look for Indian Steve and get out as soon as possible. He said later that as he rode away he could imagine guns aimed at his back, making his flesh crawl, but he escaped unmolested.

Word was soon sent to the camp that Steve had better give himself up before there was more trouble, and on January 5, 1891, he surrendered to the sheriff in Conconully. He was placed in jail and Judge Price, who knew Indian ways and thinking, started an investigation before trial. The next week the Ruby *Miner* was to print this ambiguous note:

"Last Thursday morning twenty horsemen galloped through Ruby, the soft white snow muffling the sound of their horses' hooves and the slumber of the camp was not disturbed by their movements. Death was in their hearts and they sped remorselessly onward." Jailer Thomas Dickson had been warned by the judge of the strong possibility of a lynching and when he saw the mob approaching, he hid the cell key under his mattress. The mob soon found it, opened the door and dragged Indian Steve to his death. This item appeared in the Ruby *Miner* the following week:

"Trouble is on foot and danger stalks abroad. It is principally owing to the lynching of Steve that this condition exists—but there are many supplemental reasons. George Monk accompanied by Smitkin started to convey the body to the Indian Mission. The Indians claim that Monk, when he started out, was sitting on the corpse which was wrapped in a blanket and carried on a single bobsled. The appearance of the body was the signal for the start of a big dance. For two days the body was kept while the Indians stimulated themselves at the bier."

The lynching did intensify matters. It was now rumored Indians were gathering in the mountains for mass attacks on Conconully. Another report had it that every man, woman and child would be killed and scalped in vengeance for the deaths of Johnny and Steve. Alarm grew to the point that citizens appealed to the U.S. Army for help.

In response, on January 17, 1891, Gen. A. P. Curry arrived with a detachment of soldiers and an arsenal for use of residents in case of attack. One hundred eighty rifles and 3,000 rounds of ammunition were stacked in the courthouse. When no raid developed, the guns were stored in an unused room where they gathered dust for many years.

In the beginning, Indians trapped beavers in the area, selling the pelts at a good profit and calling the valley Sklow Outiman or Money Hole. The first whites were prospectors who founded Salmon City on Salmon Creek.

In March of 1888 the newly organized board of Okanogan County Commissioners met in a log barn

OVERALL VIEW OF CONCONULLY taken about 1905 as shown in old newspaper, Conconully *Record* in real estate plug with list of merchants. Main business section is at lower right, courthouse at base of hill, left of center; public grade school at left. Salmon Creek is seen flowing parallel to road in lower right. Site of hanging of Indian Steve is along same road at extreme bottom center. Church shown here just below courthouse was destroyed by fire, replacement built on same site shows at lower right of modern photo.

on the farm of John Perkins at the head of Johnson Creek near the booming mining camps of Ruby City and Salmon City, four miles apart. George Huley, later mayor of Ruby City was one member, Guy Waring, pioneer merchant of Loomis, another. Next day, the 7th, another meeting was held at which members read petitions from both towns pleading the right to be the county seat. Ruby City won out and the committee left the log barn to meet in Ruby. By November, Salmon City had changed its name to Conconully and, the population of both towns having swelled enormously, an election was held to decide which city should now have the county seat. Conconully got 357 votes to Ruby's 157, and the commissioners again switched locations.

About 1900 there was a strong movement to change the seat to Riverside, that town doing the promoting and Conconully sitting back. The latter town had an elegant courthouse, built by the famous Steven Cloud and sheltering a safe that weighed a ton and a half with a time lock unequalled in the country. The Riverside effort failed.

One of the first county treasurers was Andrew J. Nickel, earning $125 a month, his wife having campaigned with him and getting $75 as deputy. Mrs. Nickel had spent several months driving around the county in a light buggy drawn by ponies Peter and Peggy, had talked to every man encountered on the road, passing out campaign literature and a card. After the election, she related her embarrassment when the newspapers in 1914 with the local high school footponies continued to stop at the sight of every man on the road.

A freighter named Brown used a buggy with two horses when the load of supplies and mail was light. On the road steeply descending to Conconully by a series of switchbacks, his progress was blocked by a snowslide. As he unhitched his horses to lead them around, one struggled into the deep snow and vanished. Brown led the other one down the hill and just before arriving in Conconully, met the other animal which had floundered safely down.

A stage line ran between Conconully and Oroville with bearskin coats and foot warmers as standard equipment to keep passengers from freezing to death in winter. But in November of 1904 which had been deceptively warm, the driver did not take the coats and warmers along. A large group of teachers took the stage in Oroville for Teachers' Institute in Conconully, all wearing light clothes. During the meeting the temperature plummeted to below zero. On the way home men and women teachers had to huddle together under a few blankets and at each way stop to change horses on the eight-hour trip, they were taken into the stage depot and thawed out.

Disastrous floods and fires plagued Conconully as well as avalanches and Indians. Superstitious residents recalled the invective screamed from the knoll above town by a bitter miner who had been rolled in a bawdy house. "Curses on you, damned Conconully! May you burn, be drowned and burned again!"

In spite of the silver panic of 1893, the town kept going in a limited way. It made headlines in area newspapers in 1914 with the local high school football team called "Terror of the Okanogan" but other headlines the same year proclaimed the end of the old camp. The proud position of county seat was surrendered to the now more prosperous town of Okanogan.

The old courthouse was torn down, the lumber used to build a little city hall. The jail was removed, leaving on the site the two concrete and rock vaults— and now even these have crumbled to a large extent. One has visible evidence of bars which were used as added protection for legal documents. Visitors and prowlers for historical remains are usually happy in the delusion they have found the famous Conconully jail which actually was a frame structure.

A third substantial vault remaining near the present little post office belonged to the bank which bandit LeRoy was so intently watching before he was caught. The huge livery stable stood until about 1958 when it was razed. A tiny, false-front, one-room building which served as a plant of the Conconully *Record* was torn down about the same time.

The area is now a State Park with a fine campground having all modern facilities even to automatic laundry machines. It is situated in an aspen grove on sand brought down the canyon by Salmon Creek in flood times. In the center of a landscaped park is a replica of the little log cabin in which the original county commissioners met. Trout fishing in the lake and reservoir is rated among the best in the state.

FAMOUS HOOSEGOW in Conconully, long since vanished, was butt of ridicule because of frequent prisoner escapes but did keep many prisoners in custody. Was located near courthouse which can be seen in overall photo of town. Section at left confined prisoners; quarters for jailer, at right.

PIT HOUSE. CONCONULLY, WN. FRANK MURSUROS PHOTO.

ORIGINAL PHOTO OF CONCO-NULLY COURTHOUSE was picture post card taken in 1905 by little Japanese photographer, Frank Matsura; property of Mrs. R. Brunke who still lives in old silver camp. View from balcony was superb, looking out over piney mountains and Conconully Lake. In winter, when frozen, lengthy stretch of water served as part of highway to "outside," eliminating difficult and dangerous avalanche-beset road.

STONE HOUSE dates from Conconully's early roistering days as does tenant. He walks down steep trail to tavern each day, wearing pair of six guns as he has for fifty years. These are checked at door, returned when old gentleman leaves.

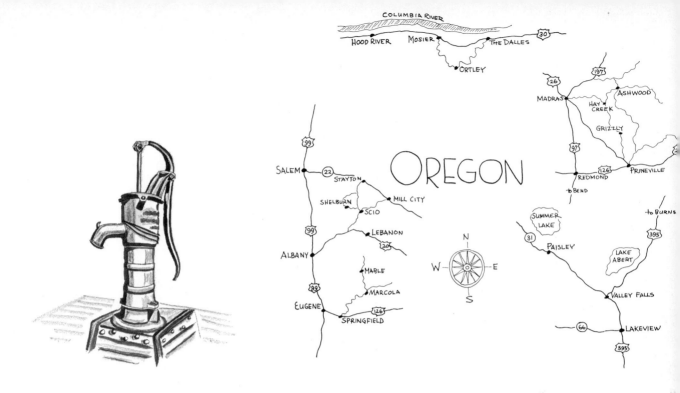

PAISLEY, OREGON

All is quiet on the Paisley front. With the sawmill shut down, the general lethargy of the little town was sharpened to the edge of frustration. Credit at the general store became a problem although people did seem to have enough money to drink at the tavern. But idleness was only incidental the day big trouble came. It started at the post office, shattering the quiet with gunfire and murder.

Postmistress Mrs. Anita Bannister, a grandmother at forty-one, saw the two men come in the door. "They were dressed like cowboys," she said, " and seemed drunk, asking silly questions. They both carried guns and I was worried."

The men staggered through the knot of loungers, then suddenly one of them stiffened, shifted his gun and demanded the "payroll." The second man, Jesse Thurman Hibdon, who had formerly worked in the Paisley sawmill and was unaware that it had closed and there was no payroll, moved back toward the door. One of the trapped onlookers was too quick, breaking outside.

"The first bandit was still threatening me," recalled Mrs. Bannister, "and kept shouting, 'I'm goin' to blow yer brains out.' I told him there was no payroll and I guess he finally believed it, poking me and saying— 'You want to see yer family again? Give us all the the money you got.'

"He jabbed the gun barrel into my head and told me not to look at his face. I gave him everything, our V.F.W. money and even the postal orders. He handed it all to Hibdon who ran to the door and

yelled—'Let's get out of here! One of them's escaped already.' But the man holding the gun at my head didn't go. He said, 'I'm goin' to think about this a few minutes' and I was sure I was going to be killed."

Now there was a shotgun blast outside and Donald Lee Ferguson who was still holding his gun at Mrs. Bannister's head, dropped it and ran outside. A man lay bleeding in the doorway and from the car with motor running Hibdon screamed—"Come on, hurry up!" Ferguson piled in and the car took off.

The man who had escaped from the post office earlier saw 65-year-old Troy Lawson with a rifle. It was the deer season and the plumber, like every other man in Paisley, was never far from a gun. Lawson ran toward the post office and, about to go in, turned to warn a woman—Mrs. Norman Carlon with baby Lana in her arms—"Get away or you'll get hurt!" The hesitation was fatal. As Lawson turned, he exposed himself to Hibdon in the car and received a shower of lead pellets in his abdomen. As he dropped, a second blast from Hibdon's gun ripped a big hole in the side of the building. Mrs. Bannister had followed Ferguson outside and later recounted: "Although the women inside were crying all the time of the holdup, I didn't—until I went outside and found Troy dead."

All available townsmen quickly gathered into a posse, every member armed with a deer rifle. One remained in town to telephone Summer Lake Lodge, thirty miles up the road the car had taken, to arrange for a roadblock.

When the bandits came to the makeshift barricade

they swung the car off the road in a desperate effort to clear it, but crashed into the boulders below the rimrock about a hundred yards from the highway. Then the posse arrived, swarming up the hillside. Logging truck driver Doug Houston, 25, sent a shot that nailed Ferguson behind a boulder. "I told him to come out but he fired and almost got me. Then he stepped out and I let him have it in the arm. He was thirty yards away and I could have killed him but didn't have the nerve."

Houston then ran up to the wounded man who had dropped in a pool of his own blood and was trying to reach his gun. Houston kicked it away as his grandfather came up. "Ferguson made a pass for grandpa's rifle and I hit him over the head with the butt of mine. He didn't go down so I hit him again. That's all there was to it."

Hibdon had escaped into the sagebrush and disappeared into the juniper-covered, boulder-strewn hills. Next day at dawn an armed group made a systematic search of Paisley on the chance Hibdon had circled back to get some shelter and food. The hunt widened into the surrounding area, every farm combed, every haystack stabbed with pitchforks. Famed bloodhound man, Norman Wilson, brought his dogs from Dallas to help and once one of them seemed to have picked up a trail but no lead developed.

All this time Hibdon was slogging over the hills to the northeast, keeping out of sight of the highway. Nearing exhaustion and starvation, he reached the Jack Pine Motel about ten miles south of La Pine. He asked the proprietor, William Schabener, if he could rent a cabin, saying his car had broken down. Suspicious of his appearance and actions, Schabener refused and alerted the State Police. Officer William Aveline tried to follow Hibdon's trail through the brush but lost it.

The robbery and murder had taken place on Thursday. The next Tuesday, Harold J. Broderick, 50, fire chief of Hammond, was hunting deer in the area with his two sons, Harold, Jr., and Pat. They had worked north from Paisley where they learned of the trouble. Broderick was about three-quarters of a mile from the Jack Pine Motel when he saw a man walking furtively among the pine trees. "He must have heard me," Broderick said of his experience, "and started going faster, almost breaking into a run. I had my rifle aimed at him and shouted to him to halt." Hibdon did and, surrendering, allowed himself to be walked back to camp where he was given the drink of water he asked for.

"He must have gulped down a quart," said Broderick, "like a horse in the desert." The fire chief had a siren on his pickup and wound it up. The boys came running. Tying Hibdon to the tailgate, they drove to the motel and called the State Police. Hibdon

MAIN STREET OF PAISLEY conforms to State Highway 31, only road through town. Peaceful setting was scene of violence when post office (center) was held up and citizen shot to death. Jagged hole in wall made by second blast can be seen in lower boards at left of deposit box. Post office saw lighter incident later. For more than 20 years after-hours patrons had dropped mail in slot in building front. Some letters, instead of sliding completely through, fell to floor between walls, accumulating until October, 1961. Then R. G. Greene was hired to modernize mail deposit and on opening wall, discovered old cards and letters. When Anita Bannister, postmistress, was told of it "she darned near fainted" said Greene. Her comment: "I thought everyone in town would be mad at me but they took it right good." Postal authorities made effort to deliver lost mail even though postage had become insufficient. At least one letter would be late, regardless. It was from a mother who wrote her daughter 20 years earlier just before Thanksgiving Day: "Please bring the cream for the pie."

offered no resistance, obviously at the end of his endurance. He had walked over 150 miles in common oxford shoes over a rugged terrain. When asked what he had eaten, he said: "I had a quart of milk" but that was the only question he would answer. That evening he was back in Paisley where he was identified by burns on his legs received in a gasoline fire some years before.

He joined Ferguson in the jail at nearby Lakeview and later confessed it was he who had fired the shot that killed Lawson. Both men were sentenced to life imprisonment. After its brief excursion into violence, Paisley dropped back into its rut of peace. The townspeople still patronize its general store, post office and tavern and do not expect to see another holdup.

WALL OF PAISLEY POST OFFICE is still scarred by effects of shot gun blast, one of two fired by would-be bandit. First was lethal, second hit wall.

TOWER CARRIES BELL rung in all emergencies, particularly fire. Paisley Mercantile is only store and, like old Chewaucan Hotel, shows signs of decay. Town was plagued by spring floods when rising temperatures released ice-blocked Chewaucan River. Ice would jam against bridges, divert rising waters into farms and town. *Morning Oregonian*, Portland newspaper of Feb. 4, 1951, said: "The ice-jammed waters of the Chewaucan River have been channeled back into the river bed and this Lake County community is totaling the flood damage. The Forest Service blasted a channel from near the Adams Mill bridge to the Z.B. ranch. . . . Icy waters that covered pasture lands and flooded homes did considerable damage, Bob Parker of Paisley Mercantile said."

MILL STREET runs at right angles to Main, between post office and Chewaucan Hotel. Hostelry, long unused, was named for marsh and the river emptying into it. Word "chewaucan" derived from two Klamath Indian words — *tchua*, a swamp root variously known in Oregon and Washington as *wapato*, sagitaria and arrowhead, and *keni*, a general suffix meaning locality or place. At right is post office with fraternal hall above serving several lodges. Ubiquitous poplar trees stand bare in early March, lit by near-setting sun.

MABEL, OREGON

When the Ritters arrived in Mabel in 1912 they were aghast. The little town was wide open, as the minister understood the term, composed of about five hundred roistering loggers and sawmill workers, most of them single, to whom a church meant one place where you couldn't blow off steam.

The Mabel men lived in bunkhouses and ate in several big chow houses supplied by the main cook-house. When a meal was ready the head cook would send a flunky with an iron bar to beat a tattoo on a triangle hanging outside the door, called the "gut hammer." Then the fellow would have to jump back like a chipmunk or have boot hobs up and down his spine. One flunky, it is said, varied the humdrum three notes by some jazzy tune. They were more careful of him when they rushed the door and he lived long enough to set chokers.

This was the ungodly setting the Herman H. Ritters were called upon to enlighten. He and Mary Elizabeth Nedrow were married in Illinois in 1894 and moved to Pennsylvania where Herman had his first job teaching in a country school. At the start of his four-day week, he walked nine miles to the little building, boarding with one farm family and another and then walking home Thursday evening. He taught sixty-one pupils on a salary of $25 a month. Each four days away from home cost $1.50 so it was a meagre existence.

In search of something better, the young couple migrated to Kansas, then Oklahoma and on to California. Teaching in small schools barely kept body and soul together but somehow young Ritter managed to study for the ministry and was ordained in the Church of the Brethren. His first call was the little

CHURCH OF THE BRETHREN. Brother Herman H. Ritter, with wife Mary Elizabeth, lived in Mabel 42 years, preaching last sermon in little church in September, 1953. Following January, couple was honored by community at nearby Mohawk Grange. Party planners were hard put to decide on gifts as Ritters lived austerely and luxury items would be out of place. *Eugene Register-Guard* story was written at this stage of uncertainty and item on January 31, 1954 read: "Their tastes are simple, their needs few indeed, since they have abiding faith, happy hearts and health surprising for their years, besides their own snug home and garden, fowls and a cow. (At the latest the committee seemed to favor an electric blanket.)" Reverend Ritter was ordained at early age of 18.

church in the raw timber town of Mabel and he preached there for nearly fifty years.

The place boomed during World War I, hitting a stride never again equalled. The Coast Fork Lumber Company ran two eight-hour shifts in the mill and turned out up to 180,000 feet of lumber in each. This was the wildest period in Mabel's history for the hard-working, hard-living, well-paid loggers and saw-mill men were going to relax when they felt like it, especially on Saturday nights, come hell or high water. Some went to Eugene a few miles south "to get their teeth fixed" but they could do a passable job of "blowing her in" right at home. The more genteel loggers who had regular girls in Mabel would save choice pieces of pitchy wood to take along on a courting cruise. Somehow an armful of fat pine seemed more appropriate than a handful of wild flowers and if they got the cold shoulder they could always throw more wood on the fire and keep warm.

Once settled into the community, the Ritters enjoyed learning about its history. The heavily timbered valley saw its first whites when a small party headed by Jacob Spores pursued a band of marauding Indians into the area in 1849. Losing their quarry, the men stood on a hill and surveyed the virgin stands of Douglas fir running down to the shining river. Spores, a native of Montgomery County, New York, was reminded of the Mohawk River back home and named this new one for it.

In 1870 a small clearing was hacked out of the wilderness about three miles above the entrance of Shotgun Creek into the Mohawk and a sawmill was built to turn out boards for cabins along the stream. By 1878 a community had grown up around the small mill, large enough to require a post office, the first official being Alfred Drury. His second daughter was named Mabel and so was the little town.

R. W. Earnest, now of Marcola nearby, remembers the first site of the town. "Around 1906 my parents took me as a small child to pick blackberries around the ruins of the old Fields mill." By that time the timber had been cut out and Mabel was moved to its present location. Mr. Earnest treasures memories of the area, among his keepsakes the "gut hammer" from the cookhouse.

In 1957 U. S. Congressman Norblad announced plans for closing six small Oregon post offices to save money. "A good example," he said, "is the one at Mabel, Lane County, where there are only six families to serve. The post office receipts are about $280 a year and the cost to the government $2,300."

In addition to his work as minister, Herman Ritter had taken care of the postmaster duties. When he relinquished these at 70, he turned them over to a woman who held the job for a year. Then Mrs. Mildred Gwynn took over and had been postmistress for fifteen years when the closure came. She took down the Mabel Post Office sign from the small lean-to at her residence, thus ending a service unbroken for 78 years.

MASSIVE RUINS OF POWER PLANT of huge Coast Fork Lumber Co. operated during World War I. Furnace remains, boiler and other metal parts salvaged for war effort. Built about 1910, mill was closed in '28 when Robert Dollar Co. foreclosed, third mill on this site. Earliest was Hyland, started before turn of century. It burned, was followed by Sunset Lumber Co. mill. Closure of Coast Fork operation spelled doom to Mabel's prosperity. Several other mills were active in area at various times, some with water power, one with wheel in Shotgun Creek. Larger one had saws driven by water of Mohawk River.

ASHWOOD, OREGON

"A volcanic butte and an early day family gave the ghost town of Ashwood, on Trout Creek in Jefferson County, its name," relates Phil F. Brogan, whose father owned a stock ranch seven miles east. "Near the site of the bustling village of the Oregon King mine days is Ash Butte. Settling close to it in the 1870s was Whitfield T. Wood and when the post office was established in 1898 the name of the butte was combined with that of the pioneer. The town grew on both sides of Trout Creek, spanned by a footbridge occasionally washed out by freshets, and into it for supplies and mail came ranchers from the range country.

"I remember all this as it was shortly after the turn of the century, with memories of riding into town from the east as a small boy to get the mail and pick up a few groceries. I can still hear the echoes of my horse's shod feet as we entered the big livery stable where the pony was rested and fed before starting home. When I walked past the open doors of saloons on warm summer days, I saw inside men standing at bars back of which were big mirrors. I have other memories of freight trains moving through town, headed for the end of the rails at Shaniko."

This part of central Oregon has a turbulent geological history. The area was covered at different times by lava flows and deposits of volcanic ash, layer by layer. As erosion progressed, many remains of long-extinct animals have been recovered which add to the store of valuable fossils in museums throughout the country. At the edge of one vast expanse of juniper trees, sagebrush and scanty grasses stands the prominent eroded cone which is Ash Butte, its sides covered by caked pumice and ash.

At the base of it, a promising region attracted pioneer Wood into settling there. The first spring

TYPICAL FALSE FRONTS of Ashwood's day. Saloon at left was one of several serving thirsty miners, ranch men and cattle drivers. Street once had small newspaper plant, printing weekly Ashwood *Prospector*, one of chain owned by Max Lueddeman. Editorials were embellished by florid prophecies of future wealth and productivity of Ashwood's mines and ranches. Town would grow to be "the metropolis of central Oregon . . . greatest producer of mercury ever known."

ASH BUTTE GRANGE for many years center of community affairs and even yet swept out for rare dances or celebrations. Was originally largest saloon in area, ground floor having bar on one side, small dance floor on other. Saturday nights saw wild times when cowboys, ranchers and miners "blew her in." Traces of windows upstairs can be seen. These opened into rooms for occupancy of short duration.

the little stream close by was a bountiful source of good water, the skies sunny and the soil soft and easily worked. But as spring became summer, hope became disillusionment. The stream shriveled and disappeared. The soil, composed largely of clay, turned as hard as concrete. Frosts persisted until late in the spring, freezing nights began in late summer. Discouraged at trying to farm in the face of these difficulties, Wood turned to raising cattle, a venture somewhat more successful, and soon the solitary rancher had neighbors, some as close as ten miles away.

"On a blustery March 27, 1897," recounts Phil Brogan, "Thomas J. Brown, herding sheep in a gulley leading into Trout Creek picked up a piece of quartz from a brushy, rocky slope. It proved rich in silver and free gold. Soon a mine boom town, with its frontier saloons, hotels, livery stables and stores, took shape on the floor of Trout Creek about three miles from the mine, and became Ashwood. It was not a wild pioneer town. On Trout Creek to the west, a lonely cove reminded the villagers that pioneer days were past. In that cove, the raider chief Paulina died under gunfire many years before to end the Indian unrest in the area."

The Oregon King mine gave Ashwood its start but there were other big producers in the Morning Star and Red Jacket as well as several lesser ones. With no smelters or milling facilities at hand, the ore was shipped out. There was talk of building a stamp mill and smelter, the weekly Ashwood *Prospector* pushing the project, but signs of the veins pinching out appeared and no backers were to be found. As ores became lower in assay values, and in quantity as well, the town settled into a period of doldrums, enlivened only slightly by occasional periods of mining.

Then came the discovery and working of a vein of cinnabar over Horseheaven way and since Ashwood was the supply center, it revived and sat up. But quicksilver in paying quantities did not pour forth for long. The company pulled out all its machinery, leaving the building to shrivel in the sun. The blight spread to Ashwood, which never recovered.

Brogan feels a bit wistful when he realizes Ashwood holds few of its buildings of pioneer days. "Gone are the livery stables, the hotels, stores and homes built close to the edge of Trout Creek. Most were lost in fires. Ashwood was a town of one main street with winding roads serving as side streets. One led past the Woods' orchard to the Axehandle highlands. One headed upstream to the T. H. Hamilton ranch and the big ranches near the head of the creek. Still another was routed down creek to the Columbus, Friend and Howard Maupin ranches, and up Little Trout Creek to Prineville."

Today the town has an open, sun-washed look. Magpies fly across the dirt road which is the main street and coyotes close in at night.

BLEAK, FORLORN ASHWOOD SCHOOL stands on knoll, surrounded by typical junipers, only trees of desert regions of Oregon. Cupola had bell which rang well in advance of schooltime, its peals reaching far across sagebrush hills, warning tardy pupils walking several miles. Schoolyard, surrounded by barbed wire fence, once held usual two outhouses.

SHELBURN, OREGON

In the old graveyard on the hill there are stones dating back to the 1850s, more from the '60s, the decade in which a cholera epidemic carried away so many of the early settlers in this section of the fertile Willamette Valley.

By the time the '90s arrived, the need for some sort of centralization of stores, school and a post office became obvious and several buildings were erected around the old blacksmith shop. This authentic gem of the false-front period of western architecture is still standing though the roof leaks and windows lack glass. With the establishing of a post office in June, 1890, a name for the town had to be selected.

Two of the leading citizens, Shelton and Washburn, were honored by having parts of their names spliced together to form the title, Shelburn.

Sawmills sprang up in this land of virgin fir and spruce and the railroad came to haul out their products as well as potatoes and farm produce. A large hotel was built and operated by Stanley Strylewicz who, for some reason, was simply called Stan. J. R. Moses was the lone barber for several years and if there was anything going on he didn't know about, "it hadn't happened yet," as one oldtimer puts it. A large dancehall was erected and on Saturday nights the sawmill hands and farmers performed the two-

ED ZINK, now gnarled and grizzled, was born on farm in 1879 before Shelburn was a town. With his older brother Eph, he lives in small shack built from lumber salvaged from old home which had begun to disintegrate and was hard to heat. "Eph and I worked in the sawmills as long as they were running," he says, "then did some farming on the old place. We used to think we could get jobs in Shelburn but the old place is sort of going downhill now."

step and Black Hawk waltz with their ladies. The perfect serenity of this was altered by the weekly thirst build-up. Because of a rash of accidents in the sawmill, hard liquor was forbidden there and the men slaked their thirsts at the Saturday night hoe down. Dances were often interrupted by drunken brawls and several bullet holes in the wall of the hall remain as evidence of broken romances.

When the surrounding timber was cut out, the mills began to close down. The once healthy potatoes developed a scabby disease and train stops were made only for passengers to buy bread and cheese for lunch. With the coming of the automobile, Shelburn residents went to Salem or Stayton for many of their needs and the local stores dropped away.

Today the place is almost deserted. The dancehall, having suffered ignominy as a chickenhouse, now stands empty. And yet not silent. Metal feeders, hanging on their wires, creak and groan with the vagrant winds sweeping through the glassless windows.

BLACKSMITH SHOP, oldest building in Shelburn, dates from early 1890s. Many horses in logging and farming made it one of busiest in new community. Concern also sold and repaired harness gear, saddles and bridles, later became supply center for farm equipment, growing into general store when mechanized equipment and "tin lizzie" caused blacksmithing to fall off. Little "wing" served as millinery shop, early phone office and residence. Roof is deteriorating in heavy rain of Willamette Valley, building having small chance for long survival.

MRS. BLATCHFORD OF MOLLALA, Oregon, recalls gala day when new school opened. Then Ethel Ogelsbee, she was smaller of two little girls in white Mother Hubbards at lower right. "We had two rooms and two teachers. Millie Jester, upper center, taught the little pupils; Bill Miller, right, the older ones, some of whom were pretty big. We loved them both and hoped they would fall in love and be married, but they never did."

LITTLE STRUCTURE IS NOW abandoned except as it is used for hay storage. Cupola, once adorning it, was long since blown off in wind, roof repaired. Huge oaks, characteristic of the Willamette Valley, form background.

CASTLE CITY, MONTANA

It was one thing for a Castle City joy girl to get drunk in a saloon and dance on the bar. That was accepted as normal any night. What did throw everybody off stride was to see one come into the post office cold sober just after the morning mail arrived, peer questioningly into every face and gum her wrath: "Which one of you dirty Cousin Jacks was up in my room with me last night? I lost my choppers and I want 'em back!"

It is not known just who took Mabel's teeth but it was probably not one of the four Hensley brothers who figured prominently in the early days of Castle City. Isaac H. was the first to arrive in the area, going to Fort Benton in 1875 after freighting between there and Helena and wanting to settle down on a farm. Next brother to join him was F. L. (Lafe) who had been working at the N. P. Hills smelter in Black Hawk, Colorado, acquiring some knowledge of minerals and mining. In 1877 he and Ike took up a homestead on the Yellowstone five miles below the present town of Columbus, calling the ranch "The Rapids." Next year the other two brothers joined them.

In those times when you couldn't work at your regular job you went prospecting. When the ground was frozen and the Hensley brothers couldn't farm, they took off separately to "look around." Lafe took his friend G. K. Robertson with him into the Castle Mountains, then nameless. There was little snow that winter, the ground was exposed during the week the pair were there, and one of them picked up a chunk of float which caused them to hurry to the Wickes smelter. The piece of galena was rich in lead and silver when assayed.

The discovery ridge was called Yellowstone by the Hensley brothers who now abandoned their ranch and located a group of mines on the steep slope. The

one proving most successful was the big Cumberland, with the Yellowstone, Morning Star, Belle of the Castles, La Mar and Cholla only slightly less spectacular. On top of the ridge were several domed lava protrusions soon called "The Castles" as were the ridge and town.

In the spring of 1887 the Hensleys bonded the Cumberland claim for $50,000 but when time came to pay up, only half that was available. To cover the rest, a half interest was deeded to the bondsmen, Tom Ash and J. R. King of Billings. Later the brothers disposed of their half to B. R. Sherman and Charles E. Severence.

Ores from the Cumberland and mines still held by the brothers were being shipped to Livingston by freight wagons at the prohibitive cost of $13 a ton. The Hensleys thought they saw a golden opportunity for profits and built a smelter in Castle at a cost of $25,000, but a hard and fast truth soon became evident. Coke for the smelter had to be freighted in, costing as much as to send the ore out. The smelter was forced to close in ten months but during that period it had reduced 13,000 tons of ore, producing bullion valued at $494,906.44—according to some penny-minded bookkeeper.

The usual problem of transportation was made tenable by using oxen for hauling freight. The Indians, having plenty of buffalo to eat, considered the bull teams no great prizes, so did not kill or steal them as they did horses.

Richard A. Harlow, a far-seeing man who had come to Helena a year or so before, envisioned a fortune for himself when he heard of the difficulties of getting the rich ores to and from processing plants. He started a railroad called the Montana Midland to run from Helena to Canyon Ferry on the Missouri River, then east to White Sulphur Springs, Leadboro

and Castle. The grade had been completed as far as the river when the Northern Pacific, sensing an extension eastward as a possible competitor, made Harlow a proposition—they to furnish rolling stock, rails and other equipment if he would tie into a place called Lombard, between Helena and the junction of their tracks, with the Butte branch farther south. Harlow accepted and ran tracks up 16 Mile Creek toward the booming lead and silver mines. The new railroad was first termed the "Montana," soon referred to familiarly as the "Jawbone." Financial difficulties and the tough terrain prevented the new line from getting farther than halfway up the canyon and there it ended for many a day.

While all this was going on, Castle was booming in spite of transportation troubles, soon reaching a peak population of more than 2,000. Main business district was centered along a street running parallel with Allabaugh Creek, the residential district of a plateau above. An ample timber supply and good sawmill made lumber available and most residences were of frame construction, many ornamented with fancy barge boards and the gingerbread of the day, all coming from the local mill, with the interior walls of better houses finished with lath and plaster. So rapid was the town's growth such a fancy domicile might have one next to it built of crudely cut and fitted logs dating from the "pioneer period" only two and three years earlier.

Grocers and other merchants took advantage of the returning freight teams to bring in shoes, clothing and millinery. Although Castle had its full quota of saloons and bawdy houses so necessary to mining camp survival, it had its refinements too.

There were so many social clubs editor and publisher Shelby Eli Dillard was moved to remark in his weekly *The Whole Truth* in January, 1893: "It appears that the people of Castle will be compelled to petition to the proper tribunal to have at least two nights added to the week to accommodate various whist clubs and parties, dances, spelling bees and other society affairs in our town."

There was a great deal of gambling and carousing in saloons and dancehalls especially after payday, the 20th, but strangely enough in the entire history of Castle, there never was a fatality resulting from a gunfight or other violence. Many did die from "La Grippe" in cold winters and wet thawing springs and from frequent mine accidents. Deep ruts still show along the hillside, marking the trail made by the be-plumed black hearse on its way to the old cemetery.

One story is told about a new undertaker in Castle. A man in poor circumstances had been killed in an explosion in the Cumberland. A collection was taken up for the widow and a nice funeral which included a suit of clothes for the victim. After the service the undertaker suggested postponing burial until the day following as the road up the hill might be less icy. One curious individual, wondering why another day might be better when it froze every night, slipped in the back door of the "parlor" next to the furniture store and caught the undertaker removing the new suit from the body.

Everyone expected a solid future for Castle. A two-story school was built on the "plateau," the only level spot in town, and staffed by good teachers from Helena and Livingston. Several large hotels and rooming houses went up along Allabaugh Creek, one with a room 20 x 40 feet, furnished dormitory-style with rows of cots each surrounded by netting to discourage petty thievery. This room was called the "Ram Pasture."

Editor Dillard was militant in his optimism concerning Castle and its future. In one issue he stated: "The man who thinks Castle is not destined to be the greatest lead and silver camp in the land has a head on his shoulders as peaked as that of a roan mule." When news of gold strikes on the Klondike began to disturb the even tenor of life in Castle, he apparently was getting ground vibrations that some solid citizens might leave for the gold fields. He wrote: "Castle is the lead and silver Klondike of Imperial Montana. There is no one in Castle inoculated with the virus of Klondike gold." Next week *The Whole Truth* hammered these thoughts home with such gems as: "We had rather be a livid corpse in Castle than to own Alaska and all the sordid gold in the auriferous Klondike Country!"

It was at this period that Calamity Jane came to Castle to run a restaurant. With her was a little girl, daughter of the soldier father in Texas, one of Calamity's many "husbands." Her current name was Mrs. Burke, and she may have had a legal spouse by that name. She had tried the restaurant business elsewhere, losing out because of drunken escapades. In Castle she was determined to lead a circumspect life, putting on the act for the benefit of business and daughter.

Yet she still felt the urge to cut loose and when this complusion came on she went to some nearby town for a few days. One of these episodes was in Gilt Edge. She found herself a man and was heading for a handy barn when the wife saw the pair and ran them off with a pitchfork. Calamity ended up in a saloon, always a haven, and was soon drunk. The sheriff picked her up and, the jail being full of men whose welfare he was sworn to guard, he locked her up in a shed.

Next morning a small boy came by carrying milk for a neighbor and Calamity called to him, slipping a

BETTER HOMES, built during rush of prosperity, stood in elegant district on "plateau" near level area, in contrast to simple log houses sandwiched in between. Most famous ghost would be that of Lady Rosslyn, born Anna Robinson, daughter of George Robinson, early prospector who settled in Castle in '78. In her late teens Anna worked two years as a waitress in mother's boardinghouse, then before silver crash in '93 family moved back to Minneapolis. With "remarkably sweet voice" Anna went on to sing in Charles Frohman's production of *Shenandoah*, starred in musical comedies, went to London where Duke of Manchester and King Leopold of Belgium paid her court. At height of success, she was friend of Harry Thaw but became bride of Earl of Rosslyn in London in 1905, settling $10,000 on him. Earl lost money at Monte Carlo, Anna divorcing him two years later. She appeared on stage occasionally, losing fortune as she aged. She died in state hospital for insane at Ward's Island about 1912.

silver dollar through a crack in the door, telling him to get her a bottle of whiskey. He let the bottle down to her through a hole above the door and kept the four-bits change.

Released, Calamity returned to Castle, retrieved the little girl from a friend in a bawdy house and settled down to business. And then she had a strong urge to return to Deadwood. Taking her daughter, she hitched a ride to the boom town in the Black Hills. She was welcomed but forced to turn the girl over to the Sisters of St. Martin's Academy at Sturgis. A benefit was staged for her at the most disreputable saloon and dancehall, the Green Front, a purse collected which Calamity spent on drinks for the crowd.

Meanwhile an event was brewing in Washington that had grim forebodings for the silver camp in the Castle Mountains. President Cleveland called for a special session of Congress and after a long and bitter struggle, a bill was passed in October of 1893 which, under the Sherman Act, stopped all purchases of silver. This demonetized the metal and although the struggle for its reinstatement on a bi-metal standard was lengthy and violent and echoed around the world, it was all for naught. Castle began to go downhill.

Yet through this disaster and the accompanying panic, the Jawbone Railroad was completed. One mine in Castle, presumed to be the Cumberland, had more than $240,000 worth of ore on the dump. Jawbone officials saw a good thing in this and interested the owners of the East Helena smelter in sampling the idle ore. The smelter firm agreed to take it at a set price, the ore owners taking stock in the railroad for the same amount.

The Jawbone was thus pulled along on a shoestring and its workers the same, laying rails for meagre wages which they were glad to get when others were starving. When the railroad reached a point near Castle, the ore was loaded and shipped to the Helena smelter.

With a railroad at its front door, Castle now had realized its fondest dream but the victory was hollow. It did not pay to mine silver and only lead was left. Editor Dillard doggedly assured the people that the town would survive and become greater than ever. His brave editorials continued but gradually became less vociferous. "It is serenely tranquil at the present writing but God, in His Infinite Goodness, will take care of us and see that we get our taters and bacon, whether school keeps or not. It is so serene and calm in this great silver and lead camp you can hear your thoughts walk out on your imagination and sit down on the sofa of your brain." Sometime later he wrote: "It is so quiet here in this great future camp that the squeaking noise in the prospector's coffee mill sounds like the rumblings of Old Faithful in the national park—trying to throw up its volcanic liver for the amusement of pink-foot visitors from the effete east." One of the last pathetic items was short: "There are plenty of excellent mining claims in this camp which can be leased on good terms."

When the price of lead dropped, the camp was finished. The last whistle blew at the last mine and even *The Whole Truth*, faced with a deficit of $4,000 was forced to give up. The exodus of population was rapid, every person in town leaving for greener pastures in a few months—except two faithful old retainers who clung to the vain hope that life would return.

Joe Martino was one. He came to Castle as a charcoal burner for the smelter and when it closed down he worked as a freighter out of Dorsey, later returning to Castle. The other was also named Joe—

Joe Kidd. He was a native of Williamsburg, Pennsylvania, where one of his grade school classmates had been Charles M. Schwab who went on to become a steel magnate. Kidd arrived in Castle about 1888, always working in the mines. While Martino had a little log house near the upper end of the gulch, Kidd lived in another at the lower end and was known for years as "Mayor of Castle."

February of 1938 saw the last chapter in the camp's life. Snow that winter had piled up to unusual depths and when it looked as though another heavy fall was on its way, Joe Kidd thought he had better get down to Lennep, six miles away, and stock up on groceries. With his horse he made it safely to the village but on his way back a blizzard caught him, his horse blundering away, Joe staggering on foot to Martino's cabin. He warmed up, divided his food with his friend and pushed on. His body was found in the drifts, frozen hard.

Joe Martino was now Castle's sole surviving resident and he kept up his lonely and hopeless vigil another year, finally consenting to be taken down to the State Hospital at Warm Springs where he soon died. Castle had only ghosts and memories.

CASTLE HAD SEVERAL BROTHELS accepted as necessary adjunct to mining camp. Only well preserved one is shown in background discreetly separated from fashionable residence section. Houses still standing in fair condition invariably have stone foundations as at left. All lumber, shingles and wooden ornaments came from nearby mill; fireplace and chimney bricks also of local origin.

SOME OLD HOMES of better construction are remarkably well preserved. One in center has lath and plaster walls, delicately tinted, different color in each room, now falling away in places. Doors still open and shut but rusty hinges creak, stair treads groan, mountain rats thump their tails. When breezes play through glassless windows shreds of curtains sigh, wispy shingles on roof rustle softly. Remains of boardwalks sink into moist ground; cooling chambers under kitchen floors, often full of icy water, had shelves for perishables.

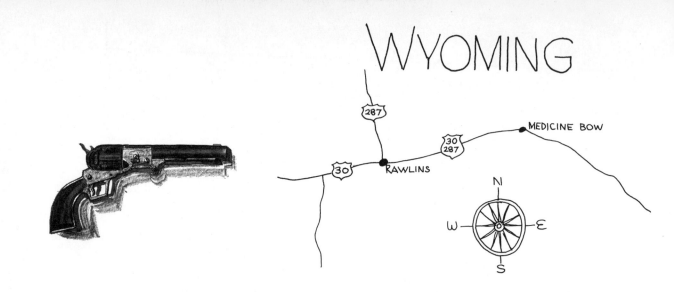

MEDICINE BOW, WYOMING

As tough as pine knots and woe be to the weakest, the tie hacks of the Wyoming woods were all that fabled lumberjacks ever were. They had hides like goats and smelled worse with long underwear buttoned up tight from freeze-up to spring thaw. In the woods they called the wild cats cousins and slammed double-bitted axes at the pitchy timber to pile up ties for the transcontinental railroad. In town this lusty vigor went to downing fiery rot gut and rowdy women.

When these men herded swarms of ties down river to the sorting booms and were paid off for the trip, they headed for the nearest saloons where all hell was likely to break loose at the sound of calks on man's shins. Irish, Swede and Norwegian tie hacks with names like Knuckles Ecklund, Deaf Charley, Syrup Strand, Cross-eyed Johnson, Lefty Hjalmar, and Whiskers Einar had money and a place to spend it. Hang tight to the bar!

Soapy Dale was foreman of a gang of them on the upper Medicine Bow River. He knew all the pokeys in towns all over the west, especially the one where they gave him no food for two days and he ate the bar of yellow cell soap.

As soon as Soapy and his fifty men had their ties safely in the corral a mile above Medicine Bow, the legend goes, they drank up their welcome in the first saloon and headed for the next. Wearing this out, they took a fancy to a loaded freight car standing alone on the tracks. Prying the door open, they started unloading when the depot agent heard the noises. He opened his window, letting out a yell, the boisterous tie hacks greeting him with balls of mud. When the agent slammed the window shut, the fun seemed to be over and the roistering crew, feeling massive pangs of hunger, swooped down on the eating house at the eastern edge of town. It was almost time for the train

crews to eat and their meals were ready, steaks sizzling and a big pot of coffee simmering on the wood range. The sides of the building bulged when Soapy and the wild bunch pushed in and loudly demanded all the food. When the cook protested, well-aimed shots punctured the coffee pot, an amber steam pouring out on the hot stove. Tables were shoved catawumpus to suit the whims of the drunken men as the trembling cook brought out the platters. The shooting continued, shattering window glass and chimneys of the swinging kerosene lamps.

Steaks were attacked with a deep-woods gusto. One man held a porterhouse at arm's length and fired several shots through it, yelling: "This critter's still alive! I saw it move!" Before the last bone was flung at the cook's head, he escaped among broken dishes and chairs, running to the depot where a dispatch for help was sent to headquarters. A special car arrived hours later by which time Soapy and his hatchet men were safely away and sobering up. But he was a worried man, realizing the jam they would all be in over the damage caused. His solution was to collect as much money as he could from the crew, dress up in his best clothes and present himself at the scene of carnage. Some railroad officials were there surveying the wreckage. "I beg yore pardon, sirs," Soapy began. "I own a spankin' big spread of sheep over yonder and I just hear some of my herders strayed off the reservation and cut up some last night. What's the damages, pardner?" Neither cook nor agent recognized Soapy in his Sunday clothes and everybody was appeased, if not fully happy. Sheep must have been in as well as on Soapy Dale's mind for at the last report he was herding them at the age of 91 in the Big Bend country.

Medicine Bow came into being when the Central

BUILDING AT RIGHT was built for Medicine Bow State Bank about 1911, was purchased in 1919 by syndicate of ranchers and stockmen and known as Stockman's State Bank until closure. Open spaces across street were once occupied by large livery stable and general store, latter with long counter which served as bed for Owen Wister during his stay in Medicine Bow while localing novel *The Virginian*. Book was published in 1902, Medicine Bow holding huge celebration on its anniversary in '52.

Pacific and Union Pacific Railroads were creeping across the vast plains of Wyoming, headed for the inviting bend of the Medicine River. Indians here found "mountain birch" excellent for making bows which were "good medicine" and the mountains were so named.

A railroad station was maintained here so water could be pumped from the river and a tank supply kept handy for the engines. The first agent and telegraph operator at the new depot was Oscar Collister. For several years he watched other buildings spring up around the station and saw a town develop as it became a shipping center for cattle and wool. Indians did not see eye to eye with the settlers and saw the railroad as their worst enemy, despoiling the ranges and streams and bringing more hated white men and their cursed sheep and cattle. Twice the raw frontier town was attacked, one siege lasting so long settlers ran out of food, finally rescued by an army detachment from Fort Steele.

At this period there were two saloons where dry-throated cowboys and herders could get refreshment. Railway men had to enter on the sly as such emporiums were off limits. The first general store was owned by J. L. Klinkenbeard and a small hotel was put up. It had a small dining room, the overflow of customers being taken care of at the eating place in the Union Pacific station. Medicine Bow was incorporated in 1909 with August Grimm as the first mayor, the town having a drugstore owned by Thomas Johns. The Hotel Virginian was erected in 1913, the finest hotel in the state with wall decorations done by cowboy artist C. M. Russell, the opening in September of that year. The main event of the gala affair was

an all-night ball and the next morning saw Medicine Bow with a gigantic headache. A sawmill was built at the edge of town and nearby a lumber yard.

The place seemed to be hold-up prone, among those recorded being a saloon and train robberies. In the first "a big fat man" was drinking with the others in the Home Ranch saloon and he suddenly pulled a gun. He ordered the bartender to hand over all the money in the till, gathered it up, backed out the door and was never heard of again.

Less fortunate was William Carlisle. He escaped from the state penitentiary after serving a few years of a life sentence for holding up two different trains. On November 8, 1919, he tried it again, robbing No. 19 when it stopped at the Medicine Bow station. He got his money and made good his escape. For the next two weeks the town seethed with excitement, curiosity seekers thronging in, taxing the hotels to the utmost as they were already full of law men. Train officials and police tried to get clues with little success and even the army stepped in, a company from Fort D. A. Russell riding up ready to pursue the miscreant. Everybody went home several weeks later when it was learned Carlisle had been apprehended on a ranch in the Laramie Mountains and returned to prison.

Medicine Bow will always be proud that Owen Wister gathered atmosphere and data there for his book *The Virginian*. He rode for the Two Bar ranch long enough to get the feel of the wide open spaces and the background that helped make his book so popular. The town still has some population but the wild old days are gone.

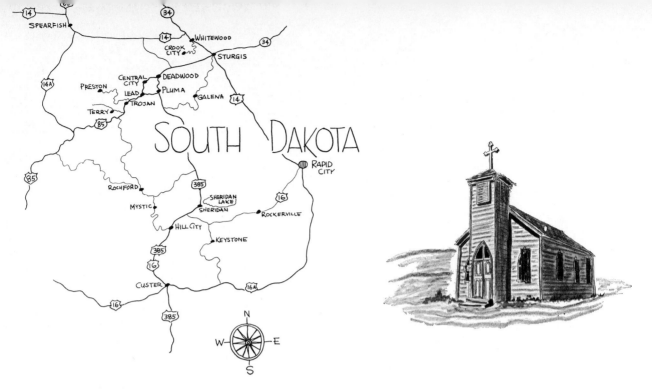

CROOK CITY, SOUTH DAKOTA

On a hot August day in 1876 a wildly yelling band of Indians rode into Crook City. They charged down the main street, raising great clouds of dust and screaming like banshees. All untethered horses jerked away from the water troughs and oat buckets and galloped for the hills. The Indians then rounded them up and vanished.

Most miners were working their claims but those in town who were prudent enough to have hitched their horses quickly organized a posse and went after the raiders. One of these was young Felix Rooney from Pennsylvania. Always a maverick, Felix did not join the main group of pursuers but took a boy with him on a private search on the hill opposite. He soon spotted what seemed to be a band of several Indians on the next ridge and sent his young companion back to Crook City for his field glasses. Then an old bullwhacker friend came along and the two squatted in the tall grass to watch.

Suddenly Rooney's horse snorted. Both men jumped up to see a Sioux brave attempting to drive the animal out of cover, apparently thinking the horse was one of those stampeded from town. In Felix' words: "The Indian already had a Colt in his hand and aimed at me. Before I could draw my gun I heard a blast and thought I was hit, sprawling on the ground. In an instant I realized I was not hurt, drew my gun and sprang up. The Indian was on the ground, dead. The report I heard was not from his gun but from my friend's, who had dropped the redskin before he was able to fire at me." By this time the boy came up with Rooney's glasses but the figures

on the other hill had gone. The three whites left the dead Indian where he was and continued their search for others.

While the brave's body was still warm, a Mexican prospector came riding by, dismounted and cut off the head which he fastened to the horn of his saddle. He hurried on to nearby Deadwood expecting to collect a bounty and being greedy, schemed to get more.

At the head of Deadwood's main street he spurred his horse to a gallop and shouted that an Indian massacre was on its way. This was all it took to gather a crowd sensitive to the red scares. The Mexican told of meeting a Sioux party on its way to ravage Deadwood, of killing the leader, whereupon the others had fled to regroup. He held up the head, still dripping blood as proof. Grateful citizens soon had a hatful of money collected, some $60.

The swarthy prospector then repaired to the nearest saloon where he bent his elbow as long as he could keep it on the bar. His new and grateful friends helped him on his horse and he started back to Crook City. But he had taken one too many for the road. His bleary eyes failed to spot a band of redmen near the trail but it is likely he felt the arrow. It entered his chest to end his short career of high finance.

When Gen. Crook had camped on the banks of Whitewood Creek the previous winter, one of his men reported gold in the stream and the town had grown up in a few months. Before two years had passed Crook City boasted a population of 2,000, several hundred houses whacked up from whipsawn lumber, logs or native stone. There was even a newspaper, the Crook City *Tribune,* and in 1879 it stated the placers in Whitewood Creek were "inexhaustible. Crook City is destined to become the first city of the Black Hills." Later it clamed: "The projected railroad to Deadwood will come directly through Crook City."

Such optimism was unfounded, for when railroad surveyors looked over the terrain they discovered the high ridge which separated the city from Deadwood, which isolated the camp and made it such an easy chance for Indian attacks, also prevented the building of a level railroad grade.

With their town passed up by trains and dismayed by the discovery that gold in Whitewood Creek was limited after all, people began to move to Deadwood and the newer camp of Whitewood on the rail line, and Crook City became a ghost so nebulous it almost vanished from the scene.

FIREHOUSE of Central Golden and Terraville Hose Co. stands exactly as it did in hectic period of Central City's boom days. Initial letters of formidable name are almost obliterated from front. Belfry still holds bell, hose tower stands intact. At the time, Muriel Wolle painted water color of old structure which appears in her book *The Bonanza Trail* with her description— "It was full of old apparatus, two hose carts, several long ladders, a two-wheeled dolly on which equipment could be loaded and drawn to the blaze by members of the company."

CROOK CITY SCHOOL was solidly built of native stone, taught children of farmers in area until school bus era. Community claimed the distinction of being first to make use of school system, set up by Territory of Dakota. Crook City was isolated from nearby "big brother" Deadwood's protection and constantly harassed by Indians. When men of Wagner family living near site of schoolhouse returned from working in stream bed, they found Indians had raided home, killed three members of family. Pregnant wife of one was scalped and thrown in front yard, iron ox goad driven through her abdomen.

CENTRAL CITY, SOUTH DAKOTA

Lawrence Bellevue, operating a successful restaurant in Central City, was a "burned child" when it came to fire prevention. He had good reason to be one, having lost a restaurant in an earlier gold camp which had gone up in smoke. Acutely aware of what happens when a blaze gets going in a bunch of tinder-dry, wooden structures, he kept up a constant ranting to his help to be careful about dumping ashes from the huge wood range, to be careful about storing "coal oil" for the lamps, to be careful about securing the flimsy metal stove pipes where they came up through the wooden roof.

He had business to take care of in town one day and left his eating house for an hour or so. On his return he turned the corner to see flames shooting from his building. Turning tail, he put on a burst of speed heading out of camp and never came back.

Most of Central City was razed in the resulting conflagration—a disaster, since many of the buildings destroyed were brand new, built after the savage flood in '83. In that year Deadwood Creek, fed by melting snows and warm rains, spilled out such a volume of muddy water as to wash away the placer operations and all buildings in the gulch. New structures were soon erected on any stone foundations remaining but when fire destroyed them, owners gave up. Many of the foundations can still be seen.

The town was actually kept up by several small placer diggings in Deadwood Creek. By the start of 1877 the populace was beginning to see that by combining the scattered communities, a nucleus of stores, schools and saloons could be economically built. On January 20 a meeting was held and a system of city government set up. When time came to select a name for the new camp, a man with some weight in the community was ready. He was I. V. Skidmore, fresh from Central City, Colorado. His suggestion of the same name for the raw town in Dakota Territory was eagerly accepted.

Shortly before the gold rush to the Black Hills, by way of flaunting the federal government's edict that there was to be no gold hunting in that area, a reporter on the Sioux City *Times* wrote many overoptimistic articles about the chances of fortunes to be found there. They fanned the flame of gold fever to such a white heat many a prospector rushed headlong for the Hills and fell victim to Indian scalping knives or was arrested by government authorities for defying the ban. Collins wrote that anyone could pick up nut-sized nuggets by the dozen "in any one of the clear flowing streams in the Black Hills." His dream was to exploit this gold for his Irish friends to use in throwing off the "English yoke over the old sod." The articles did incite the Russell Expedition and many smaller ones, all suffering ignominy in being recalled by government forces.

Although Collins' far-fetched schemes fell flat, his writing had so impressed his own electric nature he had to see for himself when migration was allowed into the Black Hills. He left his steady job to set out for Central City and actually did try to pan the waters of Deadwood Creek. After getting only a lame back, he gave up for the more remunerative and imaginative work of a reporter.

Although the camp was already being served by the *Herald*, published from 1877 to 1881, Russell started a paper of his own, the *Champion* which managed to keep its head above water for a year. Then came the *Enterprise*, also with a year's life, then the more enduring *Register*.

During its heyday, the town supported 3,000 people, an Opera House, several hotels and churches. It also suffered from many troubles between miners and mine owners. On one occasion when the Keets mine did not meet the payroll, irate miners took over the diggings, stocked them with provisions, ensconced themselves comfortably inside and waited for their money. When no threats would dislodge them, a detachment of soldiers from Camp Sturgis was sent for. When this proved ineffectual, the sheriff had an idea. He made up some sulphur bombs and dropped several lighted ones in a connecting shaft. Gasping and choking, the miners came out to the last man.

Injuries and fatalities resulted from other fights. One man, involved in labor troubles, lost his hearing from concussion when a set blast went off in the tunnel where he was hiding. In the same fracas a man named Tuttle was killed in an attempted dynamiting of the Keets mine.

During the boom days the main hotel in Central City was an elegant house called the Shannon, after the owner. He had long suspected his lovely, younger wife of "playing around" with a certain camp dandy, one Giddings. Shannon stood it as long as he could and then oiled up his six-shooter. Not concerned about his reputation as a poor shot, he set out to get

Giddings. Walking into the lobby one day, he unexpectedly saw his man and opened fire. Several shots missed and Giddings escaped out a side door, ran around the building and in the front door. More shots shattered the big lobby mirror but still Giddings remained unscathed.

A friend of Shannon's named Jack tried to stop the attack by stepping in front of Giddings and received a fatal wound. The pursuit continued around the corner once more when the quarry tiring, stumbled and fell. Shannon ran up, placed the barrel against the dude's chest and dispatched him. Only one more bullet remained and Shannon took it, saying before he died—"Boys, bring me a glass of whiskey."

OLD STONE AND STUCCO BUILDING has withstood flood and fire, second floor used as fraternal hall. Venerable structure is now serving as rock shop of amiable Jim Hill. One of Central City's oldest inhabitants at 80, he is still actively collecting, cutting and polishing ore and mineral specimens. Often engaging in long conversations with other rock hounds, he tells about a chunk of unlikely looking rock which served to hold the shop door open on hot summer days. "One day a prospector stopped to gas a little. He glanced down at the rock and then looked harder. Then he says, 'Jim, do you mind if we crack that in two?' So I set it on the cracking block and fetched it a good one with my sledge. Well, sir, it broke right across and guess what was in the middle of it — a nugget of pure gold shaped like a kettle complete with legs and handle. It weighed nearly three ounces."

LEAD, SOUTH DAKOTA

The original Lead (pronounced Leed) is a true ghost. The first business district is now a grassy, flowering park next to the highway, a short distance from the spectacular open cut, long abandoned. So many tunnels and workings undermined the townsite that buildings began to cave with the ground, were abandoned and razed.

The Homestake mine at Lead has been one of the largest and longest producing gold mines of the world, surpassing the output of the famed Cripple Creek area in the late 1930s. Most of the $550 million in gold produced in the Black Hills since 1875 has come from this single mine.

First discovery of yellow particles near the site gave no indication of such a potential. They were meager and disappointed the finders along Bobtail and Gold Run Gulches which drain the Terraville area, the former emptying into Deadwood Creek, the latter into Whitewood Creek at Pluma.

About the only value in the scant rewards of the creek sands was that they made prospectors search the banks for quartz leads. Two Mexican brothers, Moses and Fred Manuel, with partner Hank Harney, located the Homestake claim April 9, 1876. There were many others also, including the Pierce, Lincoln, Independence, Old Abe, Big Missouri, Golden Star, Highland Giant and within a few weeks that hectic spring so many men were at work that some system of streets became necessary. A meeting was held and Lead City was established, the "City" being dropped four years later.

That July, 1876, saw a system of government established. Since no legal status could be secured in this still trackless wilderness, a part of the Sioux Indian Nation, simple rules were set up, two officers elected—Secretary Charles Jones and Recorder James D. Coffin. A sort of universal law regarding miners' claims was recognized and simple justice carried out

OLD LUTHERAN CHURCH was ordered to be torn down and replaced by modern structure but hue and cry went up to save it. Telephoto view from open cut across canyon shows church, above it silver gray tower of Ross hoist shaft of Homestake mine. Little of mine shows above ground, many miles of shafts and tunnels honeycombing rocky earth beneath.

in cases of disagreements, thievery or murder. The simple plan had to be amplified soon, a mayor added, one Cyrus Enos. A school system was set up by Frank Abt, a bank headed by R. H. Driscoll, Drs. D. K. Dickinson and J. W. Freeman imported.

Streets were laid out and named, designations clearly reflecting the times and surroundings—Pine, Galena, Mill and Gold. Even the width of these thoroughfares was established—amply wide for two buggies to pass. Soon the road from Deadwood by way of Poorman Gulch was jammed with traffic. Pack trains of mules or oxen vied for space with stagecoaches and freight wagons. A new road had to be hacked out, called Washington Addition, emerging into Gold Run Canyon at Pluma.

It was known federal law frowned on the practice of placing townsites on mineralized ground but in the first frenzied period all eyes were shut to this attitude. When mineral claimants sought to revoke the town's patent, litigation soon clouded all titles. Difficulties were finally settled by allowing the buildings on the surface to remain in legal control of the original owners, mineral-bearing grounds underneath to belong to the claimants who had been working them who would pay for any damage to the town above, as in a case where a certain hotel fell into a hole made by miners.

Later absorption of most claims by the ever-expanding Homestake interests simplified many legal tangles. Private individuals would construct buildings on a "permit" system protecting the company's mineral rights.

While mine owners and businessmen were thrashing out these difficulties, the common miner was working and spending his gains where expected. The red-light district was in two sections, one run by the ever-present Chinese where a miner could relax on a narrow bunk and dream his troubles away with a pipeful of "poppy juice." In the other section, he could gamble at faro, black jack, poker or get roistering drunk and stumble upstairs with his inamorata. Either way he was likely to wake up in the morning with a splitting headache and his bankroll gone.

Homestake sent its shipments of gold to Cheyenne by stagecoach, value ranging from $95,000 to as high as $350,000 each. Such attractions were not overlooked by the road agents and robberies were frequent. For security, the management established a system whereby a shipment of finished gold bricks was guarded by a contingent of heavily armed men. Each brick was wrapped in canvas and sealed with proper tag, added to others under the guns of the watchmen and loaded in the coach. As many as thirteen mounted and armed guards would ride alongside and see the gold safely in the Cheyenne bank.

The Black Hills were so isolated that, as Muriel Wolle relates in *The Bonanza Trail*: "Years after trains on the Georgetown loop were hauling ore to smelters from Silver Plume, tucked in at the foot of the Colorado mountains, even after the Northern Pacific Railroad had celebrated its completion by driving a golden spike at Gold Creek, Montana, Deadwood and Lead were still without rail connection to the outside world; and stagecoaches were still dashing down the streets, adeptly weaving their way between freighters' wagon trains. For nearly fifteen years the towns in the Black Hills lived a frontier existence—lusty, exciting, discouraging, extravagant and dangerous, but rewarding."

Until the early '80s, all building in the town was with logs and lumber and then came an era of brick construction, starting with a three-story, 60 by 300 foot structure built by Hearst Mercantile Co. called The Brick Store and this was soon followed by another built by Ernest May. Yet even with all this developing of an urban aspect there were still signs that Lead was essentially a simple, bucolic sort of town. Most residents kept cows, pigs, chickens and horses in their yards. The *Lead City Tribune* in August of 1886 reported that due to the epidemic of cholera, poultry and livestock were dying in the streets.

By 1890 the town boasted 3,000 population with six churches, many more saloons and in ten years it had more than doubled. The Dakota Territory Centennial, "Lawrence County," credits much of this increase to the influx of foreign-born mine workers and their families—Cornish, Croatians, Serbs, Finns and Swedes added to the original Scotch, Irish and English. This kind of polyglot population in the usual camp caused separate foreign colonies to be set up. But in Lead, with its steeply rising boundaries there was no room for group segregation. Enforced integration soon melted all into a homogenous group with a minimum of racial difficulties.

The turn of the century saw a steady, solid growth with such innovations as telegraph lines, telephone system, then electric power and public sewage disposal. Even a disastrous fire in March, 1900, which destroyed a fourth of the town did not daunt it. The blaze, starting in the butcher shop of J. K. Searle early one morning served to erase most of the frame buildings remaining which were replaced by more substantial ones.

The next 18 years were steady, marred by some labor troubles. The Western Federation of Miners struck the Homestake, idling the mine from November 24, 1909 to March 2, 1910, working great hardship on the whole town, the issue being the union's demands for a closed shop. The Homestake had always operated on an open shop policy and after the strike it opened as a non-union organization.

By 1914 Lead had movies, libraries and traveling stock companies. The Burlington trolley had long since replaced the stagecoaches on the route to Deadwood. While cultural and educational societies enjoyed an all-time high of popularity, the dens in the bawdy house section continued to flourish unobstructed. The miner could find anything he wanted in Lead.

Now came World War I, inflation and the influenza epidemic to further decimate the population already faltering because of closures in some back-country mines. Just when Lead was in this precarious situation, cracks began to appear in the streets. Sewage lines became disconnected, utilities were disrupted and foundations of some larger buildings began to crumble. As one walked along the street he could see hollows where subsidence was occurring. Then one day a business structure collapsed with a roar, the ruins settling into a large opening. The entire area was roped off, condemned as unsafe. Evacuation and razing was begun in 1919 with construction work carried on for the next 20 years and Lead emerged with a new face and a new business district. Such famous old structures as The Brick Store, Hotel Cotton and Andrews Building had vanished with many lesser known ones.

While the "Hungry 30s" were being suffered out elsewhere, Lead was enjoying a boom of sorts. Homestake offered not only its regular quota of steady jobs but was expanding and modernizing its plants, actually adding to employment, and these jobs found ready acceptance by men out of luck elsewhere. Reconstruction of the city was still going on which added still more prosperity.

By 1940 this period of growth had leveled off and with the second World War came disaster. When the country suspended all gold mining in October of 1942, it suspended Lead's only industry. The mine closed and so did the mills after a stockpile of ore was exhausted. In a short time population dropped to a meager 3,000, most of them women and children. Many houses were deserted and boarded up and instead of having a wartime housing shortage, Lead now found itself staring at rows of empty buildings.

Homestake started up again in July, 1945, when the gold mining suspension order was revoked. It took some time to warm up such a gigantic operation, however, and it was months before full production was reached. By the end of 1950 employment and gold production were near normal again and a mild boom developed. Lead found the neglected and abandoned houses had deteriorated, many of them beyond use, and Homestake built six apartment buildings with fifty-five units as well as many single dwelling units which were sold to employees at cost. Veterans whose government loans were restricted found them guaranteed by Homestake.

The population never again reached its 1925 high of 7,000. Various factors were involved such as workers' living out of town and the mine's becoming more mechanized and requiring fewer workers. Yet the city was back on its feet and now numerous improvements show a healthy condition. New schools, buildings, recreational facilities and expanding parking lots indicate a stable economy.

With all this the city stands on a foundation of gold and the vagaries governing the value of the metal. Its price has been fixed for a long time, since January, 1934, while costs of production and living go steadily upward. Since there is no income for Lead other than that coming from the Homestake, the future is insecure. Closure of this one industry would result in Lead's becoming a virtual ghost town, comparable in size to Jerome, Arizona.

FANTASTIC OPEN CUT at Lead was original mine of Homestake Company. Nearby is site of original business district, now park maintained by Company, often called "Sinking Gardens." Park is centered by plaque bearing short history of cut: "The open cut was once a solid mountain on which Fred and Moses Manuel with Hank Harney located the Homestake Claim, April 9, 1876. Of the estimated 48,000,000 tons of rock removed, approximately 15% was gold-bearing ore. The remainder, waste rock, was used in backfilling underground excavations. Operations ceased in 1945." Backfilling was improperly done, resulting in earth slippage and sinking, causing damage and collapse of buildings on original site and subsequent razing.

TERRY, SOUTH DAKOTA

In a country like the Black Hills where heavy snowfall and cold weather are accepted like taxes, the winter of 1903-4 had been notable. Snows were many feet deep and a late spring had delayed melting, usually completed by March in town and the end of April at higher elevations. In Terry there was still snow in the streets at the beginning of April and the higher reaches of the mountains lay blanketed all through May. With the first of May came a heavy downpour of rain throughout the Black Hills and cold torrents continued until the snow on Terry Peak and other mountains was saturated, carrying a load of water almost beyond holding.

The 9th of June brought a sudden rise in temperature, the driving rain so warm it melted the snow with a rush. Freshets came down Fan Tail and Nevada Gulches which swelled to brown, swirling waves several feet high.

Just below the Golden Reward, Terry's biggest mine in Stewart Gulch, there was a settling pool for tailings called the Horseshoe. Horseshoe Dam was never built to stand such pressure and when water piled up to the top of it, the concrete suddenly let go to pour the entire accumulation of debris-filled waters into the unprepared mining camp.

Most residents had been warned but those in the Jenkins Saloon were contemptuous of any alarm,

TOPS FROM CYANIDE CONTAINERS made unique siding for cabin in Terry. Little structure is one of few remaining from days when street was solidly lined on both sides, standing beside route where Deadwood Central puffed up to head of Fan Tail Gulch. One Labor Day excursion train carried 415 excursionists from Deadwood at 50 cents a head for 20-mile trip.

swaggering it off with a "Let 'er come!" The flood struck the building, carrying it piecemeal down the draw. Everyone in it except Matt Miatinovick and his friend George Erack managed to survive, somehow reaching the banks and scrambling out.

In an hour the inundation drained off except for a sullen brown stream running through the main street, now gouged by holes some eight feet deep. The Deadwood Central tracks which had run through the town on the main street were a twisted mass of wreckage.

The bodies of Matt and George were at length discovered in the ruins of the saloon. There being no suitable place in Terry for the funerals, they were held in Lead. The hearse carried the bodies back to Terry but stopped short at the bottom of the one street, the only route to the cemetery two miles up the hill. Since it was obviously impossible to drive the black, glass-sided and betasseled vehicle through the holes still full of water, the pallbearers picked up the heavy caskets and made the long trudge, picking their way between piles of lumber and debris, around small lakes in the torn-up street.

Damage from the flood was soon repaired, the street holes "filled with rock and broken porphyry and Main Street was soon much better than before, almost like concrete." Repairs were completed just in time for the huge 4th of July celebration when every dry throat in town was well moistened with the special brand of refreshment known as Black Hills Lightning.

Terry's heyday saw many mines operating all over the canyon sides, it being said—"The area about Terry is now and always will be more vertical than horizontal. There are mighty few garden patches organized in the area which is largely rock outcropping and trees, withal a quite picturesque country except for the potentials from minerals and logging, not so good."

First and largest mine was the famous Golden Reward, the Company buying up several claims in 1887 when it was founded. One of the largest units absorbed was the Deadwood and Delaware Mining Co., smaller ones including the Mogul, National Gold and Silver, Isidora and Billie, Tornado, Double Standard, Welcome and Ben Hur, Mikado, Belle, Daisy, Dark Horse and many more with titles equally intriguing.

The Golden Reward stood at Terry's upper end, at the head of the gulch. It was served directly by the Deadwood and Central Railway, this line and two others extending narrow gauge tracks all over the mountainsides to reach the multitude of smaller mines up and down the canyons.

Annie Tallent, early historian of the Black Hills, says of Terry "like Topsy, it just growed." Although reaching the population of 1,177 in 1910, the place never had a mayor or town plat. It was widely spread out in the Ruby Basin Mining District, with what passed for a Main Street lying along the narrow bed of Fan Tail Gulch, houses perched precariously on the canyon sides nearly to the summit. Most prominent feature on the horizon was Terry Peak, named for Gen. Alfred H. Terry, Custer's immediate superior in the fateful campaign of 1876.

The town got along without a post office for a number of years, the mail coming in on the stage from Deadwood. There were probably earlier postmasters than Michael A. Isaacs but he was appointed April 18, 1892, dying in 1906 and being buried in the old cemetery high in the hillside.

The post office was in Quillan's Drug Store. An old map or plan of Terry shows a double line of establishments facing the tracks, their sequence significant: Miners' Union, Quillan's Drug, Kosh Market,

Mills and Brica Saloon, Saloon, Kenefich Hall, Saloon, and Barber Shop, Chinese Laundry, Bakery, Dakota Annex, Dr. Richards, School, J. Backford, Blackford's Barn, Black's Cow Barn, Saloon, Pelham's Livery, K of P Hall with Terry Record Offices. Altogether 100 businesses are listed including the ice house and several indicated as ? ? ? The mystery of these will probably never be solved as only a scattering of buildings remain.

Fraternal orders and societies were numerous, among them Knights of Pythias, General Terry Lodge No. 69, Degree of Honor A.O.U.W., Welcome No. 86, The Ancient Order of United Workmen, Bald Mountain Lodge No. 137 of I.O.O.F. There were several Temperance societies struggling to combat the evils of the dozen or so saloons. One, the Finnish Temperance Brothers No. 58, met Sunday evenings in the Stewart Building. Other organizations had unexplained objectives such as The Lemon Club with Bertha McKim as president which met monthly at members' homes. There were several Fire Department Hose Company organizations and numerous Miners' Unions.

The Terry *Reporter* listed baseball games to be

OLD LOG BUILDING stood about midway along Terry's one street, its original use uncertain. Section of harness hanging on extending log may indicate later use as horse barn. Boards were scarce, logs plentiful in early days and house builders often used what lumber they could obtain, finished with logs.

played "over at Ruby Flat" and stated there would be a presentation of the play "Dora Thorne" at the Miners Union Hall for the benefit of the baseball players. A display advertisement informed the public that the first moving pictures to be shown in Terry would be brought over from Lead, July 20th, 1908.

Terry's first disaster, other than the flood from which it quickly recovered, was the burning of the giant Horseshoe Mill on the slopes of Terry Peak. This was a severe blow to the town, throwing many men out of work. Several mines failed in the period after 1908. On Oct. 9, the *News-Record* carried an item showing optimistically that the Alpha Mine, a property of the Golden Reward, was equal if not superior to the Ben Hur, having a vein twenty feet wide and ten thick and was producing fifty tons of ore a day for the cyanide plant.

At the same time it carried notice that a number of mines were closing and one ominous note was sounded when the paper complained that advertising was falling off. And some of those appearing had never been considered necessary before. Mrs. Thomas Hoaglund, for example, desired boarders for her Double Standard Boarding House where a good bed and three square meals a day could be had for $30 a month.

About the same time the Burlington Railroad, which had taken over the Deadwood Central, removed its tracks on the Nevada Gulch route and in 1914 took up those in the Fan Tail. The Elkhorn Branch of the Chicago and Northwestern persisted in serving Terry until it gave up in 1924. Then in 1933 the C. B. and Q. took out its Spearfish line to the camp and Terry was dead.

TERRY HAD EXCELLENT BAND which gave concerts on pleasant summer evenings. Bandstand was porch of this house, home of superintendent of largest mine, Golden Reward. Structure stands near site of Quillan's Drug Store, which also housed post office. Store advertised in 1906 it had just secured "shipment of cameras of a type anyone can operate."

ROCK WALLS OF OLD GOLD REFINERY, showing about a foot above ground on hillside for years, were ignored in area full of such remnants. When roadside lunchroom in Pluma expanded into large restaurant and needed increased parking space, bulldozing exposed extensive ruins. Research shows that while immense workings of Homestead mine above Pluma at Lead overshadowed smaller mines, aggregate output of these required milling also, was refined at cooperative mill of which these are remains.

PLUMA, SOUTH DAKOTA

A brilliant full moon of March shone down on the Cheynne-Deadwood stage as it threaded the dark canyons of the Black Hills. The trip had been a wearying one, the eleven passengers afraid every moment either bandits or Indians would attack them. But now they were passing through Pluma, only two miles from Deadwood where the ride would end, and most of them had relaxed into troubled slumber.

The sudden stopping of the vehicle jarred them awake and with the sharp bark of "Halt!" came the realization that what they feared had come upon them. The stage was being held up.

It was carrying $15,000 in gold and driven by one of the best men in the Hills, John Slaughter. He was trying to stop the horses when he received a blast of pellets from a sawed-off shotgun held by one of the five bandits and pitched off the seat to the ground. Now thoroughly frightened, the horses bolted, carrying the stage full tilt down to Deadwood and safety.

One of the passengers had seen the face of the leader in the moonlight and another had heard his voice. Both were sure he was Sam Bass, the notorious bandit. The fact that so dangerous a character was now known to be working in the area delayed the forming of a posse, no volunteers eager to make themselves available. By the time a party of pursuers did set out, the holdup men were gone.

Slaughter's name was perpetuated in a way he would have liked. A new stage was built to resist attacks by highwaymen and called the Johnny Slaughter. It was armor plated, protected by steel sheets 5/16 of an inch thick, with rifle ports on both sides. The gold box was heavily weighted and bolted to the floor. An armed guard rode inside, two more perched on top with rifles across their knees. This predecessor of the modern armored car was put into service in September of the same year Slaughter was murdered—1877.

PRESTON, SOUTH DAKOTA

The old mining camps of Trojan and Preston were only four miles apart and sometimes were considered almost as one since many mines and cabins were strung along Annie Creek in the basin between. But in reality there was a great difference between the two. Trojan was situated on the narrow summit ridge of Bald Mountain, leading to the 7,071-foot Terry Peak, named for General Terry and the fourth highest point in the Black Hills. Preston was placed in a boggy hollow at the bottom of a steeply inclined road dropping down from Trojan at a point between the town and the old Portland mine.

But these were not the major differences. Whereas Trojan was peaceful to the point of dullness, Preston was continually being torn apart by strife of one sort or another, all sharpened up by frustration due to the steep road out of camp, often impassable. Men couldn't get to Lead to let off steam and cabin fever turned man upon man to result in many a fracas at the mine or town saloons.

The main source of trouble, however, was the system used by absentee owners, Golden Reward Co., which controlled some four thousand acres in the vicinity, of leasing out good ground. Each lessee watched his neighbor closely to see if he struck a better vein than his own. If so, he would likely attempt to claim the ground as his own and then trouble would break out. A man finding an extra rich lead might sit on the tailings dump with a loaded rifle or shotgun to protect it. The leasing system also resulted in the practice known as "gutting." A rich vein would be followed to its end regardless of con-

LITTLE PRESTON SCHOOL stands decrepit and forlorn, children's shouts at recess long faded away. Some desks are still in place, others burned for firewood. Chalk and eraser shelf at bottom of blackboard now holds bird's nest, little yellow bird startled by photographer waited on windowsill before returning to eggs. Small addition at front of building was common in snowy areas of Black Hills, served as vestibule where snow could be stamped off boots, shaken off clothing.

ONE OF TWO REMAINING HOTELS shows characteristic vestibule. Chimney is only one remaining in town and it is falling, brick by brick. These and other building materials were hauled down on narrow gauge railway, route of vanished tracks indicated by narrow, deeply rutted dirt "road." Site of Preston is partly on swampy ground, making driving impossible. Wooden walks were elevated over ooze, can be faintly traced. Main buildings were on more solid ground.

MAIN STREET is defined by only a few remaining buildings including two hotels now separated by open space which was once solidly filled in with saloons and stores.

servation policies, resulting in improper shoring of tunnels or no shoring at all. When stopes were exhausted they were allowed to collapse, sometimes even before workers were out and men were often imprisoned with little hope of rescue. The only ones willing to work under such irresponsible conditions were habitual drunks or renegades from legally operated mines who were excluded by owners or unions.

Three Norwegian brothers—Algot, Paul and Ole Westerlund—formed an unholy alliance, hiring out as thugs to do any job, including murder. Their names became synonymous with highjacking, robbery, claim jumping and abduction. They were never apprehended but Paul was in trouble once for some minor misdemeanor and even jailed. His brothers broke in and removed him at gunpoint, the jailer recognizing them and prudently offering no resistance. After several years of terrorizing the town, the brothers disappeared completely.

LIVERY BARN dating from Preston's wild days still stands, weathered boards showing beautiful texture and grain, Dutch doors swinging in breeze.

TROJAN, SOUTH DAKOTA

John Marsh lives quietly in a cabin among Ponderosa pines on a hillside near the old cemetery above once-teeming Terry. Nearby are the ruins of the old Horseshoe Mills and the Golden Reward mine shaft. John's main concern now is to get his wood supply dry enough to put it in the shed but during the fifteen years he was foreman of the old Dakota mine at nearby Trojan, his worries were more serious. Forty men worked in the Dakota, men from many walks of life and backgrounds. In the close confines of the enclosed shafts, friction among them was almost constant, a situation aggravated by surreptitious drinking.

When John took over at the Dakota he had already acquired long years of experience in the Trojan and Two Johns mine at Trojan. He says the ore from these was never spectacular—there was no blossom rock, only steady, low-producing material that paid smelting costs as long as labor was not too expensive and parts could be replaced reasonably. With the silver there would be "maybe ten ounces of gold in five tons of ore."

Silver would assay half a pound in one ton "then we'd go through several assaying only a few ounces." Much ore was sent to Deadwood and Lead on the narrow gauge lines, dim traces of which still show as scars on the hillside, the local mills refining mostly by the cyanide process.

ONCE BUSTLING PORTLAND MINE is silent, weeds submerging buildings which are falling into decay on mountain aerie at Trojan. Silver was the precious metal dug here although considerable gold was encountered infrequently, with some lead and zinc. These were ignored except during short period when it appeared a bonanza of always valuable lead seemed evident in main vein. This proved only pocket, soon pinching out.

Men and supplies were dropped down the 640-foot shaft and instead of hauling the ore up, it was chuted farther on down an inclined shaft which came out at a lower level, thus explaining the absence of ruins at the lofty site of the Trojan itself. The "muck" was collected into several ore bins of 350 tons capacity and the complicated refining process from rock to concentrated sludge began.

First came the crushing, not by stamp mills, but by a pair of giant iron jaws, the upper mandible of which was connected to an eccentric gear, causing it to rise and fall against the lower, crushing the material into two-inch bits. These were reduced in a Symons cone crusher to one-half inch. These fragments were in turn tumbled around in a huge drum filled with rolling steel balls about the size of small cannon shot until the ore was a fine powder and ready to be soaked in a series of chemical baths, including that of cyanide of potassium, causing the silver, gold and several other metals in lesser quantity to become a gray, sludgy soap. Into trays of the sludge rolled the edge of the huge heated drum covered with canvas. As it revolved the sludge dried to a cake of solid material which was scraped off by a set blade before the drum revolution was complete. This cake material was the end result for the mill—the concentrate. This step of refining was accomplished at Trojan, the concentrates usually being shipped for finishing at Lead or the cooperative refinery at Pluma.

Ores of higher assay values might have kept Trojan and its mines going longer. The biggest blow to the town came in 1947 when the huge boardinghouse was torn down and the final one in February, 1960, when all operations were closed down. Everybody then moved away from the camp on the mountain ridge except a few older people with no place to go.

MAIN AND ONLY STREET OF TROJAN, never a real boom camp. Town grew slowly serving several mines as supply center. Big Trojan mine was reached by road winding into hill at left. Several saloons along street were well patronized but for big pay-day busts men descended mountain to Lead or Deadwood which offered bigger ways to "blow 'er in."

DEADWOOD, SOUTH DAKOTA

"There was a matched jig between a brace of 'the girls' last night at a certain place in town," ran a lively item on an early-day strip tease in the Gulch Hash column of the Deadwood *Times*. "They danced an hour. It was a question of endurance with them and as they became warmed up they began to throw away their surplus toggery. This was kept up, our informant says, until one was barefoot to her ears and the other was dressed about as much as a boy would be with only a pair of suspenders on."

"The Gulch Hash" writer also had this to say: "One of the new girls who arrived in this camp from Cheyenne this week was out on the street between two and three o'clock this morning with her little gun aching to perforate the anatomy of a certain young man. She was gathered in by Officer Graham and put in her little bed. . . .

"A certain schoolmarm in the Hills for the amusement of her pupils stands on her head during recess . . . .

"Trixie, the female sinner whose house was demolished by the wrath of heaven the other day, has contributed a slang phrase to the rounders' vocabulary. After the destruction of her 'ranch' she returned to the ruins and, finding a pillow, held it up and remarked—'There's a part of my kit.' Now the boys, when they find anything belonging to them, claim it as part of their kit.

"Coon Sing's washee house is still located in the middle of Deadwood Street. The residents on that wonder how long it will be allowed to remain there . . . .

"The miners who have engaged in digging up Sherman Street have quit. They were convinced that businessmen and property owners have some rights that miners are bound to respect. . . ."

All this was in famous Deadwood which Ed Murphy, in a party of prospectors, set in violent motion. Disgruntled with their failure in Montana, the men made a foray into the Black Hills in the fall of 1875 hoping to get some idea of the possibilities along Deadwood Creek before winter set in. Apparently they were encouraged. Murphy and John Hildebrand worked the hardest and John made the first real find in the earliest thawing of the stream next spring.

Like a flash flood the excitement swept down the canyon where Deadwood Creek meandered. Its banks were so clogged with dead timber, the aftermath of a fire, the first men to lay out claims skipped the area and staked out their holdings immediately above it. Many haphazard markings bounded the limits of the first claims, one was a scrap of paper tacked to a spruce tree. It read, "We, the undersigned, claim 300 feet below this notice for a distance of 900 feet or three claims above this for mining purposes. Signed Frank S. Bryand, William Cudney, W. H. Coder."

The confusion was so great there were many more takers than claims and the winning names had to be drawn out of a hat. These men started to build crude cabins immediately, often finding it difficult to select level spots, so that no actual street existed, little shelters being placed all the way from the creek bank to some distance up the steep canyon side. In a short time all available cleared area was filled and latecomers had to be satisfied with the section filled with silvery-white dead trees. After removing this tangle, the men were delighted to find their ground richer than that above.

The clusters of shanties were developing so fast they acquired such designations as North Deadwood, South Deadwood, Montana City, Fountain City and Chinatown. To avoid further confusion, a meeting was

ORIGINAL MONUMENT over grave of Calamity Jane since hacked to bits by souvenir hunters. Memorial seems to have once been lawn ornament with its four grinning satyrs' faces and flower container. Actual marker was laid at base, bears out death date of Aug. 1 which disproves some stories giving date as Aug. 2 to agree with death anniversary of her friend Wild Bill Hickok whose grave is immediately below on hillside.

held and some sort of order created. A lariat was used as a makeshift surveying instrument and the townsite laid out April 26, 1876, by popular vote named Deadwood City. Among the organizers were Creighton (sometimes appearing as Craven) Lee and Isaac Brown. The first mayor was E. B. Farnham.

The new boom town lost no time in becoming the wildest place in the West. Gold dust was the accepted medium of exchange since everyone had it. Sack-like buckskin pouches carried the big money, vials or small bottles the chicken feed. All articles in stores were marked with two price tags—one for dust and one for greenbacks which were valued at 10% less.

Deadwood's first newspaper, the *Black Hills Pioneer*, started by W. A. McLaughlin and W. A. Merrick on June 8th, had this to say on the 24th: "Six weeks ago the site of Deadwood City was a heavy forest of pine timber, now it extends nearly a mile along Deadwood and Whitewood and contains nearly 2,000 of the most energetic and driving people on this continent. Every branch of business is represented and many of them are overdone. Houses are going up on every hand, immense trains are constantly arriving loaded with goods of every description. Business is rushing and bargains are driven here that would put Wall Street to the blush."

And the *Pioneer* thus described the first years: "Hustle and confusion is prevalent. Each day and almost every hour witnesses the arrival of parties of gold seekers who search for some suitable location to corral their wagons and pitch their tents. They immediately mix with the throngs and become one of us. Growing reports fill the air, placers yielding fabulously and quartz is bright with gold. Everyone wants to buy real estate and all do who can.

"Speculation on town lots amounts to a furore of the wildest kind. Building is at its height, taxing to the utmost Boughton and Berry's Sawmill which stands on Sherman Street and is in continuous operation. Help of all kinds is in constant demand and he who can saw a board or drive a nail can command his own price. Saloons multiply astonishingly and gambling is carried on without limit, in fact, at all hours. Day and night are alike is the motto of those frequenting these dens.

"Hotel business is booming too. C. H. Wagner has opened his Continental, Jim Vandoiker his I.X.L. Both houses have done such a good business from the start that it is considered a luxury by the late arrival to be permitted to occupy an office chair for the night."

Deadwood's first theater, if it could be called that, was a frame building with walls part way up, the rest and roof of canvas. On July 27, 1876, before completion, the performers were ready and anxious to give their first show. The eager audience filled not only

MARTHA JANE CANARY, called "Calamity Jane" for her raucous laugh. She tired of whipping individuals who compared it to that of a "mountain canary." Name is given in flamboyant, ghost-written autobiography as Canary and tells probably invented tale of origin of name Calamity. "It was during this (Muscle Shell Indian outbreak) campaign that I was christened Calamity Jane. It was on Goose Creek, Wyoming, where the town of Sheridan is now located. . . When we were returning to the post we were ambushed about a mile and a half from our destination. When fired upon, Capt. Egan was shot. I was riding in advance and on hearing the firing I turned in my saddle and saw the captain reeling in his saddle as though about to fall, I turned my horse and galloped back with all haste to his side and got there in time to prevent his falling. I lifted him onto my horse in front of me and got him safely back to the fort. Capt. Egan on recovering laughingly said — 'I name you Calamity Jane, heroine of the plains.'

the building but the space around it, the fresh air group looking over the board wall. About the middle of the performance a heavy rain drenched them, the *Pioneer* reporting: "All concerned stuck it out for a complete success."

The years 1876-78 were the most flagrantly lawless years with frequent killings. When Jerry McCarthy shot Jack Hutch he escaped to Fort Laramie but was foolish enough to go into a bar there, was recognized, arrested and brought back to Deadwood. The trial was held at Gayville, just above, where there was a court if not a courthouse. Proceedings were in the open air, Judge A. S. Simons ordering a guard of twenty men around the prisoner, exposed as he was to possible lynching. When Jerry was pronounced "not guilty," the guards closed in and at gunpoint held off the mob clamoring to get their hands on the defendant. He was escorted to the jail, led through the front door and while the sheriff harangued the populace on law and order, McCarthy was whisked out the back door and smuggled back to Deadwood. Commented the newspaper: "The prisoner was given a horse and told to leave town. He sprang on the animal's back, let out a farewell whoop and a holler and disappeared full speed down the Gulch."

The cost of living in Deadwood was considered high, hotels and boardinghouses charging $8 to $10 a week for bed and board. Flour was $11 a barrel, potatoes $1 a bushel, eggs 40¢ a dozen, pork $30 a barrel, "common" butter was 15¢ a pound, "good" 30¢. Coffee was 30¢ and tea 65¢ a pound.

Though not a true ghost town but a shadow of its former self, Deadwood harbors some of the liveli-

est specters known to Western history—those of Preacher Smith, Wild Bill Hickok, Calamity Jane and the fictional Deadwood Dick.

Fort Laramie is often given as Calamity Jane's birthplace although she always claimed it was Princeton, Mercer County, Missouri, the records showing she was about five years old when she arrived there. Her father, Bob Canary (Calamity added a middle initial H in her autobiography) had picked up a girl named Charlotte in an Ohio bawdy house and married her, Calamity being their first child and named Martha Jane—the "Calamity" being applied after she acquired a reputation. She ran wild in the woods around Princeton, usually with a gang of older boys who taught her the facts of earthy life.

After about eight years there, the family began to gypsy from one place to another, a habit Martha Jane never outgrew. The first stop was near an army base where Charlotte publically disported with a young soldier and as this activity spread to several others, the Canarys moved to Virginia City, Montana, where little Martha Jane spent her time in bars and gambling houses becoming further enlightened. When it came to profanity, her mind was a sponge and was frequently squeezed later on.

Somewhere along the way the father was lost and Charlotte earned the family living, easy enough in Virginia City until advancing age and illness made inroads on her charms and she had to take in washing. She died shortly after starting a laundry in Blackfoot and Martha Jane was on her own.

Aged fifteen in 1867, she had coppery red hair, was tall and handsome—some legends even have her beautiful—a buxom eyeful. She formed the habit of establishing herself near army forts—first Fort Steele, then Fort Bridger where, one historian says, she was "ruined" by the soldiers. One of her more steady friends was a Lieut. Somers who was the father of a son born to Calamity and who saw to it that the baby was placed out, an arrangement made with more of her progeny as time went on. With this easy virtue, she established a pattern with men in general and soldiers in particular. She once said soldiers were just like the boys in Princeton, except that they had more to offer.

During the boom days of railroad construction she established another habit, that of wearing men's

GAY NINETIES BUILDING showing expert cutting and fitting of native stone in telephoto view. Structure stands between site of colorful Chinatown and Chinese cemetery on Mt. Moriah. Funeral processions were almost gay, brass band preceding marchers with white-gowned mourners scattering bits of perforated paper in belief devil would have to work way through each hole which delayed him in pursuit of dead soul. Old cemetery now holds few bones, most having been removed, each wrapped in paper, for proper burial in home soil.

clothes since she was less conspicuous in them while holding down jobs in the camps. She also took to wearing a gun on her hip. Possibly the first of the hundreds of anecdotes about her concerns the time a ballad singer known as Darling Bob McKenzie made some disparaging comment about her clothes at a bar in Dodge City. He probably regretted it instantly as that soon he acquired bullet holes in his hat through which a stream of oaths whistled, the experience giving him sudden maturity.

As the railroad boom tapered off, the army organized forays into the Black Hills and who should go along but Martha Jane. Of all her current lovers she took especially to soldier Frank Sechrist who was attached to the expedition headed by Lt. Col. Dodge about to leave for the Hills. Martha managed to stow away in one of the wagons.

When she crawled out of the straw in Deadwood, the town was frantic for gold. There were only about 600 people in the boom camp and Martha saw there would be great possibilities when it grew some. To put in time while this was happening, she rode to Fort Laramie, attached herself to a bull train in an effort to reach and join Gen. Custer's column. After swimming the Platte River while "carrying important messages to Custer," she caught pneumonia and was returned to the hospital at Fort Fetterman. Had she reached the column she would have been the only woman casualty in the disastrous Battle of the Little Big Horn!

The cold bath did not give Martha Jane a trauma about swimming. She joined another army column as bullwhacker and went swimming with soldiers in Hat Creek near Sheridan. Everything was going just fine when one of the stuffy high command saw her and did a double take. Martha was escorted under guard and "disgrace" back to Fort Fetterman. She may have decided by this time that Deadwood had grown to fit her demands because she was to stay there longer than in any other spot in her saffron career—and to make a more lasting impression.

Hundreds of stories are told of her exploits and antics in Deadwood which point up the many facets of her character. She attended the opening of the Gem Variety Theater dressed as a man, escorted the girls to the bar and danced with them. She was friendly with the madames of the various red-light houses and was said by one of them to be "attractive either as a man or woman." She was hailed into court for rolling a miner who had spent the night at her house and stealing some $30 from him. Her defense was: "If I hadn't done it, some other girl would have and, anyway, I used it to pay the hospital bill of another dancehall girl who was sick and broke."

A. J. Toomey tells this incident. "In her younger

JAMES BUTLER HICKOK, better known as Wild Bill, was born in Troy Grove, Ill., in 1837. Before joining gold rush to Deadwood, he had been trapper, stage driver, army scout, Union spy and buffalo hunter. Six feet tall and handsome, he was much admired by Calamity Jane. Wild Bill often cautioned gamblers with enemies never to sit at cards with back to the door, but made same mistake himself, was shot in back by Crooked Nose Jack McCall. He was paid $300 to get rid of potentially dangerous Hickok who was up for appointment as Marshal. When shot, Wild Bill was holding black aces and eights, afterwards known as "dead man's hand." Murderer was tried, acquitted, later caught in Yankton, retried, judged guilty and hanged. Wild Bill was first buried in old cemetery on Whitewood Creek, later moved to Mt. Moriah.

days in Deadwood, Calamity was the floor manager of a variety house and wore evening gowns there. I never saw her in men's clothes. I had a little farm at the edge of Deadwood. It was the habit of Calamity and some of the others at the dancehall to wind up the night's work with a horseback ride and about six o'clock in the morning they would come whooping and hollering past my place. Well, one time the rain washed out a big hole in the road and when I heard them coming I rushed out and stopped them. They were too drunk to notice the hole and Calamity told me I saved her life. After that whenever I would visit the Music Hall with some friends, she would stop the music and shout to the musicians: 'Strike up the Potato Digger's Quadrille! Here come the Potato Diggers!'

"Years afterward, when she had spent several years away from Deadwood and had returned a drunken old woman, I met her again. I was in a clothing store buying an overcoat. Calamity came in drunk and carrying a bottle of cheap cologne. The proprietor, to get rid of her, said: 'Calamity, there's a friend of yours at the back of the store.' She rushed up, threw her arms around me and then opened the

PREACHER SMITH came to Deadwood from Cheyenne with Capt. Gardner's overland freight train, was well liked in camp. On Aug. 20, 1876 he decided to walk to Crook City to preach there against advice of friends aware of Indian menace. Body was found short distance from Deadwood, Bible clasped to breast, scalp unmolested. Friends organized posse which included Charles Holland, Isaac Brown, C. Mason. Men were ambushed by Indians, three of them killed, Indians escaping.

bottle and poured the contents all over me. I was on my way to meet my wife and had a hard time explaining things to her."

When her good looks were gone, her jobs were as cook, household helper or swamper. For a brief time she was a waitress in a restaurant and on one occasion it was temporarily out of tea. Out of habit she asked a customer from the East whether he'd like coffee or tea and he specified tea. Calamity was a little drunk as usual and spat out at the startled man: "You'll take coffee! That's all you'll get, you son of a bitch!"

Walking along a muddy street one spring day she came upon a team of oxen, stuck fast. The bull-whacker was laying on the lash unmercifully and cursing the helpless animals. Calamity strode up, grabbed the whip and flogged the driver until he couldn't stand up, at the same time piling on a stream of profanity such as he had never heard. She drank more and worked less as time went on, a habit encouraged by people sorry for her and "loaning" her money for drinks. She managed to work as a makeshift cook and maid at a bawdy house in Crook City, one of her last jobs.

Toward the end of July, 1903, Calamity Jane boarded the ore train at Deadwood, riding in a converted boxcar at the tail. Her reason for the trip is not known but she was a rover, unable to stay long in one spot even in her state of advanced alcoholism. Arriving in Terry, she made a beeline for one of the saloons and ordered a drink. As soon as she had downed it, she had a violent vomiting spell. The bartender helped her get a room at the Calloway Hotel and called in Dr. Richards. The hotel proprietor, H. A. Sheffer, and his wife took turns nursing her. The doctor reported Calamity had severe inflammation of the bowels and pneumonia and was suffering from "general dissolution."

On Saturday, August 1, hard-drinking and hard-living Calamity Jane died. Deadwood's undertaker, Charlie Robinson, came to Terry and took her body "home." There she was placed on pagan display in his establishment, propped up in a semi-sitting position. Long lines of the curious filed by and several women armed with shears cut off locks of hair for souvenirs. A wire cage was then put around the casket until time for the funeral. She was buried next to the grave of Wild Bill Hickok, as she had requested, in the Mt. Moriah Cemetery on the hill overlooking Deadwood.

ALMA, COLORADO

In the center of a dozen gold diggings was Alma, which like Silverton, was the place the miners went to buy supplies and what it took to break reality into something livable. One of these camps was called Buckskin Joe, of which nothing is left but a history as ripe as the long unwashed bodies of the miners and their women.

One of its former log buildings was a combination store and boardinghouse, one of several presided over by Horace Tabor and wife Augusta. There were several saloons, three dancehalls and a theatre where, during Buckskin Joe's heydey, a negro minstrel troupe put on a continuous show.

During this period, in the early '60s, Father Dyer, the "Snowshoe Itinerant," was a familiar character in the camps. Constantly on the gospel trail, this Rev. John Lewis Dyer starved, froze his feet, slept in snow-banks but always responded to the call to reform the rowdy "congregations" in Buckskin Joe, Montgomery, Divide, Breckenridge and other spots of sin.

Dyer kept a diary and in it stated he persisted in preaching in Buckskin Joe "in the face of every kind of opposition, at least two balls a week, a dancing school, a one-horse theater, two men shot, and yet, we had a good meeting." When snows were deep, he made his way over the passes on long Norwegian skis, which in those early days were called "snow-shoes." His traveling equipment included "a buffalo skin and quilt, some crackers, a piece of bacon, coffee and sugar, with some dried apples, a tin cup, and an oyster-can; in all, thirty seven and one-half pounds

MONUMENT TO FAITHFUL BURRO. Prunes had worked for many prospectors at most of mines in district, was last owned by Rupert Sherwood. When too old to carry burdens he had freedom of town, would panhandle food at any doorway, was beloved by everyone in camp. At his death, citizens buried him beside main street, erected monument. Prunes' last master left request to be cremated and buried in same grave which is immediately behind monument. Colored marbles originally outlined inscription, were pried out by vandal souvenir hunters. Case at left contains Prunes' harness, at right pictures of Sherwood and other mementos. At base are ore samples from mine where shaggy little animal worked.

ALMA WAS CENTER OF MINING DISTRICT, so cold in winter many nabobs built elegant homes at lower altitude of city. Most are crumbling but some still display gingerbread trimmings of another day. Mt. Silverheels is northwest of town, has some snow even in summer.

CONCRETE CALABOOSE. Prisoners from Buckskin Joe, Mosquito, and Park City, were brought into Alma for incarceration in central, substantial jail. Original building was of log construction but too many escapes took place as building deteriorated. Log house became store, now both buildings are crumbling.

to pack on my back." Four months of his efforts netted him forty-three dollars in collections.

In October of 1861, two Mexicans drove a flock of sheep into Buckskin Joe. They had no trouble selling the animals for mutton and stayed overnight in the camp. One of them woke up violently ill, dying in short order of smallpox. An epidemic gripped the town and many residents were added to the cemetery up among the aspens. The women were evacuated to Alma before things got too bad—all but one, a dancehall girl known as Silverheels.

The real name of this girl has long been forgotten, but her dancing shoes with heels of silver made for her by an adoring miner gave her the name by which she was known to all. When the smallpox struck this heroic girl who had been so snubbed by the "decent women" of the camp, refused to leave, nursing many of the stricken until they died or recovered. When the worst was over, grateful miners got together a purse of money, nuggets and dust and took it to her door, only to find her vanished. Several years later and regularly thereafter, a heavily veiled woman was seen walking among the graves in the aspen grove, then leaving without speaking to anyone. It was thought she was Silverheels, that she had contracted the smallpox, and would show her once beautiful face to no one.

A mountain, 13,825 feet in elevation and snowy most of the year, now bears the name Mt. Silverheels in honor of the "Angel of Mercy of South Park."

BRECKENRIDGE, COLORADO

Over the continental divide in the summer of 1859 came a horde of gold-hungry prospectors. Their camps along the Swan and Blue Rivers were temporary as they panned the sands of the streams. Then as one pan sloshed around in the Blue, a rich residue showed and this led to a more permanent camp on the little river, with others set up in several gulches, until the whole area was a maze of tents, shacks and cabins—the site of the original strike being built up into a roistering boom camp. Then the original settlers, the Indians who resented the white man's spoiling their streams and killing their game, began a series of attacks on the raw placer camps. Defenses were set at the central point, the place called Fort Meribeh.

As more and more people, businessmen as well as miners, swarmed into the diggings, a post office became necessary. To this end, a town was formed and called "Breckinridge," after John C. Breckinridge, vice-president of the United States. But when the predominantly Union population heard that the Vice-President's sympathies lay with the Confederate cause, the town's name was altered by changing the first "i" to an "e".

Doldrums set in with the exhaustion of placer gold but the development of quartz mining brought a boom. The stamp mills could crush huge chunks of gold-bearing rock into fragments, grind them into powder, the yellow metal separated by raw amalga-

mation. As other camps had found, this method was wasteful but more efficient smelters were too costly.

The camp enjoyed a huge prosperity in the '80s, a complete gaggle of gamblers and prostitutes. The miners of all the surrounding camps bore down on the dives of Breckenridge with a bang. Shootings were common but one had a comic opera aspect.

When this case was brought into court, the antagonists were told they would have to fight a European-type duel. The camp was starved for public entertainment and a civic-minded judge thought the idea sportive. The duel proceeded by the book until, at the count of fifteen paces, when each man was supposed to turn and fire, both contestants picked up their feet and fled—one west, one east—never to be seen again around those parts.

The end of hard rock mining again turned Breckenridge into a ghost town and the place slumbered until several dredges began to work the "depleted" gravels of Blue River. Again a resurgence of activity took over and a third boom was on. When the need arose for extensive maintenance of dredge equipment, large shops were built for repairs and fabrication of new parts. But eventually big-time dredging came to an end and the camp by the Blue rested on its laurels, hoping for gold prices to go up.

Owen Freeman was a patient man with an eye to the future, honest and trusting, too—all rare qualities in the slapdash boom world of Colorado gold. He

ORIGINAL FALSE FRONTS mingle with more recent shacks. Where post office now stands, old Denver Hotel sheltered drummers and itinerants for many years. It was across street from grocery store, and one winter, when snow reached depth of 13 feet, tunnel was dug and used until melted.

STABLE END OF OLD FIREHOUSE. Hose carts were in front of structure facing street, horses stabled in rear facing alley. Loft held winter hay. Stable still holds old wagons and fire equipment. Ten Mile Range, spur from continental divide, forms background.

discovered a rich lode but decided to tell no one, to keep working at his mine job until he accumulated enough money to develop his find.

The steep mountainside where Freeman found his vein was cluttered with tents and shanties grouped around the several mine heads. The timber was cut off, tree by tree, for shoring, shelter and firewood. Gradually the water was drained out of the canyon valley and Silver Plume took shape as a town in 1870. About this time, Owen Freeman caught pneumonia after being trapped in a cave-in.

Hovering near death, he asked to see his two best friends and to them revealed the secret of his lode.

Expected to die, he lay in comas and was pronounced tubercular, the end only a pick handle away. Then like a ghost rising from a grave, he made a partial recovery—and a startling discovery. His trusted friends had recorded the claim in their names only and were working the vein.

This mine, the Pelican, turned out good ore containing almost every metal known at that time—gold, silver, lead, zinc and copper. Other mines on the steep mountain slopes were the Payrock, Burleigh, Terrible Dunderburg and others. While their owners prospered, Owen Freeman went back to his sickbed and brooded his life away.

FAIRPLAY, COLORADO

Not all those who responded to the clarion call of "Pike's Peak or Bust" found gold along the eastern fringe of the Rockies. Some restless souls who were not pleased with small pickings there, moved on across South Park and into the fastness of the Rockies themselves. One of these groups found a good show of colors in a stream not far from the South Platte River. Deciding to stay awhile, they named the new camp Tarryall. News of the strike spread, newcomers sought to share the wealth and were bitterly resisted. Smarting with resentment, one larger party of would-be residents moved on to the South Platte itself, found a rich deposit of gold flakes in the gravels of that stream and established a camp of their own which they called Fairplay.

After a few years, the supply of easily obtained placer gold grew less and the town suffered a depres-

sion. When capital became interested, hard rock mining began in the lodes that had been dribbling their wealth into the river gravels. This gold was harder to get at and hard to separate from the native rock, but the supply was more steady and Fairplay prospered again. Business picked up in the many dancehalls and saloons and the town's twelve hook-joints could stop having clearance sales.

However, as costs of machinery and labor rose while the price of gold remained fixed, stern difficulties beset the place and gradually decay set in again as mines closed. A large dredge was operating in the South Platte, digging far deeper into the gravels than by other, simpler methods, and while this operation employed a number of men, Fairplay was never the same again. It still breathes and makes a show of its memories and mementos.

SANDSTONE COURTHOUSE, built in 1874, replaced original log building moved from Buckskin Joe after election of 1868. All women and children were herded into structure, in 1879, when false rumor that Indians were burning neighboring Breckenridge and scalping residents threw town into frenzy. About same period brutal murderer was tried here, given life. Irate citizens gathered at night, forced keys from sheriff, took prisoner from cell, hanged him from second-story window over doorway which then lacked present awning.

SILVER PLUME, COLORADO

Almost the only place in Silver Plume where transients could stay in 1870 was the Pelican House. The charitable proprietors kept a row of beds warm at all times, one sleeper shift flopping on them as soon as another vacated the blankets. These were boom days for the bedbugs, too.

One of the first to come to Silver Plume was a young Englishman named Griffin. He discovered the Seven-Thirty mine and profited greatly. The vein was rich in both silver and gold and the deeper it went, the heavier were the deposits. Yet instead of living in high spirits, the handsome Griffin kept to his cabin each night, making friends with no one. Then he discovered his past was following him. A rumor was circulated that on the eve of his wedding in England, his fiancee had been found dead in his room. Griffin denied nothing, acknowledged nothing.

Getting richer all the time, he did nothing with his money, not even frequenting the brothels of the town. But he did have one project—hewing out a depression in the solid rock facing his little cabin high on Columbia Mountain, directly above Silver Plume. As time went on, people saw this hole grow into the shape of a grave. Each evening, after his stint of excavating the refractory rock, Griffin would bring out his violin to play the melodies and classical music of his earlier days. One June night in '87 the miners thought he played particularly well. Then they heard a shot reverberating in the canyon. Face down in the grave with a bullet in his heart, was the gentleman from Piccadilly.

AT HEIGHT OF BUSTLING DAYS, the Plume boasted two churches, Odd Fellows Hall, Knights of Pythias Hall, shown here at right of church. Also lining street were school, theater and many stores as well as usual quota of saloons and red-light houses. Small community of Brownsville, so close as to be regarded as suburb was overwhelmed by mudslide, never recovered.

GEORGETOWN, COLORADO

For many years Georgetown enjoyed the distinction of being the most important silver camp in Colorado, at length deposed by the even more fabulous strikes in Leadville in 1878. Gold, however, brought about the birth of the city and caused one of the biggest booms in the early mining history of the state. The yellow metal was found glittering in the gravels of the several streams gathering in the canyon's depths in 1859 by prospectors dissatisfied with what they found as latecomers to the Denver area. A discovery under similar circumstances and in the same year had started the fabulous careers of the related towns of Black Hawk, Central City and Nevadaville, but there, gold held out and sustained the economy of the gulch.

In Georgetown, on the other hand, large lodes or outcroppings of gold were never found, and although lode mining in the '70s was sufficient to boom the town a second time, this too tapered off. The town went through all the discouragements suffered by other camps in trying to extract silver from refractory ores. Poor communications, the worst kind of terrain and almost impossible travel, kept methods of getting at the shiny metal crude and costly. The margin of profit in silver, comparatively speaking, was never that of gold until several methods were compared and the best features of each combined. Part of this agony had been already toughed out by the camps in Georgetown's category when Leadville's star began to shine, materially stimulating silver extraction methods there.

PROMINENT LANDMARK remaining from days when fire was ever threatening. Shadowy interior still houses antiquated equipment. Tower was built especially for gift of 1,200-pound bell. In 1880 Hose Company won many prizes in State Firemen's Tournaments, including silver tea set and brass cannon. In background at left is Grace Episcopal Church, built by townspeople even before rector was assured. Completed in '69, it was blown from foundations by gale, dragged back, bell anchored in separate belfry beside structure. Bell bears inscription "St. Mark's, Black Hawk, Colo. Terr." Intended for church to be erected there, Georgetown salvaged it when plans fell through.

THIS LITTLE GEM is sole survivor of fire which devastated most [of] block. When this building [w]as erected, famous Georgetown [–] Silver Plume Loop was being [b]uilt. Ore had long been hauled [d]own valley in wagons but had [re]ached proportions beyond ca[pa]city of horse-drawn rigs. When [ra]ilroad was completed it followed ["]Loop System" unequaled in its [d]ay. Tracks folded over them[se]lves to gain altitude, reaching [th]e Plume and completion thus [fa]r in '82.

But while Georgetown struggled to get on its feet as a silver camp, whiskey flowed in a never-ending stream. One saloon proprietor hired a sign painter to embellish the front of his establishment with a sign calculated to stimulate sales. He wanted a good job done but refused to pay what the painter asked, and the resulting legend read, "We sell the Worst Whiskey, Wine and Cigars." Unable to read but pleased with the attention his new sign created, the proprietor paid the painter the rest of his money, later discovering he was being laughed at. Nevertheless, the publicity so stimulated business the sign was allowed to remain for many years. Another story is told that the townspeople felt that they should have a cemetery like any other city, were frustrated by the healthfulness of the climate there, and at last had to hang a man to get things going. Although the camp attracted as many undesirables as did any other, there were fewer killings and other forms of violence.

In the late '70s the following appeared in *The Georgetown Miner*. "For a period of about sixteen years that enterprising individual, the 'honest miner,' has prospected and dug for the precious metal in our county with that energy and tenacity which is a distinguishing characteristic of 'miner men,' and, to some extent, is born of the circumstances under which he is placed. He has lived hard and worked harder, and with an undaunted brow has often faced the bitterest and sternest realities of life. He has gazed down the misty avenues of probabilities until what appeared to others to be the vaguest outlines of chance were to him an absolute certainty of all his hopes. He has acquired a fortune with a few weeks' or months' labor, and often, with a generosity bordering on recklessness, he has squandered it again in but less time than it took to accumulate it. On the one hand, he has toiled incessantly for years without taking out a single

OLDEST FIREHOUSE in town has lacy balcony and elaborate belfry, still retains picturesque emblem of crossed ladders and fire hook. Organized in 1870, Georgetown Fire and Hose Co. stands on Alpine Street, across from Louis Du Puy's Hotel De Paris.

LOUIS DU PUY'S HOTEL DE PARIS was most celebrated hostelry west of Mississippi during '70s and '80s. Born in Alencon, France, Du Puy was a hater of women, yet left all he had to one. He was a despiser of his guests yet made them comfortable in an opulence undreamed of in a wild mountain silver camp. Eccentric, unpredictable, he had squandered an inheritance in France, arriving in Georgetown to recoup his fortunes in '69, and four years later was injured in mine explosion. Displaying heroism in rescue work of disaster, he was rewarded with collection taken up by families. With this, in '75, he bought Delmonico Bakery on Alpine Street, remodeled it into Hotel De Paris. Lavish in furnishings, exotic in cuisine, hotel accepted as guests only people passing close scrutiny of Du Puy, many being turned away for no apparent reason. Only one woman gained his second look — a widow, Sophie Galet. She was taken in at husband's death, made comfortable and was bequeathed entire establishment at Du Puy's death in 1900.

'red,' but his faith still continues unshaken and his perseverance unimpaired. He has accomplished labors compared with which the cleaning out of the Augean stables would be but a before-breakfast chore. He has penetrated to the very foundations of the eternal hills, and the innermost recesses of 'earth's gigantic sentinels' have echoed with the sharp ring of his steel-impelling strokes and bellowed back the infernal roar of his fiery persuasion. He has carved his way through sullen solitude in search of metaliferous wealth, and a liberal and enlightened civilization has followed close on his heels. If he has not discovered the secret of transmutation of metals, he has discovered the secret of their hiding places; while mechanical and chemical science have sprung to his aid and rendered indispensable assistance in their extraction. The brave and persistent miner has accomplished all this and much more, not with the wand of an eastern fairy, but with a striking hammer weighing from six to eight pounds, and other implements necessary to his vocation."

Georgetown could have faded into decay but the town continues to live with pride. Its buildings are kept in good repair and a hard surface road brings many tourists every year to view the monuments to a glorious past.

BLACK HAWK, COLORADO

Drama rode with every gold mine mule, came bucketing down every crooked lane between the miners' shacks. Black Hawk wallowed in it from 1867 to 1879 and for some years it went under the name of Doe.

Gregory Gulch's first gold was discovered at Mountain City and from this camp grew the settlement of Black Hawk which was soon enough swallowed up by bigger ones above and below. The whole Gulch area produced most of Colorado's gold for three years after 1867.

Black Hawk then began to have trouble. As the shafts went deeper the granites and porphyries grew more obdurate. Soon only 15 to 40 percent of the assay could be saved, the rest swept downstream and lost. Such a situation was tolerated as long as costs of labor, supplies and materials were at a low level, but as these advanced the waste became disastrous. The harder the rock, the better the milling machinery had to be, and this transported over the plains through the hazards of Indian wars. Operations almost ceased, saved from death throes by a Professor Hill who secured the cooperation of Boston and Colorado Smelting Works in putting up a huge smelter at Black Hawk in '68. All good ore was then sent through the smelter, low content rock treated by raw

amalgamation in the quartz mills as before. The rehabilitation was further aided by the construction of the Colorado Central Railway up through the mountains to Black Hawk. This sparked life into many neglected and flooded mines.

In July of 1877, a pair of newlyweds arrived at Central City on the narrow gauge—a Mr. and Mrs. William H. Doe, Jr., the husband known as Harvey. The little blond wife had been Elizabeth McCourt back in Oshkosh, Wisconsin, two weeks before, and was already nicknamed "Baby" Doe. She was excited, sure that her Harvey would make a mint of money out of the Fourth of July mine, which his father owned and he was to manage. When time proved that father had all the business acumen, Baby Doe became impatient, donned pants and went to work at the mine to speed things up.

Then father Doe came out to Colorado to take over and ousted the young bride from the mine. Disillusioned and bored, she took long walks around Black Hawk where she and Harvey had taken rooms to save money. During the course of these strolls she walked into the clothing store owned by two Jewish merchants, Jacob Sandelowsky and Sam Pelton. Drama was now hovering low over her head and the handsome, curly-haired one of young Jacob. There were more meetings

DOWN ON FLAT, near Gregory Creek, stands old blacksmith shop. Built after one of Black Hawk's fires to replace wooden structure, it stands precariously, cracks having developed all through brickwork. Door was widened for automobiles, original horseshoe replaced above it.

BLACK HAWK STREET fronting on creek was once solidly lined with ornate houses. This one with fancy carved barge boards is one of few survivors. Baby Doe, on her lonely walks around town, often passed here.

between the two which increased the already rampant town gossip. And when the Does attended the opening night at the Opera House in Central City as the guests of the partners, tongues flapped like shutters in the wind.

Now Baby Doe found she was pregnant and afraid to tell her husband. He learned of it from snoopers and flew into a tantrum. His taunt—"I hear you're going to have a Jewish brat," provoked a furious quarrel and bitter recriminations on both sides. Time passed in this strained manner until the baby was born, prematurely and dead. Harvey's rage was softened at Baby Doe's grief and he relented, a certain kind of peace being declared.

Harvey had lost out at the Fourth of July altogether and was forced to take menial jobs, going deeper and deeper into debt. The gulch itself was

suffering a depression, not so much for lack of gold but because the population was being lured to a brash new camp, Leadville. And this was where debonair Jacob Sandelowsky went, changing his name to Sands and opening an elegant branch store. He was still very much in love with Baby Doe, flooding her with letters entreating her to join him.

One cold day in December, 1879, she walked up the hill to take a long, wistful look at the Fourth of July which had now been declared worthless. To those who saw her she looked dejected and beaten down, yet the next morning she was her bright, vivacious self—when she took the little train to Leadville.

(Author's note: The rest of Baby Doe's story is told in *Western Ghost Towns*, the first of this series, under Leadville.)

119

CENTRAL CITY, COLORADO

"The richest square mile on earth" was to have a theater. And no less a personality than dancer Mlle. Haydee, with her Troupe, was coming to play in it. Major Hadley told the people of Central City it was all true. That was why he was fixing up his old log hall. And the brothel girls wondered just what kind of troupe this "Mlle." had.

This was Central City in the first summer of its gay day, 1859. April saw John Gregory locate a gold ledge and fight a blizzard. May saw many more claims in the gulches, the boom on its way. June brought 3,000 people and the next month Central City had 30,000.

All this lightning development came after the placer discoveries in Little Dry Creek where Denver would sometime be. John H. Gregory was not satisfied with the "chicken feed" there and with a pick and a prayer, grubbed around in the gulches looking for the source deposits of gold. In a stream flowing down through the Kansas Territory Rocky Mountains, he found grains instead of flakes and was further elated

when he located the ledges they had come from. A snowstorm almost defeated him, but grubstaked by David K. Wall, who raised vegetables for the miners and sold milk from his cow for more than whiskey cost, Gregory organized a party of veterans and greenhorns and found his yellow treasure on May 6. The spot was first called Mountain City but it lost its identity as Black Hawk below and Central City above gained attention. Meanwhile, William Green Russell, found grains instead of flakes and was further elated when he made the Little Dry Creek discovery, a rich strike in a gulch parallel to Gregory's. Above Central City the mining locality came to be called Nevada City, then Nevadaville.

The whole area became interlaced with workings and small towns and known as the "richest square mile on earth." Gregory sold his claims by the end of May for $21,000, a small fortune then.

As in all camps when gold was first discovered, panning was the sole method of recovery. Soon rockers were built and, while wasteful, were more

VIEW UP EUREKA STREET shows several famous Central City structures. At immediate left is Teller House, opened on June 24, 1872 with large dinner, and concert of "exquisite music by Prof. Barnum's Orchestra." Publicity stated "the majority of rooms are without transoms, ventilation being obtained by the use of adjustable windows. Guests may therefore lie down to peaceful slumbers undisturbed by apprehensions of getting their heads blown off or having their valuables lifted by burglars." Just above is Opera House, across street is Courthouse (with two towers), next this way is St. James M. E. Church, organized by missionaries first summer of camp's existence. First services were held in home of "Aunt Clara Brown," a former slave. This building was begun in 1864. Next is City Hall, then Williams Stables.

MOST POPULAR STABLE OWNER was big, jovial and beloved R. B. Williams, who was also the sheriff. Williams was murdered in 1896, by a man gone berserk over his wages being garnisheed. Opera House was only hall in Central City big enough to accommodate friends attending his funeral.

productive. Then Long Toms, enlarged versions of the rockers, appeared up and down the streams. By the second summer most of the placer gold was gone and more hard rock mining was enforced. This was where the real wealth lay, in the vertical or nearly vertical, metaliferous veins. In the Central City area these lodes were granite or gneiss, or a combination of both. The upper, exposed ends were more or less weathered and crumbly, were easily worked, but as the mines sank deeper the granite became increasingly refractory and the boys were separated from the men. Quartz stamp mills began to appear, purchased by companies of miners banded together. The day of the individual claim operator was gone.

The first quartz mill to operate here was also the first in Colorado. Set up by Prosser, Conkling and Co., this noisy contraption was small and crude but worked well, and was followed by a rash of similar—larger and more refined—monsters which split the air day and night with their din. Over a hundred mills of five, ten and fifteen stamps were erected in Gilpin County in the first years. Some wore out and their replacements were even bigger and noisier. A system was soon worked out to avoid the stamp mill waste to some extent. The ore of a given mine separated into lots, the few tons of very rich material being sent to the smelter, the remainder, perhaps thirty times as much, crushed in the mill.

The first summer in Central City saw all the excitement of a typical boom town. Almost all the 30,000 in the district were established miners, hangers-on or prospectors looking for a claim and moving on as they found the good ones already taken. Among these last were the Tabors—Augusta, Horace and baby—camping and prospecting in the mountains for many heart-breaking, privation-filled months, then after a short rest moving on toward Leadville and destiny.

When the first flakes of snow fell many decided to return to home and families for the winter, and Central City was down to some 1,500. They worked their claims during open spells, particularly where rockers were still in use, as these did not freeze so easily. One man, left alone, took out some $2,400 during the three coldest winter months. When his partners returned after a winter of ease and carousing, broke and expecting to share in this hard-won wealth, they found it was not being passed around. Next winter they stayed but snows were so deep from November to February no one could work.

But that first year—and Mlle. Haydee's artistic troupe of players. Major Hadley readied the big log building in the gulch, the ground floor of which was fronted by a row of stores, saloons and a barbershop. The theater would be in the upstairs loft where supports for candles were nailed along the walls, one row

121

VISTA DOWN EUREKA STREET shows area almost completely destroyed by fire in 1874. Sidewalk in front of Teller House (next after Opera House on right) was paved with silver bricks on occasion of visit by President U. S. Grant in '73. Silver was borrowed for event, gold being too common in Central. This same gold kept gulch going, even after collapse of silver which ruined Leadville and other camps, but by 1914 Central City was nine-tenths ghost.

placed crosswise near the far end for footlights and before it all the benches in town.

What difference did it make if the "madamoiselle" was from Missouri? Half the men in town fancied themselves in love with her and called her "Miss Millie." She ruled the males of the gulch and that meant almost everybody as there was only one "straight" woman, Mary York, and a dozen prostitutes. Later a permanent theater, The Olympia was built for the players above the Veranda Hotel. When a report got around that gambler Tom Evans had been seen to force Miss Millie into a buggy and depart with her, whipping the horses to top speed, a posse of furious would-be lovers was made up but had no place to go as no one knew where Evans had taken the dancer. A week later came the awful truth. The couple had wed in Denver. The posse was dismissed.

Mary York had been the first woman in the raw young camp and defended her virtue against all comers. She became so adept at this that she set up the first boarding house. Among her guests was a young miner named Billie Cozens. He was the first man she had ever looked at twice and when he proposed Mary gladly accepted him.

Before long Billie was made sheriff, and one of his problems was holding prisoners, there being no jail.

On one occasion, he arrested two men in the evening. Mary had just given birth to a new son, and was still confined to bed. Billie dragged the prisoners into the bedroom, over Mary's weak protest, and chained them to the bedstead. They were forced to lie on the floor, Billie theatening the two with violence if they disturbed the new mother or baby. They were model prisoners and in the morning were hustled off to court. When Mary regained her strength, she made her young husband's life so miserable over the incident that he soon managed to get a jail built.

The next years were ones of prosperity for the gulch inspite of many troubles such as the over-exploitation of mine stocks by New York tycoons who had bought up most of the larger mines. The Gregory lode sold for $1,000 a foot and at this high peak of manipulation, the boom collapsed, plunging the camp into a deep depression. Then came a period when many of these absentee owners came out to run things themselves, only to do further damage through ignorance. But the "square mile" survived, and had some more good years, the best being the '70's and '80's. There were the usual big fires, sweeping flimsy wooden structures before them, but even these catastrophes had good results, solid brick and stone buildings going up—the ones that make Central City the fascinating monument it is today.

APEX, COLORADO

Apex is the story of a man who found true gold in the veins of the Pine Creek hills—and none in those of his fellows. The discovery and disenchantment made Apex a part of Colorado mining history, even though brighter parts were played by Black Hawk, Central City and Nevadaville.

Sometime in the '70's, Richard Mackey made a good though not exciting strike in the Pine Creek mining district. He sold it while the selling was good and the new owner soon did the same. This went on until a man named Mountz got hold of the lode—and he was serious about working it. From his mining experience Mountz was sure this was a good vein. Just where it went from its first indication he was not so certain. The main trouble was that he was broke.

Talking up his property, he secured a partner who seemed equally enthusiastic about the Mackey and together they raised enough money to get going. Almost immediately the two struck good pay ore though the main vein still eluded them. In no time the partners had stacked up a tidy $30,000. Then, one fine morning, Mountz woke to find himself alone, his part-ner and the money vanished. Despondently plugging along alone, he decided to try for the lode and to that end persistently drove his tunnel in what he hoped was the right direction.

One day he was forced to take stock of his situation. He was down to his last dollar, almost out of food and there still was no sign of that vein. His decision was to stack his last several sticks of dynamite in the bore at the terminus of the working, light the fuse and the hell with it.

Next morning he slept late, finished a good breakfast of all the food that was left and went to have a look. The shattered pile of debris was all rich ore—and there behind it was exposed the shining lode! A sample rushed to the assayer in Black Hawk proved out $1800 to the ton but everyone was sure there must be some mistake. A second sampling verified the good news, and the rush to Apex was on. No other such bonanza was ever found there but the Mackey continued to produce so faithfully that it justified the building of a mill, just for the one mine.

EXCITING STRIKE BY MOUNTZ sparked real boom and town of Apex came into being in the '70s. Main street was lined solidly by saloons, stores and hotels in '80s.

WARD, COLORADO

Prior to the '60's, prospectors had been pecking around on the steep, heavily timbered sides of Left Hand Canyon, which was named for a south-paw Indian. Every pan dipped in the creek at the bottom of the canyon had yielded a rich residue and there was interest in finding a vein somewhere above. Then Calvin Ward struck it. In his joy at the discovery he called his claim the "Miser's Dream."

Ward's find tended to confirm the belief that a lode must lie somewhere above and the excitement began early the next year when Cy Deardorff chipped off a piece of float that showed the location of the main vein. This was to be the Columbia Mine, which in its period of productivity, turned out $5,000,000 in ore. Later the big producers were the East Columbia, Ni-Wot Utica, Baxter, Boston and Idaho.

Even on foot a prospector had a hard time making his way up the sides of Left Hand Canyon, but that going was easy compared to the troubles encountered when wagons became necessary for hauling equipment. First the trees had to be cut down in a strip wide enough for a road. Rocks had to be blasted out of the way and dirt filled in. Grades were so steep that teams of oxen and horses could just get up the hill with the wagons. The first trees cut were dragged to a sawmill but the mill burned to the ground almost before it had

ONCE WARD WAS LIVELY. Work was started on Congregational Church in same year town was incorporated, 1896. Although Ward's big fire destroyed fifty-three buildings with a property loss of $85,000, the church was seared only on one side. Large false-fronted structure at upper left is C. and N. Hotel. In later years Mrs. Thompson operated hotel in summer only, she herself stayed on in big front room and kept hot fire going in big stove. Artist-Author Muriel Wolle spent part of one winter sketching in Ward, stayed in upper frigid room, slept in sleeping bag on floor, woke up at night to see stovepipe, going straight up through room, "glowed dull red from heat of the banked stove below and vibrated back and forth whenever a particularly strong blast struck the building." Corner of building at extreme left is remnant of store. Long structure in center dates from later period, was Small's Garage.

produced any lumber. A second was built immediately and it turned out the material to shelter the first miners and construct several stores. By 1867 some two hundred people were living in new frame houses in the Columbia district. When the Ni-Wot built its small mill, total population was about six hundred.

By the 90's the town was fllourishing and was incorporated. In 1897 a railroad was brought up to Ward from Boulder. The twenty-six mile right of way climbed 4,100 feet to reach 9,450 feet in elevation. Officially the Colorado and Northwestern, the route was known as the Whiplash and Switzerland Trail. The long switchbacks took the train past one high point called Mount Alta and at this point the company built an elaborate resort with a dancehall in the hope of attracting tourists. June 28th, 1898 saw the "Formal Opening to passengers, traffic and business of the Whiplash Route from the verdant Valley of Boulder to the Cloud Kissed Camp of Ward."

The first train stopped at the mouth of the mine tunnels to allow the passengers the thrill of entering. To make things more homelike for them, boards were laid over the puddles and a long line of burning candles dimly lit the way. About the time the excur-sionists were all inside and more than a little apprehensive, the miners added thrill to excitement by setting off a blast of dynamite in a side tunnel. How were they to know the resulting rush of air would blow out all the candles?

There had been thousands of tons of low assay ore accumulating on the dumps around Ward for twenty years, its value more than offset by the high cost of wagon transport. Now that the railroad had come there was jubilation—the waste would now be converted to cash. But the optimism was not justified as the ores proved to be extremely refractory.

Then, at the turn of the century when the mine production was slackening, disaster was added to disappointment. Fire nearly destroyed the camp. The *Ward Miner* of January 26, 1900 stated that "not a store, hotel, saloon, restaurant or a business house of any sort escaped the flames. If the life of the old town depended wholly upon the profits taken over the counter and the bar, its destruction would be complete, and the little basin in which its business houses once stood might be abandoned for the home of the chipmunk and the coyote."

ONE OF DEARDORFF'S DISCOVERIES was Utica Mine. It became leading workings of camp, began to pay off in 1888 and by next year had made a million dollars. Its stone mill, shown here, is one of oldest still standing, was originally run by water power. Pipeline brought water five miles over hills. Main shaft of mine was destroyed by fire in 1898, forcing temporary closure, suspending monthly income of $10,000. Ore assayed $200 to $500 to the ton.

ALMA, NEW MEXICO

Into Alma's brief period of life was crowded more turbulence, murder and bloodshed than fell to the lot of any other comparable town in New Mexico. Apaches almost continually harassed the village; any brief respite from Indian raids was filled with internal strife between ranchers and holdups by bandits.

The original plans for Alma were more than peaceful; in fact, the town was laid out along communal lines. No mining was involved at first; this meant no influx of single men to allow for saloons and brothels. Only families would settle here in the fertile and well-watered "Frisco Valley" and farm the land. Cabins would be built close together for better protection from Indians; the farms would surround the homes; everything seemed ideal.

Maurice Coates, one of the dreamers, was born in Canada in 1856. He was a drifter and in his wanderings became a friend of James Keller who also was heading westward. They stopped in Prescott, Arizona, for a while where they decided that farming was their forte, then retraced their steps to the San Francisco Valley, New Mexico, where they found land that was suitable at the edge of the Mogollon Range, named for Don Juan Ignacio Flores Mogollon, Governor of the Province of New Mexico, 1712 to '15. Together with two other interested men, Capt. J. G. Birney and

Robert Stubblefield, they laid out plans for the town and called the place Mogollon. The same year, 1878, control of Mogollon was bought out by Capt. Birney. Since he had never liked the name Mogollon, he rechristened the infant settlement "Alma" for his mother.

And now the bloody period began. W. H. McCullough, a native New Mexican, was the first man to sell the founders on the idea of settling in the state, and had been one of the original farmers of the valley. Almost immediately after the change in ownership, he, with Birney and Prescott, were slain by a party of sheepherders which included whites and two Pueblo Indians. The sheepherders had learned that the Alma men were going to the Adams diggings in Arizona to see what was going on there, and an ambush was laid for them on the assumption that they would be carrying quite a lot of money. They figured, rightly, that Navajos who had recently been on the warpath would be blamed. The true story came out in '86, when the remains were found and one of the Pueblos, conscience stricken, confessed to the deed. He was convicted of murder by the tribal council and put to death by his own people. Before he died, he implicated the other members of the party and they were pursued by the sheriff but never caught.

Although trouble with Pueblos and Navajos continued, the real terror was furnished by Apaches. One evening five of them made a raid on James Keller's ranch and killed several of his cattle. Infuriated, he swore to kill every one of the Indian party, and started after them, alone. When he caught up with them unobserved, he thought better of it and returned to Alma for help. Reinforced by several men, he took the trail again, and since the Indians had not suspected they were being pursued, they were soon overtaken by the avenging settlers. The tally at the end of the battle, three warriors dead and one wounded. The latter died while fleeing the scene, his body found the next day. The raid had been a costly one for the Apaches, but the significant factor in the whole episode was that one of the slain Indians proved to be Toribo, son-in-law of notorious Victorio. His slaying would not go unavenged.

As soon as the news reached Victorio, the Chief began to lay plans to wipe out the entire settlement of Alma. He went to the camp of a sub-chief called Steve to enlist help. When Steve refused, realizing that slaughter of the whites would soon bring the wrath of a battalion of soldiers on his head, the furious Victorio retreated far enough to assemble his warriors and then attacked his erstwhile friend. The battle of Apache against Apache ended in humiliating defeat for Victorio, and in addition the loss of several of his best braves. Smarting, he killed and scalped the first two white men he ran across. Their names are not known, but two of the same party escaped— George Mehams and Eli Mader. These men made their way to the nearby mining camp of Cooney and spread the news. The founder of this community, Sergeant James Cooney, with a couple of miners named Chick and Brightman and other man unnamed, took off after the Indians. In the meantime, Victorio had found more willing allies than Steve's warriors, the more terrible Geronimo and Nana. Their augmented force was too much for Cooney's party, Brightman and the unidentified miner being killed and scalped. Cooney and Chick fled to Alma, arriving there in the dead of night.

Alma now made preparations for an almost certain attack, and agreed to make a fort of the Roberts home, that being the most likely to resist a siege. Cooney, having alerted the settlers in Alma, was anxious to return to his own town and with one volunteer, left for the camp named for him.

BLACKSMITH SHOP under large trees at outskirts of Alma where travelers stopped to have wagon wheels fixed, horses and mules shod. Dry climate most of year often made iron tires come off wheels. Tire was laid on ground, elevated about eight inches by rocks, fire built under and around. When metal was well expanded, tire was slipped over wheel and hammered on. Blacksmith shop was owned by partners, Dan Russell and William Antrim. Antrim had courted and married Katherine McCarthy, mother of Billy the Kid, in Sante Fe, March 1, 1873. Billy was then 14 years old and extremely fond of mother, resented intrusion of Antrim. Two got along in armed truce. The Kid hung around the blacksmith shop and affection of a sort grew between them so when Garret killed the Kid everyone thought Antrim would go gunning for the killer. He eventually went to Adelaide, California, died and was buried there. Shop was converted to garage in earliest days of autos, "antique" pump added to front of old smithy.

They got safely away about eight o'clock. At ten, Apaches appeared on the hillside east of Alma and opened fire on the Roberts cabin. One wagonload of four whites, the Meador family, had just arrived at the refuge and had not yet entered. They were unable to get out of the wagon because of the firing by the Indians. Suddenly to everyone's astonishment Mrs. Meador grabbed a rifle and began returning the fire. In the resulting momentary confusion, a woman opened the cabin door, and all slipped in, though not before Mr. Meador lost a lock of his hair to a bullet whizzing by. Another missle went through the bonnet of the lady opening the door. The river was on the opposite side and the women managed to get some water collected in kettles and pans before they were spotted and fired upon.

The siege was now on in earnest and firing was general. The first Indian casualty resulted when a brave couldn't resist the temptation of a beautiful horse tethered in the open. When he exposed himself to reach for the bridle, a well-aimed shot from the gun of Jim Keller felled him. One of the men in the cabin, a Mr. Wilcox, made the mistake of standing up to make sure the Indian was really dead and was himself slain by a bullet through the heart.

It seemed necessary to summon aid some way, so Keller and Pete Carpenter managed to slip out as soon as it got dark and made it to Silver City, unharmed. From there a rider was sent to Fort Bayard where a rescue squad was organized and joined by a reinforced group of civilians from Silver City. The men rode the seventy-two miles when they were forced to rest their horses. They then made the distance to Bush Valley where they expected to change horses, but were dismayed to find that Indians had run off all available mounts, some thirty horses. They were now out of provisions as well and managed to collect three days supply while their horses rested. At last they reached the outlying ranches near Alma on May 14th, 1880. The next day they forced the besieging Indians to retreat to the mountains, and the first siege of Alma was over. Altogether thirty-one whites had been killed in the area during the uprising. These figures included Sergeant Cooney and his volunteer, who had been waylaid on the return to Cooney and killed. Their mutilated bodies were found by the rescue party. Cooney was buried in a solid stone "tomb" close to his mine and town.

As soon as Alma had a chance to relax a little it went ahead. July of '82 showed a population of more than three hundred. A school was built, taking care of sixty-eight children. James Meador built the Hotel de Brunswick. An organization called the Minute Men was set up and the men trained regularly so as to be ready for the next Indian attack. Church services were held in the schoolhouse by a circuit rider, and later by ministers from neighboring Cooney and Mogollon. One of the residents wrote a letter to the editor of the *Albuquerque Journal* in 1883, stating "our town is made up of thirty-five houses well constructed of adobe and lumber. We have two business houses doing general merchandising business and in connection with the same a good saloon and card rooms. . . . Two saloons, one owned by D. A. Bechtol who smilingly caters to his many friend's desires in the shape of liquid refreshments; the other mentioned above." Two blacksmith shops and a large general merchandise store in a newly constructed adobe building completed the inventory.

The same year saw another Indian attack. This one was on a ranch near town and Judge McComas and his wife, who had stopped there overnight on a trip from Silver City, were killed and their six-year-old son carried off. The boy was never seen alive again although many stories persisted about him. One was that the boy's head was bashed in when it seemed certain that the party would be attacked by whites, another that the chief of the Indian tribe in later years had red hair and blue eyes and was presumed to be Charley McComas.

In another siege most of the settlers remained awake all night waiting for an imminent attack—all but a Mr. Herr who slept with a large revolver under his pillow. Circumstances, however, weren't conducive to anything but the most restless slumber, and his turnings worked the pistol out from under the pillow. When he arose in the morning, he knocked it down. It fired and sent a bullet through his head.

At various times troops were stationed in Alma to guard against Apaches. During the worst of Geronimo's raiding, two troops of the 8th cavalry made their headquarters at the big W. S. Ranch, remaining for some sixteen months.

Before and after, never during, these occupations the town became the hangout of the notorious "Wild Bunch" made up of Butch Cassidy, Tom Ketchum, Toppy Johnson and the others. William Antrim, father-in-law of Billy, the Kid, was a resident of Alma and the Kid stayed there with him for a time. Another familiar figure in Alma was that of "Mountain Man" Ben Lilly. He was supposed to have killed 110 mountain lions during his time there, earning for himself $55,000 in bounty money.

All these legendary figures, ferocious Apaches, farmers, saloonkeepers, their shelters and places of business are gone with the wind now. Only one adobe building and the tiny cemetery filled with victims of Indians and murder remain.

MOGOLLON, NEW MEXICO

Young Sergeant James C. Cooney was one to keep his eyes open and his mouth shut. When, in 1870, on a scouting expedition out of Fort Bayard he found a rich ledge from gold bearing float was crumbling, he kept the discovery secret until his hitch was over. This feat is unparalleled in the history of most mining towns. Whiskey usually loosed the tongues of those finding gold.

As soon as Cooney was mustered, he confided in several men he could trust, among them Harry McAllister, forming a partnership to explore the possibilities of his find. The area was in the mountains called the Mogollons (pronounced muggy owns), thickly infested by hostile Apaches. Cooney's party was attacked by Indians so continually that, after establishing several locations, the prospectors retired to Silver City to nurse their wounds. Two years later, with augmented defenses and supplies, the men again set out for the claims. Two ox-drawn wagons carried their equipment and food.

The first place to be established as a camp in the Mogollons was Claremont but this one was short-lived. Then a camp in Cooney Canyon was started

and flourished as a typical rough-and-ready camp for a brief period of glory.

Indians were a constant menace and on one occasion when it was rumored the redskins were about to attack the camp was evacuated as usual. A couple of miners named John Lambert and George Doyle were hiding in the bushes just above the houses when the Indians came down the trail. The white men had their little dog with them and he began to growl. Fearful of attracting attention, they choked the animal to death. The Indian party ransacked the house, one squaw coming out with a full length mirror tied to her back. She was followed by a retinue of delighted youngsters who vied for positions to see their reflections.

At about this same period nearby Alma was established and shared attacks by Apaches. In one of these, James Cooney was killed and his camp at Cooney taken over by his brother Captain Michael Cooney.

In the spring of '83 the Captain grubstaked a man named Turner. Rumors persisted that Turner found a bonanza but the man himself vanished. In '89 his body was found in Sycamore Canyon, waylaid by

PLANK PORCHES ALSO SERVED as sidewalks over stream bed, show wear and tear from use and weather. At about this point on one street of town, during Presidential election in fall of 1896, large picture of William McKinley was suspended from wire stretched across street by Republicans. Returns began to come in indicating candidate was losing. Portrait was lowered by Democrats, black cloth draped over it, and again elevated. Late evening stage came in with word that McKinley had won. Everyone, regardless of affiliation, got drunk, then went home to sleep it off.

ever-present Apaches. Captain Cooney determined to find the supposed wealth that was legally his if it existed. He started out in the fall; next spring *his* body was found where he had frozen to death, only about 100 yards from where that of Turner had been found.

In the meantime, the new camp of Mogollon had been started in the bottom of Silver Creek Canyon, a short distance from Claremont and Cooney. The first mines developed there were the Maude S., Deep Down, Little Fanny and Last Chance. It is the history of the Little Fanny that permeates the history of the camp itself.

Mr. Friolo was a resident of Mogollon all through its best years and still lives in the crumbling old camp, the only "bona fide" resident, the few others being summer campers. The old gentleman tells of how miner's consumption, so called, and "miner's con" in

his words, took a ghastly toll of men working in the Little Fanny. The jack-hammers used in breaking the quartz for removal from the mine made a cloud of gritty dust which affected the lungs, some miners lasted only three years or less. If they did not die outright they were relegated to lighter jobs, but even this did not save them. Water hoses were provided them by the company for wetting the rock to reduce or prevent the dust, but this procedure soaked the men too. They refused to work wet all the time, perferring the dust. Finally, in desperation, the company worked out a system where the water was squirted along with the air-pressure. From then on the toll from "miner's con" was cut down and the town's three physicians, Drs. Feel, Kern and Parm, had a respite.

At the time the Little Fanny was developed the population of the camp was about 2,000. That was in 1909. Two years later the number of people had

FACING J. P. HOLLAND GENERAL STORE is group of buildings constituting main business center of camp. At extreme left is tiny saloon, next is Mogollon Mercantile, then Annex to larger Holland store, specializing in furniture and "notions" after period as post office. Large stone structure at extreme right was Howard's Drug Store, with doctor's offices above. Upper floor was gained by outside stairway, now smothered by "Trees of Heaven." Structure served as grocery store later, as town declined and adobe buildings disintegrated. Patch of mullein weeds in foreground is at edge of area once constituting red-light district.

IMPOSING ADOBE served Mogollon as roominghouse, was "respectable" since brothels were segregated, confined to flat at lower edge of town. Smaller "dobe" at left was grocery store. One road to mines wound up gulch back of buildings and many small cabins still perch along route.

expanded further and there were fourteen saloons, seven restaurants, five stores, two hotels and the usual brothels.

The sixth annual edition of "Mogollon Mines" pointed out that "there is room for and an absolute necessity for the establishment of a Society for the prevention of Cruelty to Animals in Mogollon. Scarcely a day passes but what a cruel and heartless driver abuses his animals. Whether in a team or a burro heavily laden with wood, both are subjected to knock-out blows with cordwood or loaded whips. It is not uncommon to see an animal devoid of one eye, and frequently this is in a bleeding condition, and the poor, suffering brute has no way to relieve itself of the constant annoyance of myriads of flies. . ."

By 1915 the camp's payroll was between $50,000 and $75,000 every month. Gold and silver bullion were shipped out regularly to Silver City. The distance was ninety miles and in bad weather the ore teams required ten days for the trip. Even in the most favorable weather, fifteen miles was a good day's average because of the frighteningly steep grades encountered. Ordinary harnesses were not used for the long line of 18-mule teams. A center chain ran the entire length, each team harnessed with hames and collars, belly bands, back bands and chain tugs, with the exception of the two wheel horses. Metal doubletrees were hooked to each section so the teams could pull. The teamster rode the right wheel horse with a saddle, and guided the teams with a jerk line which extended the entire length and was snapped to each team. On

the steep curves the mules stepped right or left over the chain as it rubbed against their legs. Ordinary brakes were ineffectual. Rough locks with heavy timbers were dropped by a lever in front of the rear wheel of the train wagons. On the steepest grades the strings of wagons were separated into smaller groups.

The end of the haul at Silver City would see the 300-pound bars of gold and silver stacked in front of the Silver City National Bank, the return trip made with heavy loads of crude oil for the diesel engines at Mogollon. In 1912 when a flywheel weighing 12,400 pounds was hauled up to the Little Fanny, a 24-horse outfit was employed. The rigs were owned by W. A. Tenney, and operated from 1910 until the opening of World War I. Trucks took over but the camp was tired and beginning to drag its feet.

There was less and less of that famous "blossom rock" from which little nuggets could be shaken. What remained assayed poorly, was refractory and hardly paid costs of milling and refining. Several mines closed down entirely, others operated on a part-time basis. When the Little Fanny quit, so did the town. The Black Jack Gang, so belligerent at the turn of the century, was already long since tamed, holdups along the steep and rocky road to Alma and Silver City had become less frequent. Gunshots ceased to echo from Jimmy Johnson's saloon or the similar emporium of Pedro "Pete" Almeraz where the notorious Cosmo Zapata had been killed. Mogollon shriveled as people moved away, sighed and lay down to sleep.

ELIZABETHTOWN, NEW MEXICO

This is the country of "The Big Ditch"—and traces of it still show after almost a century. A rare visitor may stand in the deserted ruins of Elizabethtown, where it nestles in the high bowl between the peaks of McGinty and Baldy Mountains, and visualize activity when they brought water to Humbug Gulch.

The gravels of that mountain gash were rich in gold but water was either too scarce to work them or flash flooding in the spring damaged equipment. "We've got to have an even and regular water supply or quit," the miners said. So they did it the hard way, digging the eleven miles of "The Big Ditch" by pick and shovel and a few sacks of blasting powder from the source of Red River. It cost $280,000 but saved the camp.

On July 9, 1869 when the first water hit Humbug Gulch there was a wild celebration but it was short-lived. The flow slowed to a dribble with dozens of leaks showing up along the route. Patching remedied the loss temporarily but crews had to be established at intervals along the waterway with cabins for living quarters to make constant repairs to insure the steady flow of 600 inches. And even then it became necessary to divert more water from Moreno Creek and Ponil River.

Elizabethtown is situated five miles north of Eagle's Nest Lake and some forty miles northwest of Cimarron. The boom began in the middle 1860s when Ute and Apache Indians were relatively peaceful, wandering over the slopes of Baldy and McGinty Mountains. One of them showed up in Fort Union with a specimen of float so rich it set off a rush of the first magnitude, swelling the town on the slopes of Baldy to 5,000 people.

The first men to track down the location where the sample had been picked up were William Kroenig and William Moore, whose small copper mine was named the Mystic Lode. While that first sample of rock was rich copper ore, and the first diggings had been for copper, this find of gold changed the whole scheme of things. The original metal was forgotten and from then on, E'town was all gold.

By the spring of '67, locations had been made at Michigan Gulch, Humbug Gulch and Grouse Gulch,

LOG BUILDING was erected at time of E'town's greatest expansion, when group of five men with sluice 90 feet long were taking out $100 a day in gold for each man, worth $20 an ounce just as it came from dripping gravels. Quartz lode assayed $2,000 per ton and no one bothered with anything skimpier. Almost all frame buildings in town have crumbled away.

the latter containing the phenomenal Spanish Bar. All measurements were made from a large willow tree on the banks of the central stream. The town was named for the eldest daughter of William Moore, Elizabeth, who later became a schoolteacher in the town, shortened to E'town. The camp grew so rapidly it was soon the seat of Colfax County, an honor lost later to Cimarron.

During the best years there were three stagecoach lines, to Springer, Trinidad and Questa. There were saloons and three dancehalls, two hotels, five general stores and later several boardinghouses. One hotel operator was a Henry Lambert who had once cooked for General Grant and Abraham Lincoln. In the fall of '71 he went to greener pastures in Cimarron where he opened the celebrated St. James.

In 1868 the editor of the *Sante Fe Gazette* wrote: "The first house (in E'town) was built by John Moore who furnished the miners with provisions on credit, thereby enabling them to open up the country. Elizabethtown now has 100 buildings." A later article stated: "The new city of Elizabethtown continues on its course. The weather is cold; the cool winds from the snowcapped peaks cause us to huddle around the blazing pitch-pine fires of our fellow townsmen, Messrs. Sears, Pollock, Draper, C. E. Pease and Harburger. Occasionally, we find our way to the Mayflower Saloon, where we warm the inner as well as the outer man. So pass the long winter evenings. Prices are very reasonable for a mining town. New arrivals are an almost everyday occurrence. Denver and vicinity are well represented among the new arrivals. I perceived Doc Howe of prospecting celebrity whose manly form and gentlemanly address is truly an honor to the place he has left. There is very little mining property for sale. Claim owners generally think we have a good enough thing to warrant them to suffer a New Mexico winter in order to be on the ground when the water comes . . . . A stage line has been established between Elizabethtown and Maxwell's by V. S. Dhelby and Co. who intend to commence running a tri-weekly line in a few days." Toward spring came optimism and some advice: "Elizabethtown contains fifty or sixty houses, some of them like the Arkansas Traveler's house, roofless, for the weather is too severe to complete them . . . . There is considerable bustle and business in the air to be seen and especially should you go into Abor's Saloon you will be convinced that it is a stirring place. There are several stores, two restaurants and many saloons, as also a drug store, a billiard table, a barber shop and gambling houses where a miner can deposit all his hard-earned earnings of weeks in a few hours. That house across the street in which you see two smiling faces you will do well to give it a wide berth, as you will be richer in pocket, better in health and wiser in mind."

Those early days of the boom town were filled with such robbery, murder and pillage as have rarely been equalled. One badman was Long Taylor. He stood six foot seven inches, was easily identified but not often caught. In '73, in company with one Coal-Oil Johnny, he held up the Cimarron stage in the narrow passage known as the Palisades, escaping with some $700. George Greely ran one of the most profitable saloons but was constantly in trouble because of a hot temper, taking no "guff" from anyone. On Independence Day, 1886, he called a customer on the carpet for a fancied insult to one of his several "lady friends." Infuriated, the man rushed out, returning in a few minutes with his Winchester. Firing point blank at Greely, he turned to make his escape but was stopped by a flying tackle at the door, later serving time for murder at the penitentiary in Santa Fe.

Perhaps the most gruesome episode was staged at the height of the town's heyday when rooms were scarce and no questions asked about them. A stranger would come into camp, rent a room in the boardinghouse operated by Charles Kennedy on the side of a steep hill, and disappear. Since no one knew such newcomers, they would ordinarily not be missed. But one was and his friends went to Kennedy's place. They were met halfway by the proprietor's distraught wife, a native New Mexican, who had decided to confess everything.

The Vigilantes were sent for and they slipped in the back of the house. There was Kennedy bending over a fire, burning dismembered sections of the visitor's body, his valuables set to one side. The town had a stout timbered jail but when the murderer was taken to the courthouse for trial, the outraged citizens seized him, tied a rope around his neck and threw him to the ground. Then one man got astride a horse and dragged the unfortunate miscreant up and down the dirt streets until long after he was dead.

McKenna, in his *Black Range Tales* recalls: "Myself and three other men who were footloose and without families pitched together and hired a bull team. Loading up what we needed in the way of food and blankets, we pulled out for Elizabethtown, a gold diggings in the main Rockies, a hundred miles west from Trinidad. It took us about fifteen days to get there, the bullwhacker being in no hurry, for the bulls were poor and the grass was good . . . . It was there I panned my first gold . . . learned what was meant by diggings and stored up bits of mining lore from veteran prospectors. I was told that Elizabethtown was tame when compared to the days of the big rush, when shootings were as common as meetings in the street and saloons. I sat for the first time before a golden

campfire and listened to blood-curdling tales of raiding Indians, of heartless cutthroats, of daring outlaws, of dashing cowboys, of painted women, of dead shots and regular old sourdoughs and desert rats, some good, some bad . . . ."

And there was the building of the dredge *Eleanor*. In 1901, E'town was still a busy place, its seven saloons always crowded and hotels full. Eastern capital was still interested in organizing companies and gold was still so plentiful it was being weighed out in troy-weight in exchange for such necessities of life as— whiskey. But here and there were reports that a certain placer was petering out, that expensive stamp mills were working on a part-time basis. Some people were even expressing the opinion that E'town might one day be a ghost town. Loud and derisive boos might greet this kind of remark but cold figures gave it credence—that gold production in the camp was not what it had been.

The famous Spanish Bar still harbored as much and more gold in its depths than ever had been removed but getting at the deeper gravels was something else. The answer came in the Oro Dredging Co. and the person of H. J. Reiling of Chicago. He had solved similar problems in the mining camps of Montana and felt the only possible obstacle here would be getting two boilers into the camp. These would weigh a total of ten tons and the existing road from the rail head at Springer was a narrow, winding track that ran almost its entire length up the precipitous Cimarron Canyon. Machinery of lesser weight had been hauled up the road and the inadequate bridges and narrow switchbacks could be remedied.

When the first of the boilers was started on its way, hauled by fourteen head of horses, it soon ran into difficulties, a small bridge at the beginning of the route collapsing like cardboard. With this warning, spans over deeper canyons were strengthened and the first boiler was deposited on the bar in two weeks, the second in one. A side benefit of the job was the widened and improved road for daily trips of the stage. During the period the dredge was being hauled two stages had been shuffled, one running above, one below, since there was no passing.

The camp turned out in a body to dedicate the new dredge in August of 1901. Incongruous were the "outfits" worn by members of the party from the effete East who had shuddered their way up the raw canyon. After all, their money had built the dredge, now so proudly floating on its own pond at the lower end of Spanish Bar, and they felt they should be on hand to see it put into operation.

A bottle of champagne was broken on its bow by Mrs. W. A. Moughy of Wooster, Ohio. Since other bottles had already been opened and emptied in more conventional fashion, champagne for the Easterners and whiskey for the men responsible for the hauling and assembling of the *Eleanor*, the celebration that followed the christening was the wildest in the history of the town.

The first few years of work for the big dredge went according to plan. Values of the gravel in Spanish Bar were about $2 per cubic yard and the machine was capable of biting off 50,000 cubic yards a month. Part of this material was from the bottom of the pond and the rest from the banks. Operations were on a round-the-clock basis to make up for complete closure during winter.

The high and mighty days gradually came to an end with the failure of easily obtained gold in the gravels. Hard rock mining became more and more expensive in proportion to profits, replacement machinery and labor costing more while the price of gold remained static. The fate of the big dredge paralleled the demise of E'town. The *Eleanor* slowed down and for a few years operated on only one shift, then there were complete shutdowns for a month at a time. The company was extending its operations to the town of Breckenridge, Colorado, and needing more money, mortgaged the *Eleanor*. It was gobbling up the gravels but there was not enough river gold to meet expenses. At last the mortgage was foreclosed and the dredge sold at a sheriff's sale to two optimistic gentlemen named J. Van Houten and Charles Springer. For eight years they paid a watchman to live on the gold boat, hoping that one day the metal would advance in price.

As the machinery rusted and the dredge began to settle into the gravel, she was at last abandoned, as was the town itself. Several years later the pilot house was all that was showing above the sand of Spanish Bar. Now even that has disappeared.

MOST PICTURESQUE RUIN in E'town, perhaps in all New Mexico, is old gambling and pool hall. Upper floor housed girls who entertained miners for a price. Each had room, went downstairs to attract business on dance floor. Structure was gutted by fire, picture made from inside catching afternoon light to give effect of Roman arches in lonely New Mexican ghost town.

MINERAL PARK, ARIZONA

What the Hualpais Indians of this part of Arizona were usually called cannot be printed here. It was only when the early whites felt charitable they referred to the low-grade tribespeople as simply "Wallapais." The Mineral Park *Mohave Miner* constantly complained; "There are more drunken Wallapais women on the street than there are drunken Wallapais men." The best that could be said of them was they were peaceful when sober and never attacked the citizens of the remote mining camp in northwestern Arizona.

Mineral Park's other newspaper, *Alta Arizona*, ran a news item January 28, 1882, concerning a near violent encounter between Wallapais Charley, by way of being a minor chief of his tribe, and Jeff, another Indian. Ordinarily the best of friends, they imbibed too much firewater and when an agrument developed, Charley drew his pistol. Before any blood was shed, Under Sheriff Collins intervened, dragged the pair into his office, gave them a good talking to

HOME-MADE HEATERS were popular in country where stoves were all but impossible to obtain due to expensive transportation. Juniper trees were main fuel, hills near camp cleared of them.

and confiscated Charley's precious gun. The next day Sheriff Robert Steen received this contrite letter:

My Friend Bob Steen

Won't you be so kind as to send me my pistol. I will not carry it into town any more and will behave myself and be a good Indian. Tell me where I can come into town and oblige

Your Friend Wallapais Charley

The first prospectors in western Arizona were soldiers attached to Fort Mohave on the Colorado River or disappointed miners from the California gold fields. Some of them found gold in the blistering foothills, one discovery located where Oatman later mushroomed. The Moss mine developed there and among others those at Gold Road attracted a rush of hopeful, would-be miners. Many found treasure there, others reaching out to make discoveries nearby.

These activities were in the early '60s and a few years later several mines were located at the site of Mineral Park but were not worked extensively as the hostile Hualpais, who were picking out some turquoise, forced the miners to flee. Later some whites took out limited quantities of the semiprecious gemstone.

Ten years later, so many whites had infiltrated the area a truce of sorts was established. Before long, rich silver deposits were uncovered in the Cerbat Range, the mines centered in a beautiful parklike, juniper-covered bench on the western slope, the name Mineral Park as apt as any given to western mining camps. Not only were gold, silver and lead deposits rich and varied in the "Park" but the stream flowing through the town was so permeated with mineral solutions and salts it was unfit to drink. Potable water had to be hauled from a canyon several miles away. By 1874 Harris Solomon was running a regular mule train carrying the supply from Keystone Spring.

Once established, Mineral Park boomed. By 1880

ADOBE RUINS BLEND WITH BACKGROUND, sun-baked bricks matching color of parent earth. This material was much used in areas of scant timber, little lumber available and that high priced. Cerbat Range in which Mineral Park lies is rich in cacti. Shown in foreground is patch of prickly pear, *Opuntia engelmanii*, bearing yellow, water-lily-like flowers, deep red pears which are edible. Behind these are clumps of staghorn chollas (choyas), *Opuntia versicolor*, whose main characteristics are barbed spines with easily detached joints often adhering to stock animals and carried away to start new plants where they drop.

there were four saloons, a restaurant, blacksmith shop, hotel, school and several stores, the earliest influx from less glamorous camps nearby which were soon all but deserted. Anyone wanting to get to the camp

from the east was faced with a formidable problem of transportation. He had to travel across the northern part of the United States on the Union Pacific to San Francisco, get down to Los Angeles and overland to

Yuma. Here he would transfer to one of the flat-bottomed steamers which paddled up the Colorado River as far as Hardyville. If lucky, he would not have to wait more than a week for the stagecoach to Mineral Park. And this ride was not exactly luxurious, the roads only dim trails over sand or rock and cactus-studded hills where in summer it was well above 100°.

Supplies had to be sent over this same circuitous route or transported more than four hundred miles over alkali and sand deserts. It is no wonder commodity prices were so high. Bacon cost $1 a pound, sugar 35 cents, flour 50 cents in a day when the miner earned $3 for ten hours' work.

And occasionally prices were used as weapons by saloons. At one time when most of the saloonkeepers tossed a quarter into a lard can for a shot of whiskey, one rebel was charging only half that, Spanish *real* with a value of twelve for a dollar. These "pieces of eight" were commonly called "bits," accounting for the western use of "two bits."

Two of Mineral Park's merchants were always at each other's throats in this same manner. Krider Bros. openly advertised they would not only equal other prices but undersell anything offered by their aggressive competitors, Welton and Grounds, and carried on a running feud with merchant J. W. Haas. Being postmaster and having the post office in his store from '79 to '86, W. M. Krider had a distinct trade advantage.

In casting around for an excuse to quarrel with Krider, Hass accused the postmaster of withholding his mail, this openly in front of the store. Insulted and infuriated, Krider lifted his cane and fetched Haas a smart one on the cranium. Haas went berserk, drew his gun and fired wildly. Krider returned the fire and also missed. In the post office at the time, Sheriff Steen ran out and grabbed both contestants by their collars, marching them to the calaboose where the pair passed the time arranging lawsuits for assault with attempt to commit murder. Both were released on $3,000 bail. The *Mohave Miner* which chronicled these events failed to tell the rest of the story.

By 1884 there were 500 registered voters in Mineral Park with, no doubt, as many women and children. The Chinatown had several opium dens, as well as stores and laundries. At first the opium houses were ignored, then tolerated with distaste and finally a marked increase in young addicts was detected, the greatest evil being they were spending their money with the Chinese instead of the white saloon and bawdy house keepers. The white madames, some car--rying considerable weight in town politics, demanded that boys who smoked the poppy stay away from their girls.

In July of 1884, the *Mohave Miner* was needled into carrying scare headlines: "This Menace To Our Youth Must Be Stopped." It is to be assumed the opium dens were closed, for Wilfred Babcock, who worked and lived in Mineral Park during the period after the newspaper blast, could not recall any.

The town continued to grow by leaps and bounds. Lumber was always scarce and high priced, a great drawback to progress. There was a sawmill in the Hualpais Mountains forty miles west of the Park but by the time this essential material reached its destination, the cost was $125 a thousand. In spite of this, building went on apace and Mineral Park could boast of several hotels and office buildings to house "the many professional people who have moved here from Cerbat, Mohave City and Hardyville," as the newspaper had it. It soon took over as county seat from Cerbat. A fine courthouse was erected and, beside it, the jail. Wilfred Babcock remembers the jail doors did not open or close easily for some time.

First newspaper was the *Wallapais Enterprise*, started June 1, 1876 by John Leonard and Chauncey F. Mitchell and dying soon. Two later ones, the *Alta Arizona* and *Mohave Miner*, were contemporaries for a time and bitter rivals for subscriptions. The former was beset by a plague of drunken printers, the two who

OLD CEMETERY retains original juniper trees spared from axes. Some graves date back to '70s. Enclosure in center is unique in style. On grave in foreground grows beavertail cacti, *Opuntia basilaris*.

drank only water from the spring getting the type set and keeping the presses going. After a few spirited years of refuting each other's statements, the *Alta Arizona* left the field to the *Miner*.

Issues of this paper in '84 stated in glowing terms the many plans for expansion. A new hospital was to replace the one that had burned. It was hoped all patients could be kept and treated under one roof where part of them were cared for in the Palace Hotel. The old school building had been purchased by the school board to make an expansion possible, including a 220-square foot extension for the teacher's platform so she could look over the heads of her older and taller pupils.

Because of the price of lumber, many buildings were made of adobe. The locally popular Sheriff Steen's family had one of these for their home. Early one morning during a rare rainy spell, the Chinese cook at the Palace Hotel passed the Steen house on his way to work and saw it had collapsed in the night. Frantic diggers found the small girl of the family still alive, her younger brother almost doubled up under the weight of the adobe bricks but still breathing, the remainder of the Steens dead. Both children survived.

It cannot be said religious influence was very strong in the Park. There never was a regular church, traveling ministers sometimes preaching in a pool hall or hotel. The community did make one gesture heavenward by organizing a non-sectarian Sunday school. The *Mohave Miner* beamed paternally: "It is very important to the children as well as the community whether they shall be trained to be gentle, kind and good or allowed to grow up in evil, vicious habits, a curse to themselves, their parents and their country."

A bank was also missing from the camp. Miners had a haphazard system of leaving part of their money with storekeepers for safekeeping. In 1883 the *Miner* agitated for a bank with a capital of $50,000 to $100,000 but no bank ever appeared. Another plan for the building of a toll road from Mineral Park to Free's Wash, southwest of the present Kingman, also came to naught. It was to be called the Mineral Park and Wallapais Tow Road, the idea proposed by R. H. Upton and S. Owen who got as far as drawing up a partnership February 1, 1875 but built no road. However, several stage lines were eventually established, two of them running between Prescott and Hardyville on the Colorado River, making Mineral Park a station. Hugh White and Co. ran a small express and passenger service from Prescott to Mineral Park, Mohave City, Hackberry and Hardyville. A. L. Simonds advertised his Mineral Park and Kingman Stage would transport passengers between the two towns for $2, a four-hour, fifteen-mile trip.

The town which had been so hampered by transportation problems was thus overjoyed when in 1880 there were rumors that the Atlantic and Pacific Railroad was being put through northern Arizona. The rumors became facts and in '83 the railroad passed a point within fifteen miles of Mineral Park. Plans were carried out to improve the road to this point so as to take advantage of cheap rates for shipping ore and concentrates. Where the new road ended at the tracks, a depot and loading platforms were built, additional buildings put up for stores and a hotel. Several Mineral Park business concerns moved there, others establishing branches in Kingman, the new station stop.

When Kingman began to be noticeable as a town, the *Miner* predicted caustically the place would "soon be taken over by the horned toads." After a few months it took a neutral attitude and soon it was carrying more ads and news from Kingman than

ORE CAR abandoned beside narrow gauge tracks once carried quantities of rich gold- and silver-filled rocks. Prior to building of stamp mills, ore had to be rich to pay for immense cost of shipping overland to Colorado River, thence by barges to Port Isabel at mouth of river on Gulf of California, down Gulf to Port Arena and up coast to San Francisco where it was shipped to Swansea, Wales. When Selby smelter was built in San Francisco, shipping costs were reduced to $125 a ton. On February 12, 1876 a five-stamp quartz mill was put into operation in the Park, could get high price for crushing. After other mills were built, prices were forced down but never to low level, partly because of water scarcity for wet operation to reduce dust hazard.

NAMES OF MINES around Mineral Park include the whimsical Metallic Accident and Woodchopper's Relief as well as Lone Star and Fairfield. Keystone was first important lode, found in 1870 by Charles E. Sherman, producing gold and silver, giving name to Keystone Springs, only source of good water for town.

from home. In 1887 the paper moved to Kingman where it still operates.

Before long there were many vacant buildings in the Park. Several structures were burned and others vandalized, some adobe buildings collapsed for lack of repairs and Mineral Park took on the aspects of a ghost town. Kingman had been agitating for some time to get the county seat position and in November of 1886 a general election to decide the issue gave 271 votes for Kingman, Hackbarry 132, Mineral Park 99 and definitely out of the running. The town would not give up, however, especially since the supervisors had been so slow in calling for a recount of votes. Official results were not presented until December 31, on demand of County Supervisor Samuel Crozier.

What happened next spelled the final doom of Mineral Park's status as county seat. Shortly after midnight a party of Kingman men, their patience exhausted over the obstinate refusal of Mineral Park to comply with orders to give up the records, piled into a wagon and set out on the four-hour trip to the dying town. Arriving in the early morning hours, they proceeded to the courthouse and broke down the doors. They loaded all essential records into the wagon, returned to Kingman and set up the legal procedures necessary to the operation of the county seat.

Population in the camp was now further depleted and only a little mining activity remained. Even this went out in time and Mineral Park was very dead for many years as all buildings fell away, were burned or wrecked for valuable lumber.

At present one mine is again functioning across the creek of the bitter waters, near the old cemetery so picturesquely hidden in the junipers. These old trees and the fence posts near them, full of hollows and holes, make good nesting places for the profusion of Western Bluebirds which have forsaken so many other areas.

JEROME, ARIZONA

The little movie house was well filled that night some twenty years ago. Every now and then a jolting motion shook the building, an effect to be taken as an earthquake anywhere else. The patrons here paid little attention to shuddering floors and when the show was over they headed for the exit doors. The sidewalk which had been only a few inches above the doorsill when they entered was now nearly two feet higher, or more accurately, the theater floor was that much lower. A few of the more elderly had to be helped up to the higher level but no one was unduly excited, the phenomenon of sliding and moving buildings being too ordinary an occurrence in Jerome.

The jail had started to behave the same way a few years before, settling a few feet downward, the little concrete building pulling away from the sidewalk. Steps were made down to the new level while the now sobered drunks inside talked about their free ride. Then with more slips and slides the jail was so far below the street, a new street level had to be established. As the years went on, successively lower street levels had to be made until the calaboose was closed. However, this was not because Jerome was tired of building new streets for it but because there were no more prisoners among the few Jeromans.

What caused all the shimmeying of the earth?

HIGHWAY BELOW is only "through street" in Jerome. High school on point in middle distance, once filled with local youngsters, is still used by 850 students coming by bus from communities in Verde Valley — Clarkdale, Cottonwood, Clemenceau, etc. Top buildings are 1,500 feet above lowest. Smelter in Clarkdale may be seen in distance, Oak Creek Canyon visible on clear day.

JEROME as seen from below shows fantastic panorama of deserted hotels, theaters, schools. Good stand of pine trees once surrounded city, killed by fumes from smelter which has since been torn down, replaced by huge one in valley. Adobe structures once swelled limits of town, ruins of some seen at center and lower left.

The geological reason was Jerome's situation directly upon the large Verde Fault, a major cause of subterranean movement. Then the town was undermined with a complex of more than 85 miles of mine tunnels.

Add to this the fact that the "overburden" of loose rock and soil on top of a solid layer of rock which lay under the town was penetrated by heavy winter rains and leakage from the aging water supply pipes, with all the water collecting in a saturated layer on the rock. And compounding the natural earth shocks were those from frequent explosions in the mines and one mammoth one in the powder house. Small wonder Jerome progressed downward as well as ahead.

John Figi, custodian of the Art Gallery welcoming Jerome's visitors, says these movements are trivial in light of what went on in former ages. "At one time Mingus Mountain, on the side of which Jerome is built, was 12,000 feet higher than it is today. A prehistoric cataclysm flung the top off and pitched it into the Verde Valley, the sandstone and rock hills you see there being the result. The plant down there is making cement for the dam in Glen Canyon and if removal of material is carried on at the present rate for fifty years, they will reach the layer thrown off from here, the top of Jerome's mines, so to speak, and

it will be a tremendously rich layer of copper as exploratory diamond drillings have shown. The large Daisy mine which used to produce so heavily is probably the top of the decapitated vein."

The earliest use for the colorful ores of the Jerome site was by Tuzigoot Indians in 935 A.D. These aborigines found vivid surface outcroppings in blue, green and brown which, when powdered, made fine war paint and in times of peace was useful for pottery coloring. The first Spanish explorers centuries later were friendly with the natives and shown the deposits. It was tough going up the steep sides of Mingus Mountain but the Spaniards were spurred on by thoughts of gold. When they saw the deposits owed their color to baser metals, they turned back in disgust, giving the country "back to the Indians."

A later visitor to the site was Indian scout Al Sieber, who in 1872 found evidence of Indian mining in the primitive rock tools and crude ladders made of juniper pegs. Sieber, however, was no miner and made no effort to capitalize on his find.

In January of 1876 a small party of prospectors from Nevada headed by Capt. John Boyd and John O. Dougherty arrived in nearby Prescott and listened to the tales of copper wealth on Mingus Mountain. They reached the place but seem to have been unimpressed with the area that was to yield half a billion dollars in copper with gold and silver paying the refining cost. Later that same year came more curious and enterprising visitors, ranchers John Ruffner and his friend August McKinnon. Although the two did stake out several claims, they were primarily ranchers and snapped up a buying offer from Territorial Governor Frederick E. Tritle of $2,000 for the claims, getting $500 cash, the rest to come.

Even now there was no development rush, Tritle finding it took more money than he had to open up the claims and get going. But about the time he was ready to throw up the sponge he met an angel in the form of a New York lawyer, Eugene Jerome (who was the grandfather of England's Sir Winston Churchill). Jerome had money and was willing to sink it in a rocky hole on Mingus Mountain but there was a string attached. He was positive a town would develop there and he thought it would be fitting and proper to have it named after him, and so stipulated in the contract. Tritle was willing, or felt he had no choice if the mine was to be developed.

Yet nothing much happened. It seemed necessary to build a smelter to refine the undeniably rich ore and an impossiblity to get such a thing hauled that distance over rough or nonexistent roads. But in 1882 the Santa Fe came to Ashfork and Tritle, with the lawyer's money, built a wagon road from the railhead 60 miles to his property. Parts for the smelter at last arrived and a fabulous mining town was born.

In 1893 the United Verde Copper Co. was incorporated. At this time the town had four hundred people and six saloons. For years an almost continuous wagon train brought food, water, fuel and mine supplies to the settlement that was progressing as it clung to an all but vertical mountainside. In 1900 a contract was let to supply Jerome with water on a regular basis with a 200-unit mule team. The contractor? Pancho Villa.

The population was cosmopolitan to an extreme. Represented by closely knit groups were Italians, Mexicans, Swedes, Yugoslavs, Bohemians and Welshmen. A large English-speaking section was squeezed into a small space on the red splintered rocks of Yeager Canyon, Slavs filling the Hogback and Mexicans overflowing their adobes along Bitter Creek. No

HUGE OPEN-PIT OPERATION of Phelps Dodge Corp., part of old United Verde workings shown behind buildings in telephoto lens. At left center is "Traveling Jail" which has slid downhill from street above and right. Front center is unique church built by Mr. Sabino Gonzoles, Mexican Methodist minister, who felt "urge" to construct building of any material available including railroad ties, powder boxes and old mine timbers. Construction was from 1939 to 1941. Rev. Gonzoles preached last sermon late in 1952, just before mines were closed down.

JEROME
POPULATION
15,000
10,000
5,000
1,000
GHOST CITY

matter what group or location a man lived in, he had a magnificent view of Verde Valley with its red backdrop of Oak Creek Canyon or could look directly down on his neighbor's roof, perhaps scratch matches on his chimney, and on the other side would be the basement of the next house. Only one main street existed, wrapping itself around the crest of the ridge and most cross streets were steep stairways. Some so-called ones were almost impossible to negotiate—and there were no busses or streetcars.

Jerome suffered from labor troubles. The first strike was in 1907, a success for the men which reduced the ten-hour work day to eight and raised wages to $2.75 a day. The next disturbance was not only unsuccessful but took on some comic opera aspects. In 1917, just before the United Verde was bought out by the huge Phelps Dodge Corporation, the I.W.W. started a strike. The men not only ceased to work but staged demonstrations and street battles. The trouble ended when several hundred miners and imported agitators were taken out of the company-owned houses

on the hill, loaded on boxcars under the persuasion of guns and other weapons, hauled out into the southeastern Arizona desert and left to sizzle with their sins.

1925 was the top year for Jerome, after which production began to shrivel, closing several of the smaller mines which could not afford operation without rich ore, and then some of the larger ones. In 1953 Phelps Dodge permanently closed the big mine and that was the end of Jerome as a city. Only 100 remained of the 15,000. After this low ebb a few tourist attractions were organized, such as an art gallery, restaurants, etc. The post office is still active, the figure of 300 accounting for all residents now.

Visitors arriving from either end of town, from over Mingus Mountain from Prescott or from Verde Valley, will find the big camp most rewarding. The streets are still such in name only and could lead the unwary motorist into some cul-de-sac of a yard too narrow to turn around in, such as the street leading past the Catholic Church. The automobile should be

JEROME JAIL has slid dowhill nearly 300 feet by stages, each new location requiring new street for access. Original level is at upper left, part of street showing. City had ample water supply, enough to keep several swimming pools filled in heyday. Leakage from pipes from artesian springs 14 miles away on Mingus Mountain was partly responsible for unstable ground, a handicap added to natural earth fault and mine explosion.

parked at the bottom of town with wheels against a wall or curb and excursions made on foot, return to the car then being downhill. Otherwise the experience is like descending into Grand Canyon with the return all uphill.

As John Figi said: "Of course if mining should be revived here people would not build on this steep mountainside, but settle on the level ground below. Modern cars would easily reach the mines where the haul up the road used to require at least one team of horses, several with a good load."

In 1884 Senator William A. Clark of Montana showed an interest in the properties since they had begun to pay off. He took a lease on them long enough to assure himself that he had a good thing, then he bought the project, lock-stock-and-barrel. Clark poured a million dollars into the development of the copper mines during the next twelve years.

Now tier upon tier of houses was glued to the 30-degree angle of the hillside, for married men and their families, the immense stone Montana House housing a thousand single men—the largest building in Arizona. Even so, a large number lived in tents and shacky houses of bone-dry lumber. Most of this section went up in smoke in the last series of fire ending in 1899. That same year Jerome was incorporated as the fifth largest city in the state. The mine was to become one of the largest individually owned copper mines in the world.

Near the immense Verde development another vast copper deposit was opened up, the faulted top of what was to be the famed Little Daisy. The ore body was located by George Hull and J. Fisher in 1912 and the richness of the Daisy May was almost unbelievable. Where ore at a value of five percent paid well, here were 300 feet of rock with an assay of fifteen percent at the 1,400-foot level of the mine, then 40 feet of forty percent and at the 1,500 level, five feet of ore with a fantastic copper content of forty-five percent. The Company—The UVX—built a smelter at Clemenceau in the valley and by the end of 1938 production had grossed $125 million.

By 1929 the population of Jerome was 15,000 and included a working force of 2,345 men. More copper was coming out of Arizona than any other state, the Verde operation alone producing as much as $29 million a single year. Gone were the days when building brick was hauled by four and six teams of horses up the single steep road from the kiln in Verde Valley. No longer was it necessary to use the ingenious but inadequate system of converting surplus steam into power to drive the dynamos for electricity. Jerome never had gas. It jumped directly from kerosene to electricity.

Culture was not lacking during the halcyon days.

The miner could attend a lecture by Miss Hollister of Phoenix under the auspices of the W.C.T.U. or a box social put on by the Ladies' Guild of the Episcopal Church. Better attended were the less socially accepted functions.

OLD MOVIE HOUSE slides downhill at rate of inch in two months, may remain stationary for long period, then skid twenty inches in short time.

STATELY COLUMNS STAND at entrance of immense grade school, are slowly crumbling. Structure was closed when large mine operations ceased.

COLOMA, CALIFORNIA

In any tale of the California gold rush and particularly of Coloma where it all began, Johan Sutter's name looms large even though his part in the discovery was inadvertent and his actions antagonistic. He must have known his troubles were back to dog him when his foreman James Marshall found those fateful flakes of gold in the mill race.

Sutter had trouble in his native Burgdorf, Switzerland, where he was a merchant. Debts and women disrupted his life and he deserted his family, heading for America and landing in Santa Fe, New Mexico. In 1834 he heard glowing reports of wealth to be made in the fertile acres of the pastoral Sacramento Valley.

His course there was roundabout, by way of Fort Vancouver, thence by sailing vessel to the Hawaiian Islands and from there to San Francisco. His record stalled him in that booming city but Monterey gave him a better welcome.

By exercising some imagination he became "Captain Sutter" and was granted a tract of land on the Sacramento River for colonization purposes. An entry in his diary of August 13, 1839 reads: "Today with the help of my ten Kanakas and three white men I founded a colony called New Helvetia." As soon as an adobe fort was built the colony developed rapidly, soon having a bakery, blanket factory, kitchen and dining room for the help and luxurious quarters for the master.

During the war with Mexico Sutter managed to be a friend to each side and when it ended in 1847

and formal transfer of the territory to the United States was consummated by the signing of the Treaty Guadalupe Hidalgo in February, 1848, Sutter's land was left unaffected. He could concentrate on the affairs of his colony which gave the farm the most productive period in its existence.

Six years before, in 1842, Mexicans had found gold in the sands of dry Placerita Canyon near Los Angeles, the first known discovery in California. They "dry panned" the gold-bearing dirt by filling tightly woven baskets and tossing the heavy contents upward in the breezes, deftly catching gold and gravel which were then separated by hand. All this human labor made little impression on history and started no major rush.

Neither did an incident at the mouth of a small stream emptying into the South Fork of the Yuba River. Joseph Aram and wife were members of a party of immigrants who had left New York for San Francisco. Now nearly at their goal, Mrs. Aram went to the creek to do her laundry. The water was too shallow so she scooped out a hole in the bottom and uncovered a small nugget. No one was greatly excited although after the Coloma news, a few staked out claims.

Toward the end of August, 1847, Sutter and James Marshall formed a partnership to build a sawmill at a place called Cullooma by the Indians. It was to supply lumber for Sutter's Fort started about Christmas, 1847, and after seeing it underway, Marshall went to the Fort to oversee the fabrication of mill

EARLY APRIL OF 1851 SAW hotly contested race for honor of El Dorado County Seat between Coloma and Placerville, Coloma winning by act of Legislature April 25th. Until this time Coloma had struggled along with log jail from which prisoners made easy escape. New status demanded more secure hoosegow; $16,000 was set aside for construction, stone jail was built within year. In '57 Coloma was forced to relinquish position of County Seat to more flourishing Placerville, expensive and "escape proof" Coloma jail continued to serve El Dorado County until '62. It was then sold to its former jailer, John Tensher, for building material. Partially wrecked structure still offers imposing and picturesque ruin.

irons, leaving instructions for a ditch to be dug to carry water for the race. On his return he found the job being bungled by inept workers trying to dig the waterway from the upper end instead of the lower, the ditch filling with water as they progressed.

Marshall employed a handyman named Wimmer whose wife was an energetic woman doing much work around the property as well as her household chores. She was later to write: "They had been working on the mill race, dam and mill about six months when one morning about the last days of December, or about the first week of January, 1848, after an absence of several days at the Fort, Marshall took Wimmer down to see what had been done while he was away. The water was entirely shut off and as they walked along talking about the work, just ahead of them on a rough, muddy little rock, lay something bright like

gold. They both saw it but Marshall was first to stoop and pick it up." Doubtful that it was gold, he gave it to the Wimmers' little boy and told him to have his mother throw it in her soap kettle. Later the nugget was retrieved from the kettle untarnished by the "saleratus water" and all had to admit it was really gold.

The fat was now in the fire and Sutter was well aware the event would mean the ruin of his dream of empire. Without much hope his words would have any weight, he asked Marshall to keep the business quiet. Instead, his partner went to Sacramento to display the nugget and was laughed at as a crackpot trying to pass off a chunk of pyrites as gold. Had everyone laughed, the rush might have been delayed, although it was not likely all the gold later found could lie undetected forever. The believing one was

Sam Brannan, a San Francisco publisher on a business trip to Sacramento. Brannan looked at the nugget through eyes trained to minerals and publicity values. He went home, spread the news to the world, and in a year or two the world came to the Sierra and reaped its harvest of wealth with neither Brannan or Marshall getting any of it.

Thousands of wildly shoving men flocked to Coloma and soon were spreading up and down the length of the Sierra Piedmont. On their ruthless way the goldseekers overran the Sutter domain, trampling underfoot all the man's vision of grandeur. Even his Kanakas and Indian help rushed to the hills, leaving New Helvetia to decay.

Forced to join the rabble, Sutter gathered up his pitiful remnant of supporters and moved to a stream in the area in an effort to share in the new wealth. Establishing a settlement called Sutter's Creek, he encountered trouble with the American way of life,

was run out of the diggings for what the Yankees called his system of "slavery."

Back in Coloma, Marshall was also having a bad time. The fact that he was not an employee but a partner of Sutter's gave him the right to claim the ground as his by mineral discovery. It also explained why Sutter went to diggings other than Coloma. The man who should have been revered as the discoverer of wealth that would change the course of history was instead hated and despised because he was forced to post armed guards to keep away swarms of prospectors who disregarded his claims. When he appealed to the courts, friends of the trespassers filled the jury box and even his attorneys turned against him in the hope of getting shares of his claims if he lost the suits.

During the next ten years Marshall was an outcast, spied upon, cheated, abused to the point he gave up mining his own property. He tried to make a

THIS WAS HOME OF JAMES MARSHALL at time of his discovery. It stands on rise directly above Coloma, across road from old Catholic Church. Latter is long abandoned, given over entirely to swarm of bees which is established in walls directly over entrance. Photographer was anxious to obtain record of church interior, nearly intact, was unwilling to climb in through window, even more reluctant to penetrate angrily buzzing bees.

living lecturing throughout the west but this effort to justify his position failed too. Twenty years after the discovery, he returned to the site to find things completely changed. Huge combines of moneyed interests had squeezed most small claims from the original settlers, the law courts upholding the consolidation in many cases. Marshall was left out entirely together with many others who had done the spade work.

In 1872 a sympathetic reporter for a San Francisco newspaper took up the cudgel for James Marshall and wrote a series of articles which so changed the mind of the fickle public the legislature was forced to appropriate for Marshall a sum of $200 a month for two years. By the next session public sentiment had cooled and relief funds were cut in half. On August 10, 1885 James Marshall died a broken pauper, was buried on a hill above and within sight of his discovery location.

DELIVERY WAGON OF "People's Store" is well preserved from early days of Coloma.

OLD PHOTO FROM California State Library shows Sutter's mill. Figure in foreground is thought to be that of James Marshall.

BITTER DISCOVERER OF GOLD in Coloma, James Marshall, pushed out of rights to mine own claims and tiring of doing odd jobs for living, went to nearby Kelsey, established new mine, the Gray Eagle. In order to provide funds for pushing tunnel, he started blacksmith shop, doing good work but made little profit. Here he died in abject poverty on August 10, 1885. Body was taken to site on hill above old home at Coloma. In 1890 this monument was erected over his grave by Native Sons of the Golden West. Marshall's figure points finger to spot of discovery so momentous to his state and world, but bitterly disappointing to finder.

ACTUAL SAWMILL BUILT by partners Johan August Sutter and James W. Marshall had long disappeared when period of exceptionally low water in American River revealed bits of timbers sticking out of gravel. Investigation showed enough remains to exactly pinpoint location and even give some idea of ground plan and construction. Other artifacts included axes, bolts and implements, now all carefully sheltered and displayed in museum in State Park at Coloma. Site of mill was permanently marked with monument.

ROUGH AND READY, CALIFORNIA

The "Great Republic of Rough and Ready" it was to be called. It was only a small mining camp and only a year old in 1850, but people in other towns had to admit the brash camp had ideas of its own and the courage of non-conformity. The scheme? To secede from the Territory of California and the United States, and to declare itself an independent country.

The hard-working miners had a point. They had laws, the mining laws they had worked out and which they figured were good enough to live by. Most of them had left Wisconsin to escape onerous restrictions and now with applications of U.S. laws about to be put into effect through territorial legislation, they were hot under the collar. They could expect all manner of irksome restraints now and, worst of all, they would be taxed the same as back home even though the basis

ROUGH AND READY IS FULL of romantic tales of heyday. Story of secession is well authenticated, less solid is story of Caroline, daughter of "slavegirl" who lived on this site. Caroline loved to ride, on one occasion came up to door-step on favorite pony, dismounted and with flourish stuck whip into ground. Whip, cut previously from cottonwood tree took root, grew to be venerable giant, was blown down few years ago and part cut away. Caroline, growing up, went to San Francisco to go into "business" on her own. She caught sleeve on fire over lamp chimney while curling hair, rushed out to well for water, in her haste fell in, was drowned. Crumbling remains of W. H. Flippin blacksmith shop show in background.

would be different. They would even have to pay to operate their own claims, their very own by legal staking under miners' law.

Seething with the thoughts of these injustices, tempers suddenly exploded when a spark was unintentionally applied by a smart aleck from Boston. One of the original miners from Wisconsin was sweating at his claim and getting little gold, about ready to quit and "maybe chuck the whole shootin' match, maybe" when he looked up to see a dude watching him intently. On impulse the miner asked: "Say, Mister, how'd you like to buy this claim for three thousand dollars?"

The man in the city clothes shrugged his shoulders, took a step forward and made a counter offer. Nobody could be expected to buy a pig in a poke so he would work the claim all the next day to see how rich it was. Everything he dug over $200 the owner could have. Anything less would belong to him. Then at the end of the day they would decide. An agreement was reached.

The Boston man appeared the next morning still dressed fit to kill but with a helper who was ready to work for a promised $8. No sooner had he begun to fling the shovel at the rock when pay dirt showed up and before the day was over he had brought up $180 in gold. The helper was paid and left. The owner of the claim protested this thing wasn't fair, that he had never found more than a bare wage in a day and he should have a share in this find. The eastern man said no, the contract agreed upon was legal according to U.S. laws and there would be no reneging now. He intended to keep his clear profit— $172.

This reasoning pleased no one in Rough and Ready. Almost every miner sided with the claim owner and got hotter and hotter about it until an indignation meeting was held. Discussion dried men's throats and they repaired to the saloon, the Bostonian conspicuous by his absence. The original group expanded to include almost every adult male in the camp and not only was this most recent grievance hashed over but every other one as well.

When the issue of an impending tax on mines and

ROUGH AND READY SCHOOL, built around turn of century replaced original which was destroyed by fire. Now abandoned because of lack of pupils, it has been put to use as "Trading Post." Identification of little "tails" strung on line baffled curious photographer, even on close examination.

DOUBLE DAFFODIL OF TYPE
popular in early days, probably
Von Zion, still blooms in grass
where house used to stand.

miners was brought up, the crowd exploded. One
miner, E. F. Brundage, by way of being a leading
citizen because of his ready and sonorous voice,
loudly proclaimed—"We've had enough!" Everybody agreed, but what to do about it? Some were
for appointing Brundage a committee of one to look
into ways and means of combating the oppressive rul-
ings and report a week later, same time, same place.
But Brundage already had a solution which he proclaimed with a bullish roar—"Secede!"

After a brief, shocked silence followed by loud
cheers, the resolution was passed unanimously and
after a long pause for a few shots of Rough and Ready
dust layer, a manifesto was drawn up. Climbing on a
table, Brundage read the document which set forth a
few complaints and ended with the resolution: "We, the
people of Rough and Ready . . . deem it necessary and
prudent to withdraw from the Territory of California
and from the United States of America to form peacefully if we can, forcibly if we must, the Great Republic
of Rough and Ready." With loud huzzas the resolution was passed unanimously, Brundage was elected
president and all had another round of drinks. A constitution of twelve articles was drawn up and likewise
approved.

The new government went into immediate action.
Delegates were dispatched to the hotel room of the
man from Boston. There was something about the

pointed guns of the group that caused him to wilt
and hand over the $172. Given five minutes to pack,
he was prodded down the stairs, escorted to the edge
of town and booted into the Territory of California.

The Republic waited expectantly for some reaction
from Washington. Would it be disciplinary after
suitable confabs? Would a regiment of soldiers make
camp outside the boundaries of Rough and Ready,
making plans to attack at dawn? The rebels organized a group of Vigilantes and felt prepared for any
emergency—but nothing happened. It felt somewhat
miffed at the complete silence, the insulting aloofness
of the government—no recognition, no invasion. But
gradually the miners settled down to their mundane
labors, unhampered by United States law under Territorial jurisdiction.

Spring came and went. The month of June began
to brown the green carpet of grass on the rolling hills.
Thoughts began to form as to celebrating the Fourth
of July in a proper way. Several miners, with others
from Timbuctoo, discussed possibilities. Then while
plans were sprouting, an appalling realization crashed
down on the heads of all. The camp was no longer
a part of the United States! Independence Day for
it was no longer the Fourth of July. If there were to
be a celebration, on what day would it be?

This was a quandary of cataclysmic proportions.
No mining camp could hold up its head without a

proper Independence Day blow-off. Something had to be done even if it meant restoring the new Republic to the United States. More meetings. More discussion. More whistle wetting. Then decision. Without asking if they might, the people of Rough and Ready voted it back into the Union. With this obstacle out of the way, plans were made for the dad-blamedest lid-lifting Fourth ever held in California.

Putting plans into effect was another thing. When they were going full tilt, on June 28, along came a disastrous fire, sweeping almost everything in town before it. Citizens did what they could with a Fourth of July parade down the little main street now bor-

dered by charred shells of once proud false-fronted businesses.

Rough and Ready was one of the first camps established in Nevada County. A party of men calling themselves the Rough and Ready Company arrived in the area September 9, 1949 under the leadership of a Captain Townsend. He had served under Colonel Zachary (Old Rough and Ready) Taylor, hero of the Mexican War. The men kept their gold discoveries secret for some time, getting out quite a bit of it before the tide of settlers and miners flooded in to make a town of a thousand by early spring, 1850.

A double row of buildings quickly formed, begin-

W. H. FLIPPIN BLACKSMITH SHOP is one of few remaining original buildings of Rough and Ready. At time of taking picture, venerable relic showed strong signs of imminent collapse. Peeks through cracks in walls revealed full complement of blacksmith's implements, forge and all.

ning at the foot of a transverse, oak-covered ridge. About twenty of them lined the camp's one street which had a crook in the middle to conform to the contour. At the end, and considerably elevated, stood an imposing church, complete with steeple and broad flight of steps. As was the custom, this elevation was dubbed "Piety Hill." If any of the founding party which had only "temporarily camped" on the spot ever thought of continuing on to Sacramento, he must long ago have forgotten it for the population remained stable for a number of years.

A Christian Association was organized during the first days holding meetings in one of the little clapboard shanties on the main street. Other religious organizations developed, generally of orthodox nature.

One "church" was headed by a "hell roaring" preacher, James Dinleavy, whose demands were greater than the satisfaction of soul saving and ran a popular and lucrative saloon on weekdays. As soon as he got together enough money, he sent for his wife who waited in San Francisco. Mrs. Dinleavy was the first woman to arrive in camp and excitement stirred the crowd into meeting her at the stage and deluging her with gifts including 21 ounces of gold dust.

The town continued to grow until about 1870. At its best period there were more than three hundred substantial houses, in spite of two crippling fires in '56 and '59. As placer deposits faded, so did Rough and Ready, and little is left of it today except the preposterous legend of secession.

PART OF OLD ROUGH AND READY HOTEL is incorporated in present conglomeration used as post office.

SIERRA CITY, CALIFORNIA

The jagged granite spires of Sierra Buttes frowned down on the huddle of miners' shacks on the broad ledge as though to sound a warning: "Thus far and no farther." The North Fork of the Yuba had willingly yielded its gravels and gold but the peaks were lofty and less charitable. When the lower creeks were raked to meager pickings, the determined miners turned upward to the giant's step on the canyon side and desecrated the mountain with a maze of tunnels and shafts.

The town of Sierra City below was founded on placer gold discoveries in 1849 and was now on the way to becoming a back country metropolis from more substantial though more difficult hard rock mining. But it reckoned without the mountain peaks. In fierce retaliation for the gopherings and pickings of the miner hordes, they held the heavy snows of the 1852-53 winter until they were of prodigious depth in early spring. Then they loosened their embrace and in a terrifying avalanche the village was completely destroyed.

The disaster was so final the place was deserted for about two years. Yet the gold remained in the readymade tunnels and the lure of it was stronger than fear of another inundation. By 1858 another settlement was established on the ledge. All buildings of the first, arrastres and everything above

ground had been wiped away but the existing shafts and tunnels were being worked.

In the spring of '50, P. A. Haven and his partner Joseph Zumwalt located among the Indians at the site. They had done some placering and preliminary prospecting on the Buttes but it was a man named Murphy who made the discovery of the Sierra Buttes Quartz Ledge. The mine started here would be one of California's biggest producers, continuing to turn out gold long after most of the Sierra mines were exhausted. This was reopened after the avalanche and another, the Monumental Quartz, was put in operation. This too was to figure in history, in 1860 producing the second largest gold nugget mined in California.

Stories of the finding of large nuggets should be assayed as closely as the metal itself. In the case just mentioned the weight and value are probably accurate. The nugget was found in a commercial mine, officially weighed and recorded at the time. In other instances, nuggets were supposedly discovered by men working for mine owners and perhaps smuggled out to be bragged about at safe distance. Even a nugget found by the owner of a diggings might be kept a secret until it could be transported beyond the danger of road agents, possibly cut into smaller pieces. In such cases no official record would be made.

STURDY OLD BUSCH BUILDING built in 1871 still stands on Main Street, though it has lost former third story which was of frame construction. Construction began with ceremonies on Fourth of July, always big day in Northern Mines. Festivities were under auspices of famed fraternity known as "E.C.V."; full title,— E. Clampus Vitus. Society had been organized in Sierra City in 1857, main headquarters were in upper floors of this building when completed. Originally a burlesque of known fraternities and strictly for fun, brotherhood grew to have more aspects such as aiding widows of miners, though these activities were never published. At top was "Noble Grand Humbug," members gathered at braying of "Hewgag" in "Hall of Comparative Ovations." Initiations were sometimes rough, such as giving intended member blindfold ride in wheelbarrow over such obstacle as length of stepladder. Membership was essential to anyone wanting to do business in town, even traveling theater group found scant acceptance until manager and male actors joined.

MINE-RIDDLED BUTTES LOOM above Sierra City. From these heights slid devastating burdens of snow, often burying portions of town. Alarm bell is mounted in tower beside comparatively young Sequoia. It announced disasters such as slides, fires, also arrival of stages and mail. Clapper is actuated by twin pull ropes while bell remains stationary. Several bells of this type persist in gold country, such as one in front of old firehouse in North San Juan.

Tales of individual finds should be tested by the integrity of the teller. The word "nugget" is defined as a native lump of precious metal, said to derive from the word "ingot" which is a piece of refined and pure metal, usually cast in some convenient shape. While an ingot would be of pure metal, a nugget might have impurities or be found with part of the matrix attached. Some of the colossal nuggets found in California's early placering period included a considerable amount of adhering quartz or the gold was attached to a much larger chunk of quartz. In the pre-record days many sizable chunks of gold were found, some weighing from five to fifty pounds, containing enough pure gold to send the most phlegmatic miner to spasms of joy.

In the verified case of the nugget found in the Monumental at Sierra City, it was described as a mass of quartz filled with chunks of pure gold. The owners, including top man William A. Farrish, sold it intact— except for several quartz crystals which were broken off—to R. B. Woodward who owned the Gardens, a popular San Francisco resort. Woodward purchased it for exhibition purposes, paying $21,636 on an estimated value of the metal it contained. After its use as a showpiece, it was crushed and the gold melted out came to a value of only $17,654.

The avalanche that swept over the first Sierra City seems to have been the mountain's only vengeance. The catastrophic fires razing so many other wooden towns never touched this one. Old age and vandalism did, reducing the original buildings to remnants. The spectacular scenery, the Buttes, the forest, the sparkling waters of the Yuba, are still there unchanged for the jagged spires look down upon them with compassion.

NORTH SAN JUAN, CALIFORNIA

The long belt of gold rush towns stretching along the western foothills of the Sierra Nevada begins with Mariposa on the south and ends in a scattered cluster of high-perched camps in Sierra County to the north. The span includes many different geological formations, all having one important feature in common— the outcropping of gold. The belt is cut in two about the middle in the vicinity of El Dorado and Coloma, the southern section usually designated as "The Mother Lode," the northern, "Northern Mines."

Mother Lode towns were often settled by Mexicans, sometimes founded or named by them, as Hornitos and Sonora. Most of the camps farther north were settled or christened by Yankees and this includes North San Juan with its obvious Mexican name.

A German miner, Christian Kientz, did the naming. He had been with General Scott's army in Mexico and was deeply impressed with that country's geography, particularly by the hill on which sat the old Mexican prison of San Juan de Ulloa. When he saw the California gold area hill just north of a bunch of shacks beginning to be a town, he called it San Juan Hill and the town also took the name. By 1857 the place needed a post office, the authorities pointing out a much older town with the name San Juan already existing in San Benito County. They solved

OFFICE BUILDING, BUILT IN 1859 contained headquarters for numerous firms operating hydraulic mines, main source of income for North San Juan after placers were exhausted. When Sawyer Act became law and washing away of mountainsides ceased, prosperity of town ended, offices were emptied. Lower floor — originally large clothing store—was given over to succession of enterprises, in later years garage occupied quarters. At last, building was sold for valuable brick it contained and scaffolding was erected preparatory to wrecking historic structure. Mrs. Amelia Cunningham, long-time resident of North San Juan was outraged, bought structure, saving it from wreckers. However, Mrs. Cunningham died before starting renovation, estate is still in litigation, fate of building hangs in balance. Many hope State will take over, make Park of old town which contains so many relics of California's Gold Rush days.

the problem by simply attaching a "North" before the name.

The famous "Deadman's Claim" also had odd naming history. In January of 1853 two young men, West and Chadbourne, discovered a rich deposit in San Juan Hill. To get a sufficiently steep pitch to carry off tailings from the diggings, they were forced to make a deep cut. They were working at it when the whole bank caved in, burying both under tons of rock and dirt. Since there were no other claims near, and the boys were known for minding their own business and not fraternizing with other miners, they were not missed for several days.

When they were, it took several shifts of men to uncover the bodies. Both West and Chadbourne were found to have brothers, who were located and informed they owned a claim at North San Juan. Neither, it seems, was interested in mining, both selling out to Louis Buhring and Peter Lassen who paid $300 for the legal right to mine the spot.

MANY BEAUTIFUL EXAMPLES OF OLDTIME ART of marble sculpture exist in cemetery of North San Juan, most dating from about 1855. During period floral offerings now called "sprays" were made as flat bouquets in style shown on stone. Represented are lilies of the valley, callas, forget-me-nots, roses, morning-glories, lilies, tulips. Roses are "cabbage" type of that period, not high centered hybrid teas of today.

The new owners had trouble with the water supply which either flooded out the equipment or disappeared and they barely made expenses, selling shares now and then to survive. Then a fluming company brought in a steady supply of water and fortunes changed drastically for the owners, now increased to seven. During the sixteen months ending in December of 1858, they took out a total of $156,000. The men continued to mine the claim by removing and washing the alluvial soil until in '60 nothing remained but bare bedrock.

What was probably the first "gold brick" swindle was perpetrated by a slicker posing as a lucky miner returned to the east from the North San Juan gold area. He announced to the New York assay office he had found a nugget of solid gold weighing 193 pounds Troy, and requested an assay. As he desired to display the chunk, he did not wish to mar its appearance and would samples please be removed at the places he indicated so they wouldn't show. Why, certainly. The assayed samples proved to be of the usual "fineness" of typical California gold.

Then the miner announced he was in a terrible predicament. He had a wonderful offer from a London firm for rights to display the nugget there. Yet he was tempted to cash in more directly by sending it to the Philadelphia mint but, in the meantime, he had to live. Could he have a loan, leaving the fabulous chunk of gold as security? Why, sure thing. The assay office advanced, the nuggeteer retreated. After what seemed a reasonable wait, the assayers dug more deeply into the glittering blob of treasure. Under a coating of gold there was a nice fat wad of lead.

HUGE NOZZLE, CALLED MONITOR spewed streams of water at terrific pressures against hillsides, washing away tons of soil, resulting gold-laden mud to be diverted into sluices where heavier gold lodged against slates or "riffles" at bottom. Several millions in gold are said to remain in hills around North San Juan, hydraulicking being outlawed.

NEAR NORTHERN LIMITS OF RANGE for *Sequoia Gigantea*, Big Tree or Mountain Redwood, stands a grove of several specimens in old cemetery at North San Juan. Trunks of these are riddled from near ground to hundred feet or more by holes made by "California Woodpecker." Birds find easy chiseling in soft thick bark of trees, ram acorns point first into holes, seemingly as winter food supply. Nuts, however, are seldom missing from storage holes, many are black with age.

AUBURN, CALIFORNIA

In November of 1855 two young easterners arrived in Sacramento. One had been getting some exciting letters from a friend in Downieville and he interested an acquaintance in making a trip west to find out if the letters were truthful or full of hot air.

It was raining hard when they set out for Downieville. Experienced westerners would have waited a few days for the mountain storm to subside, but they took the scheduled stage. At Auburn the drivers said he could not go any farther without endangering the passengers' lives, that the streams were all running full tilt and many would have to be forded.

The young fellows killed time by drinking in saloons and playing poker and when the storm broke, so were they. Deciding to walk back to Sacramento, work awhile to recoup their finances and then return, they took shovels and pans given them by saloon pals together with some advice, and started out.

About two miles out of Auburn, they came to a place where flood waters still covered the road so went up the ravine where the water was cascading to find a place to cross. They noticed a spot where water had cut away the bank and went to work awkwardly,

FLOWERING BRANCH OF FRUIT TREE offers fresh, young touch to old buildings from gold rush days.

but learning fast. In a short time they had three pounds of nuggets and returned to Auburn rejoicing. The find was worth $980.

Claude Chana was one of the workmen at Sutter's Fort who dropped his tools and headed for the gold fields. But instead of going to Coloma as did most of his fellow workers, he picked up some Indian helpers at Sicard's Ranch on Bear River and worked along the arroyos until he found gold. At this place there was no water, it being necessary to take the dirt to the river to wash it, and this seemed to be too much trouble for Chana. He left.

But others more energetic came and stayed. They thought the name should be Rich Dry Diggings or for variety, North Fork Dry Diggings. Finally a miner with some influence made it Wood's Dry Diggings.

Even that name proved impermanent when a bunch of soldiers arrived, stragglers from Stevenson's Volunteer Regiment. Most of them were from Auburn, New York, and referred to the camp as such, the briefer and more refined name becoming official. During the summer and fall of 1848 the take of a miner willing to work averaged from eight hundred to fifteen hundred dollars a day. Small wonder the camp was filled with several thousand prospectors, miners and hangers-on, all of them from California, most from Coloma.

Auburn, feeling like a town, elected an alcalde and drew up a constitution based on generally accepted miners' law. But now it looked to some as though this effort was all for naught, that the dry diggings might be worked out. Some citizens moved away but not the astute Mr. Jenkins. He reasoned there was still plenty of gold here. It just was not paying to haul the dirt to the water. So why not allow the water to come to the diggings?

Jenkins built a flume from a point above the location where the stream came closest. With plenty of water he worked his claim again but with indifferent success. Had it not been for an accident he might have been discouraged and left camp. His water suddenly ceased to flow. Investigating, he found a failure in the flume, a break in the plank bottom which allowed the water to pour out, washing a big hole in the dirt. Jenkins saw the gleam of gold there and abandoned the earlier workings. The new one yielded him a fortune of $40,000 in the next month. Naturally, everybody who had left Auburn now came back, operations shifting in the new direction.

There was a spiderweb of lesser ravines radiating from the town, one of them called Civil Usage for

ONCE PRINCIPAL STREET IN AUBURN, this virtually unchanged section is now preserved at edge of present bustling city. Attorney's offices were concentrated in block giving rise to jocular appellation, "Lawyers' Row." Two-story Masonic Building, dating from 1853 stands at upper corner. Next was hardware store, then old home of *Placer Herald*. Most early-day newspapers in mining towns shipped in four-sheet papers already partially filled with "boiler plate," usually printed in Chicago. This consisted of syndicated hackneyed material. More local, newsier items were then filled in by use of tiny Washington hand press. Earliest issues of *Herald* lacked ready-printed sheets due to difficulties of transportation, soon began receiving them as overland shipping improved.

some unknown reason. A Swiss named Schmidt built a small cabin on his claim here and being industrious, was generally supposed to have accumulated a quantity of dust. Yet when a Chilean shot and killed him, he found no gold. He fled to Amador County where he was lynched for another crime. Miners found Schmidt's body and gave him a decent burial, not looking for hoarded gold as they presumed the murderer had taken it.

The little cabin stood idle for a while and then a Chinaman rented it. He set to work mining with great industry but stopped after a few days to repair the fireplace for cooking his rice. The removal of

one loose stone opened up a cavity in which lay a buckskin bag full of dust. The pigtailed miner showed it to a trusted friend who estimated its value at about $8,000, then he decamped before the public administrator got his hands on it.

Auburn had one big advantage over towns dependent entirely on gold. Strategically placed in the center of a network of roads, it became a hub of distribution, first for mining supplies, later for more durable trade with farmers and orchardists. The present business section is higher on the hill than the old district which is confined to a block or two on the steep slope.

GRASS VALLEY, CALIFORNIA

When Lola Montez, the fiery and exotic dancer in the Latin manner, bought a house in Grass Valley and settled down there, the forthright women of the town could be expected to throw up their hands in alarm. Instead they respected her, not because they saw she was going to keep hands off their errant husbands, but because she worked diligently in her garden. It was not a gesture. She liked gardening and was good at it, transplanting such difficult subjects as the native cacti. And too, she was aware even dirty, old, digging clothes looked good on her.

A remote, back-country mining camp was not Lola's native habitat. Her beauty was far more outstanding than any extraordinary talent as a dancer,

SECTION OF GIGANTIC CORE removed from ever-deepening shaft of hard rock mine in Grass Valley during town's golden age of mining. Shaft was bored by machine directed by operator who rode in cage directly over cutting equipment. When section of core was cut, operator and machine were lifted from shaft, section loosened by driving wooden wedges around circumference. Hoist was then lowered, attached to core which was lifted out. Repeated drilling and removal of rock sections sank shaft deep into bowels of earth. This sort of mining with expensive equipment spelled doom for earlier miners with their simple pans and rockers.

yet her time was not booked solid and when she was out of audiences she retired to Grass Valley to think about new dance routines and possible engagements.

Born Eliza Gilbert in Ireland, she eloped with an army officer at fifteen and after quickly shedding him, picked up some rudiments of dancing and walked onto a London stage as a professional—the Famed Spanish Dancer, Lola Montez. Her undeniable beauty brought her to the attention of Ludwig of Bavaria, that monarch being between mistresses. She was said to have caused a revolution in that country, fled back to England and married again. This caused her some embarassment because she neglected to end her first marriage legally, but it enhanced her stage career. She was more popular and earned more money at this period than before or later.

Lola decided on a United States tour. The *New York Times* gave her so many press notices she had a public reception in her hotel suite. Joseph Henry Jackson, said of her: "There was an aura of delicious scandal about her. She was graceful and she was beautiful and that was enough." It was enough to carry her across the country, though with diminishing returns. From San Francisco she drifted to the gold camps, winding up in Grass Valley to lick her wounds and plant flowers.

The dancer liked pets, had in her collection a small bear, several parrots and monkeys. She was slightly bitten by one of her bears which inspired this verse by Alonzo Delano:

When Lola came to feed her bear
  With comfits sweet and sugar rare,
Bruin ran out in haste to meet her,
  Seized her hand because 'twas sweeter.

Legends about her concern an editor who wrote a derogatory story and received a visit from the dancer. She carried a whip with which she taught him a lesson on how to treat a lady. Another is about a preacher who let slip some slighting remark about her in a Sunday sermon. Next evening she knocked on his door, very briefly dressed in costume for her famous Spider Dance. While the "unfortunate" minister watched, she performed the dance on his doorstep.

The most important impression Lola made in Grass Valley was on a little girl who lived with her mother a few houses away—a girl named Lotta Crabtree. She was a constant guest at Lola's and it was natural enough the performer should teach songs and dances to the talented child.

When the exotic Montez left Grass Valley to return to the stage with an engagement in Australia, the residents sincerely missed her. But she returned, the tour a failure, staying only long enough to sell the house, then departing on a lecture circuit. This too was an abbreviated affair and things went from bad to worse. Broke in New York, Lola Montez died five years after leaving the mining town.

In Grass Valley little Lotta Crabtree was growing up the way the flamboyant dancer would have her. The mother, Mary Ann Crabtree, encouraged the dancing and taught her all she could. They started a tour of the mining camps beginning with Rabbit Creek where the bearded miners went wild over the lovely black-eyed child, throwing nuggets at her feet. Success in another camp was punctuated by gunshots, Lotta and her mother lying on the floor while bullets whistled through the walls as a pair of drunken miners shot it out in the street. All this was left far behind as the "darling of the mining camps" went on to

world fame. She lived to be nearly eighty, leaving a fortune of $4 million to charity.

Grass Valley received its name when a party of weary emigrants arrived there in 1849 after a hard journey across country and the Truckee Pass Trail. They allowed their bony nags and cattle to eat their fill on luxurious, waving grass on the well-watered spot. There were white men there earlier but they did not stay, Claude Chana and his party of French emigrants who passed through in 1846.

Late in the summer of '49 a party of prospectors, originally from Oregon, wandered northward from the El Dorado diggings. They searched along the streams and found enough to hold them until cold weather set in, then left for the lowlands. That same fall another party headed by a Dr. Saunders had taken the precaution to build a cabin on Badger Hill near what was to be the site of Grass Valley.

Another party settled in Boston Ravine a short

THIS HOUSE ON MILL STREET in Grass Valley was home to famed exotic dancer, Lola Montez. While licking her wounds caused by recent cool reception of her performances in San Francisco, Lola was a warm hostess to all sorts of theatrical and literary people. Here gathered such lights as Ole Bull, Stephen Masset, and two nephews of Victor Hugo, along with many others less known but equally thirsty guests. Liberal potations encouraged wild applause for Lola's performances in her parlor. New husband dancer had brought to Grass Valley was less enthusiastic, bitter quarrels followed soirees. Lola washed mate out of hair by going to San Francisco for divorce. On return to Grass Valley, parties were resumed on even less inhibited level.

IN BACKYARD OF LOLA MON-
TEZ residence is picturesque
shed topped by dove cote. Little
structure sheltered dancer's men-
age of pets including young grizzly and brown bears. Other
members included parrots and a
monkey or two kept in the house.
Animal pets were less in Lola's
affections after divorce gave her
greater freedom to fondle succession of young male guests. While
photos of Montez home were
being taken, crew was laying new
pipeline in street. One crash-
helmeted worker sauntered over
and inquired of photographer,
"Say, who the hell was Lola
Montez, anyway?"

distance away, the gulch also becoming part of the
town. The first Christian burial in Nevada County
took place in Boston Ravine. Services were held by
Rev. Cummings for an emigrant who had made it
this far only to die almost within sight of his hoped-
for destination. A dozen smaller camps sprang up
nearby, some with names of wonder—Red Dog,
Gouge Eye, Little York, Quaker Hill, Walloupa, Sailor
Flat and You Bet.

Some of the rich placers in the district were Hum-
bug Flats (first considered a failure), Pike Valley,
Grass Valley Slide, Thode Island, Lola Montez and
Kate Hardy. Hard rock mining was the mainstay

and the reason Grass Valley lived so much longer than
camps having only placer beds. The discovery of a
rich lead on Gold Hill in 1850 by George Knight gave
impetus to a vast network of later discoveries and
many crude mills to crush and reduce ore.

Millions of tons of tailings surrounding hundreds
of old shaft heads and mills attest to the huge activity
continuing eighty years with a total production of
gold amounting to more than $80 million. Under
the complex of once-active mining buildings is a vast
labyrinth of tunnels and shafts. One vein extends
almost two miles and one tunnel drops to 7,000 feet,
the bottom 1,500 feet below sea level.

NEVADA CITY, CALIFORNIA

John J. Kelly was a superstitious Irishman who worked in one of the steeply slanting shafts in the Nevada City mines. Kelly lost his partner in a mining accident and missed him sorely. This day he had been working alone and was now going to check the little wooden storeroom where dynamite and caps were kept. There was a hole in the door and it was Kelly's job to reach in and feel the latch on the inside to see that it was securely fastened.

It so happened one of Kelly's friends was in the powder room where a bucket of water was kept for emergencies, and the water was always cold down in the mine. When he saw the Irishman's hand come groping through the hole, he yielded to the impulse felt by a practical joker, stuck his hand in the cold water and then grasped Kelly's. The Irishman jumped with terror and ran up the shaft in a panic, screaming that the ghost of his dead partner had gripped his hand.

There are ghosts around Nevada City but the town itself is not dead. Its history concerns its place in the Northern Mines and it is full of gold rush color.

The first man to pan for the yellow metal in the area was the same one who first noticed flakes in the race of Sutter's Mill—James W. Marshall. His efforts at Deer Creek were disappointing and he moved on. He would later know that in the next two years there would be a rush of ten thousand miners to the area. Cabins began to go up in Gold Run just above the spot where Marshall dug in September, 1849, the first being that of Capt. John Pennington and his two partners.

A Dr. Caldwell erected a small building for a store on Deer Creek. Then as richer diggings developed seven miles above, he started a store there that became Caldwell's Upper Store, a name applying to the town also. In March, 1850, miners elected a Mr. Stamps to the position of alcalde of Caldwell's Upper Store. He was not one to put up with a name like that and taking his inspiration from the snowy mountains on the horizon, he named the town Nevada or "snowy" in Spanish.

In 1851 the county of Nevada was established with the rapidly growing city as its seat. Ten years later when the State of Nevada was formed, a hue and cry went up from the California city that it had the name first. Government officials said it was too late to do anything about the state's name but the city could add that word to its name. Citizens had to be satisfied with Nevada City.

During the first few months of the town's existence, strangers along the stream where placering was going on rubbed their eyes in disbelief—a woman was standing knee-deep in the cold water working a rocker right along with the men. The townspeople nodded and went on working. They knew Madame Penn. She worked hard and with some luck got enough gold together to start a boardinghouse, the first in Nevada City. The Union Hotel now stands on the site.

Swarms of hopeful prospectors and miners were pouring in at a record rate with all the excitement of the first placer gold, the loose stuff that could be scooped up from the creek bottoms. But this came to an end and as the old claims were exhausted and new ones impossible to find, the hard rock mining not yet started, some avid miners actually began to dig up the streets in search of gold—and found it.

One merchant, angered at the shambles in front of his store, protested to the man with the shovel: "See here—you can't dig up a public street like this!" The miner maintained he could, that there was no law that said he couldn't. The enraged storekeeper drew his gun to emphasize his words. "Very well, then—I'll make one. You git!" The miner moved operations to the next street.

A short distance from the town on Lost Hill a fantastically rich placering area was discovered. Several miners took out a quart of gold in a single day, worth $6,000. The dry gravels were covered by an overburden of soil and tunnels were necessary to get

DUMP WAGONS OF THIS TYPE were used throughout Sierra gold belt. Tree in background is also characteristic of country, though confined to medium altitudes. Called Digger Pine after native Indians, it does not penetrate loftier mining areas such as Sierra City, where it is replaced by Sequoia and other conifers. Digger Pine is distinctive, having lax, grayish needles and divided trunk. Picture taken in early March shows "candles," new growth starting at ends of branches.

at the gold-bearing material. The area became a maize of burrows and the resulting town was named Coyoteville. When it was swallowed up by the expanding Nevada City, the gravels were exhausted, but during the mad two-year rush a total of $8 million was removed.

One of the last good discoveries in the creek banks was made in the summer of 1859. John Burns, a resident of Nevada City, was walking along a ditch near Deer Creek and in crossing it, slipped on a wet plank and fell in the water. He floundered around and grabbed at the bank, dislodging a piece of decomposed quartz and exposing a yellow gleam. Burns clambered out and went home to change clothes, not because of discomfort but to attract no attention. He took a sack and shovel back to the ditch band and "cleaned out," the yield $2,000. The ditch company took over the new diggings the next day but Burns was happy to have enough nuggets for a string of wild days and nights.

Fourth of July celebrations were big days in mining camps. Two weeks before the holiday, about

NEVADA CITY IS UNIQUE in many ways, repays leisurely stroll on foot. Streets seem to have no set plan, original wandering burro trails may have influenced survey. Steep hills complicate pattern, narrow streets twist and turn unexpectedly; every angle offers architectural surprises like this "conservatory" linking hotel and annex. One house plant visible is Aspidistra, "Cast-Iron Plant" of Victorian times. Not popular or well-known these days, specimen could well have descended from lusty mining days when hotel was built.

1850, Nevada City was delighted to hear there would be a big fight between a jackass and a grizzly bear at nearby Grass Valley. The bear was billed as the most Ferocious Grizzly ever to be trapped in the Sierra, the donkey as The Champion Kicker of California, having killed a mountain lion in Hangtown and a bull in Sonora. On the morning of the festive day some two thousand miners went noisily by horse and foot to the "ring" of brush and stakes in Centerville, just north of Grass Valley.

Considerable dust was being stirred up along the way so a man carried a bottle of something to keep it wet and by the time the crowd arrived it was in a mood for anything. Every man paid his two dollars and pushed inside the stockade. There was the jackass, sure enough, nibbling at the grass at one side and there was the savage bear in a big wooden box. . . . "Don't get too close, gents!"

Then the play was ready to start and at a signal the gate was raised. The bear moved out slowly, a small brown one, timidly sniffing as if reluctant to leave the familiar shelter. A man forced him all the way out with a pole and when he saw the jackass, he ambled playfully toward it. When was the savage rush coming? The spectators waited anxiously.

Now the bear swung its head, obviously wanting to make friends. But the donkey was having none of that. He rolled his eyes, laid his ears back and when the bear got within range, two sharp hooves caught him in the ribs. Fully disenchanted, the bear slunk back and bounded over the barrier, disappearing into the chaparral. While the victor resumed his grazing nonchalantly, a thousand men set up a roar and if the promoters could have been found there might have been a lynching. A few had foreseen the outcome and were long gone for another bottle.

Something had to be done to relieve the tension so the miners who still wanted action took charge of the long-eared animal and led him at the head of a long, disgruntled procession toward, but not directly to, Nevada City. There were a lot of saloons along the way and the new hero would be welcome in all of them. None was passed up and in each he was toasted lavishly. By the time all got to Nevada City, there was only one of the crowd who could walk straight— the jackass.

The advent of quartz mining meant that Nevada City had come of age but with some placers still producing and only a few hard rock operations beginning, the transition was gradual and the camp did not suffer the setback experienced in other gold camps, notably Jackson, another Mother Lode town developing in a similar way.

In June of 1859 news came to the gold country which further depleted population and made an impact on Nevada City. The Nevada City *Transcript* of July 1 carried this item:

"J. T. Stone, formerly of Alpha but now living on Truckee Meadows, has just arrived here and reports the discovery of a vein of ore of extraordinary richness at the head of Six Mile Canyon near Washoe Valley. The vein is four feet wide and is traced a distance of three and a half miles. The ore is decomposed and works easily. It is like that from which silver is sometimes obtained. The discovery was made by a miner working in Six Mile Canyon, who found as his worked his claim, that it became richer as he approached the vein. The news has caused great excitement here."

Then the golden trumpet sounded again—far to the north. The clarion call spelled out "Cariboo" and away went the gold hungry drifters again, while the California camps were left to more decay. But Jackson and Nevada City stood out as examples of having something solid to fall back on when the bubble of loose placer gold broke.

Gold was still coming out of shafts penetrating far down into slide rock veins extending in quartz seams thousands of feet and producing if big companies were at hand to finance. Gone was the day when the individual prospector, equipped with only a pan and shovel, could stand in a stream and slosh riches in glittering gold out of the dripping gravel.

Nevada City, having successfully weathered the adjustment period, was displaying handsomely ornate mansions along Nevada and Prospect Streets, and by 1892 these homes gained further eminence with electric lights. The tiny power plant supplying this new-fangled convenience was the nucleus of the giant Pacific Gas and Electric Company.

French nurseryman, Felix Gillet, started his business in the town, perhaps the first of its kind in the west. He was responsible for the beginning of California's huge English walnut production, introducing these and other nut trees.

Nevada City is a living monument to a fantastic era long gone. If it is not in itself a ghost, it is full of the wraiths of lusty, bearded miners and of sharpies who took their gold the easy way.

FIREHOUSE BUILT OF NATIVE granite and brick about 1851 was at first simple structure, Victorian-type balcony and gingerbread added later. It is likely most beautiful of many buildings remaining from heyday. Traditional iron doors and shutters are frequently encountered, one office building, "modernized" presents shock to history-minded observer; upper floor has several windows complete with ancient iron shutters, brilliantly painted chartreuse, alternated with purple.

DOWNIEVILLE, CALIFORNIA

Juanita was a good-looking Mexican girl who entertained young miners in her little Downieville cabin . . . until one of her guests pleased her so much she invited him to move in. He jumped at the chance.

A young Australian, Jack Cannon, was not aware of these developments. Juanita had shown him hospitality on several occasions and one morning he was reeling down the street, partly supported by half-drunken companions and partly by thoughts of Juanita's charms. At the door of her cabin he told his friends to go on, that he was going to see a man about a kangaroo.

The others knew about the newly established love nest and tried to argue Jack out of his idea but he pushed open the door and went in. Instead of welcoming him with a loving embrace, Juanita slipped a knife between his ribs. Another version of the legend has Jack opening the door but heeding the advice of his comrades after seeing Juanita had a man, then returning at a later hour to apologize and then getting the knife.

In any event, the result was death for Jack Cannon

and the calaboose for the beautious Juanita. The end of the story might have been the funeral but racial prejudice reared its ugly head. Mexicans in Downieville and all California mining camps were barely tolerated. Little excuse was needed to make it rough for them. Forgotten or ignored was the fact of sex and when Juanita was found guilty of murder the same day it happened, she was promptly strung up to a beam of the bridge over the Yuba.

This was mining camp justice but California and the country as a whole reacted with revulsion. Publicity was so unfavorable that lynching even in the California camps became unfashionable for a time.

The first man to pan the water of the Yuba at the forks was Frank Anderson in September, 1949, but he had little success. A few months later there arrived a motley crew headed by one William Downey, a Scotsman. His retinue consisted of ten Negro sailors, an Indian, an Irish boy named Michael Deverney and a Kanaka called Jim Crow.

The group erected several little log cabins above the point where the North Fork of the Yuba joins the main stream. Although snow soon fell and a skin of ice formed on the quiet pools, persistent panning yielded considerable gold. Snow was brushed away from extruding quartz veins, the crevices yielding as much as $200 a day. Most surprising reward came when Jim Crow cooked a fourteen-pound salmon caught in the river. When the eaters got to the bottom of the kettle they found a sizable flake of gold.

Inevitably, a stampede converged at The Forks which was soon renamed Downieville for the leader, now respected and endowed with a courtesy title of "Major." Claims and men spread up and down both streams and by 1851 the camp had a population of 5,000.

Not all of these were miners, one authority claiming "there was only one producer to eight leeches." But the bars were long and shiny with roulette wheels spinning all night. Streets seethed with pack trains of mules, burros and freight wagons. There was no way to haul supplies and prices of commodities proved it—$4 a pound for sugar and boots $100 a pair.

When religion came to Downieville the town had no other edifice for church purposes than the Downieville Amphitheater, located on what came to be Piety

CATHOLIC CHURCH OF IMMACULATE CONCEPTION clings to steep canyon-side, seems to be all steeple, chapel is tiny by comparison. Originally built in 1852, first structure was destroyed by fire 1858. This edifice was erected on site shortly after; Fr. Dalton was first Pastor.

Flat. The intrepid preacher, first to enter the roistering camp and deliver a sermon, was Rev. William C. Pond.

Surprisingly, the miners welcomed Pond and his preaching with an enthusiasm so great funds were provided for a church. It was built in a few months but the week before dedication was scheduled, the building burned to the ground. Thoroughly discouraged and dejected, the minister opened the door of his cabin to a miner with outstreached hand who said he had walked four miles into town. "Here's a hundred dollars, Mr. Pond," he said, "to start a new church." Contributions came thick and fast and in a short time a new fireproof structure of brick and stone was ready for use.

Stories of fantastic finds of gold in and around town would make it appear more churches could have been built in record time. Weirdest is an unverified tale that on August 21, 1856, James Finney found close to town a nugget weighing 427 pounds, Troy. Even allowing for the fact that most California "nuggets" had considerable quartz matrix adhering to them, this one was worth over $90,000. It was sold to bankers Decker and Jewett and sent to the Philadelphia mint where it was displayed for several years. This would be the largest nugget found in California, the the second largest in the world.

In 1858 John Dodge, who was working the forks of the Yuba between '50 and '53, told of an experience plausible enough in view of the highwayman menace. He, said he, Bill Haskins and an unidentified Dutchman were working an abandoned claim on the middle Yuba. Digging in the bank he came to a chunk of pure gold, too large to pick up after being wedged out. Being "very excited" and fearing discovery, the men posted the Dutchman as a guard and went to work on the chunk. On complete exposure it showed some attached quartz, "not over five pounds." This was chipped off, the nugget dragged into the cabin and shoved under the bed.

The men stayed away from Downieville that night and the next day, Sunday, trying to figure out some way of weighing their find, their gold scale being capable of handling only a pound and a half. A novel scheme was concocted, weighing pieces of rock until they had enough to balance the chunk of gold, and it proved to weigh 227 pounds. Any idea of taking it to the express office was ruled out as causing too much excitement and putting the owners' lives in jeopardy. The men spent Sunday working halfheartedly as the nugget held their main attention and a decision was finally made as to disposing of it. Dodge went to town late Monday, bought a cold chisel and the men spent all that night cutting and dividing the big lump. "It seemed like vandalism," he said.

DOWNIEVILLE IS SITUATED in bottom of narrow ravine where North Fork of Yuba enters larger stream. Main street parallel to Yuba is only one somewhat level, others like this one rise steeply by means of switchbacks and terraces of dry-laid schist rocks. Near site of National Theatre was location where trial was held for miner who had stolen pair of boots. Man was convicted, promised release if he returned boots to owner, set up drinks for crowd. Prisoner was glad to comply, was so generous with drinks that judge, jury and witnesses were soon celebrating uproariously. In resultant drunken brawl, culprit re-stole boots, slipped unobstrusively out of town.

When the job was finished they caved down the workings, had a brief nap, cooked breakfast, wrapped the gold in their blankets and boarded the stage for San Francisco. The stage passed Goodyear Hill and Nigger Tent, rendezvous of road agents, without incident and after arriving in the Bay City, they caught a ship for Panama and New York where they sold the gold for cash, about $50,000. The find was made in '53 and in '58, when John Dodge told the story, he was working as a teamster in the Australian gold fields, but "had a good time while it lasted."

A claim on the North Fork of the Yuba was called Sailor's Diggings, being manned by English sailors in '51. The seamen were said to have found many nuggets from a top size of 31 pounds down. When they had enough, they headed back to England with two large canvas sacks of gold.

On a fine Sunday morning of June, 1856, Major Downey went for one of his habitual walks, this time to the top of a hill on slate Creek to look over the country. While enjoying the view, he scuffed his toe on the ground and unearthed a chunk of quartz about the size of a man's hand. He loosened it and let it roll down the slope. Some time later one of the numerous Chilean miners went up the same hill hunting quail. He shot one, the dying bird fluttering into the hole left by Downey's rock. On picking up the quail the Chilean noticed a glint. Half buried was a piece of gold and quartz which, when cleaned by the assayer in town, yielded nearly a pound of pure gold, about $200 worth. The hill was soon covered with claims and more than fifty miners made fortunes there. Far more wealth was almost discovered by Major Downey than he ever found in his claims. Disgusted, he left shortly for the Cariboo fields in British Columbia.

A middle-aged lady in pinched circumstances came to Downieville to start a boardinghouse on a shoestring. A brother there set her up a tent house with board sides but no floor over the dirt. She got a stove, a long table, some chairs and thirty boarders at $12 a week. She was raking and sweeping the "floor" one day when she noticed what seemed like a piece of gold. The chunk she picked up was exactly that and it wasn't the only one. She rushed to tell her brother who helped her move out the furniture and start panning the floor. Before the day was over they had $500 and when the boarders arrived they were told to eat elsewhere. A month later she returned to the east and told the folks her boardinghouse venture had been very successful.

After two summers of working the gravel beds at the edge of the Yuba between Downieville and Goodyear's Bar, the pickings were getting somewhat thin. The miners, confident the middle of the stream bed would yield plenty, contrived to build a flume. It was built in the spring and successfully dried up the stream by diverting the flow, but the first high water from melting snow took out the entire project and it was never tried again.

Hardly anyone was willing to admit the real glory of Downieville was fading but two events in 1865 made the fact hard and clear. Pond's church was closed for lack of a congregation—and the Chinamen came. Mr. Pond went sadly to another call in Petaluma and the church structure was sold. The Sons of the Flowery Kingdom were not tolerated except in menial capacities, such as washing dirty clothes for the miners, as long as gold was plentiful in the creeks. But as the supply grew scant they were permitted to glean the white man's leavings.

The pattern was repeated over and over in the mining camps of the west but in Downieville the Chinese put a different twist to it. They saw how the miners had tried to divert the Yuba by flume so the hard-working Orientals patiently and tirelessly carried large rocks from the edges of the stream to make a new channel. When the exposed gravels were worked out, other parts of the river were opened up likewise. The moved rocks were stacked in piles and many of these cairn-like humps remain today.

DOWNIEVILLE'S MAIN STREET remains much as it was, despite frequent fires and floods. Structure in center is original Craycroft Building, in basement was famous 75-foot bar. At intersection, road turns right one block to bridge crossing Yuba. From beam of original bridge dangled body of Juanita, only woman hanged in California.

TIMBUCTOO, CALIFORNIA

Jim Denton was a miner in Timbuctoo. His claim on the banks of the Yuba River paid him only the barest minimum in gold dust to keep body and soul together. His little cabin was furnished with only the simple essentials and he ate plain foods sparingly.

Nights along the Yuba even in June are cold and Denton was out of wood. He stopped working his rocker early one evening, June 20, 1860, and cut down the old oak near his cabin for firewood. He had planned to take it down because the aged tree had a badly decayed side and a strong wind might blow it over on his shack. He felled the tree and set about cutting it up. When he split the rotten section, he laid open a large hollow—and in it snugly reposed a buckskin sack.

As soon as Jim took hold of the soft leather, he

RAPIDLY FALLING INTO RUIN is pathetic shell of once busy Stewart Store. Patriotic groups mindful of value of historic relics have made effort to preserve old structure, placed sheltering metal roof over it. Struggle is futile against human vandals who pluck bricks and paint obscenities over old signs on building.

BEAUTIFUL EXAMPLE OF STONE-MASON'S work is crumbling rear wall of only building remaining in Timbuctoo. Native rocks, including river boulders, have been split so as to form facing. Doors and windows are lined with brick, furnished with iron shutters characteristic of period.

knew what he had and his hands trembled as he opened the drawstring and poured some of the contents into his hand. Nuggets they were, hundreds of them, with no quartz matrix sticking to them. He took the sack into the cabin and weighed the nuggets one at a time on his gold scales—total weight thirty-five pounds. He carefully counted the number of *chispas* and wrote down the figures.

An honest man, Jim took the bag to the store for safekeeping and then let out the story. He said all the rightful claimant had to do was give the weight and number of nuggets. No one in Timbuctoo or nearby Mooney Flat or Smartsville came forth and after waiting a reasonable period, Jim took the gold to Grass Valley where he sold it for $7,500. No claimant ever turned up and Jim Denton concluded the rightful owner had met with a fatal accident after pushing the bag into that hollow.

First miners to slosh gravels in their pans along that part of the Yuba camped there in 1850. In the party was a Negro, a refugee slave from the South. He had originally been captured by slavers in the French Sudan of West Africa, his native town being Timbuktu. He worked industriously in the little ravine above where the town was later built and found good colors in his pan. Happy over his discovery, he asked the others if he might call the place Timbuktu Gulch and they were agreeable. The colored man's first strike was followed by many more, news spread and a town grew up where the ground was more level. The name was preserved with American variations.

Getting started in 1855, the town grew steadily but not spectacularly. Then came the hydraulic mining era when the banks of the stream were literally washed away in a flood of thin mud and boulders. Results in gold production were so large that Timbuctoo boomed into the largest town in the eastern part of Yuba County. Churches, theaters, hotels, saloons and stores went up to serve a population of more than 1,200 people.

The flood of debris and mud soon raised another flood, that of protests from ranchers and the valley and the Sawyer Decision, 1884, put an end to this type of mining. The props that had kept up the economy of Timbuctoo were knocked out and the town quickly sank into oblivion.

SIMPLE STAMP MILL REMAINING from earliest days of hard rock mining in California. Principle is simple. Large wooden wheel is turned by power which often came from water wheel. As shaft turns, cams lift iron spools and release them in rapid succession. As spool and rod drop, bottom end equipped with heavy weight rises and falls on chunks of ore thrown in bin. Ore is gradually crushed to near powder, readying it for further refining. When this mill was in use, separation of gold and crushed quartz was accomplished hard way, in pans and back-breaking work in streams.

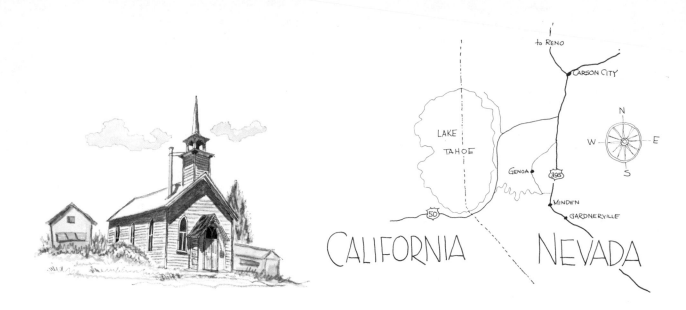

GENOA, NEVADA

"Fighting" Sam Brown of Virginia City was pure bully, although he bragged he had filled a graveyard singlehanded. For a time he ran things in the mining camp on Mount Davidson and it was at the height of his ascendancy that one of his young henchmen was caught holding up a stage and was taken to the then county seat of Douglas County, Genoa, for trial.

Sam stormed down to the picturesque Mormon town at the base of the Sierra to attend the trial, fully prepared to bluster the judge and jury into intimidation and thereby, free his cohort.

What Sam didn't know was that the county had a new District Attorney, Bill Stewart, and that young Stewart had been informed of what he might expect of the witness. Testimony at the trial had been going against the stage robber, and when it came time for Sam to testify he was boiling mad. Storming up to the stand he was fully primed with the best liquor Genoa had to offer and was prepared to bluster that young lawyer into submission. The edge of his resolution was considerable dulled when he found himself facing the muzzle of a gun held in the steady hand of the man who would one day be U.S. Senator from Nevada. Cowed, Sam gave tistimony at best not calculated to help the case of his friend, who was soon convicted.

As soon as he got out of the courtroom and away from the end of Stewart's six-shooter, Sam, regaining his courage, raging at his failure, and returning to the Comstock, took it out on an innocent Dutch farmer who lived near the road, firing several shots in his direction. His aim being as bad as his disposition, Sam missed the Dutchman, who now understandably got *his* dander up, and with considerably better aim, cut short the career of "Fighting" Sam Brown. A coroner's jury held that "Brown came to his end by the dispensation of a Divine Providence." Van Sickle, once more phlegmatic, paid little attention, having returned to his again placid fields.

Those Argonauts heading for the California gold fields that preferred going overland to an even more dangerous sea voyage again had several choices of route. Some sought to shorten the distance by crossing the terrible Salt Lake Desert to reach the Humboldt. More headed for Fort Hall and Soda Spring, thence south to the river. Some went north around the main part of the great desert, avoiding the greater part of it though still suffering their full share of hardships.

For the first few years of overland travel pioneers could count on shooting game for a food supply. As travel increased, all living creatures soon were exterminated over a wide band adjacent to the route. Those depending on the bounty of the land found themselves hungry to the point of starvation by the time they reached the Humboldt, many had even eaten their dairy cows and some of the beasts hauling the wagons.

It was only natural, therefore, that trading posts would soon be established along the Humboldt Road as the wall of the Sierra grew nearer, the travelers sometimes still having a little cash, not having had any opportunity to spend it. A small settlement grew up beside the first of these establishments. Weary, dirty families often took the rest stop as an opportunity to wash out all clothing still serviceable, hanging the tattered remnants on surrounding bushes to dry. And so "Ragtown" came into being, the name later was changed to Leeteville.

For a time this was the last settlement, then, in June of 1849 Col. John Reese, a trader sent out by Brigham Young, built a log stockade, corrals and a cabin or two at the very foot of the Sierra. At first the place was called, simply, Mormon Station, that being exactly what it was. As others became established this one needed a more identyfying cognomen and a settler with an Italian background called it Genoa. Since the earlier Ragtown never became a permanent fixture, Genoa was the first real town in the state of Nevada, although that state didn't exist at the time of Genoa's founding. For those who fol-

lowed every tenet of Brigham Young it was the state of Deseret. In 1850 the United States Government declared the area to be part of the Territory of Utah, the southern part of what is now Nevada going into the Territory of New Mexico.

An interesting sidelight on the story of Genoa is that when the first gold-hungry men who were heading for the Mother Lode and Northern Mines stopped beside the Carson River near Genoa they panned the stream and actually did find a little gold, but were too filled with dreams of the other side of the Sierra to pay much attention. Later, when the big Washoe Boom hit the Nevada side many of those same adventurers, disappointed in what they found in California rushed back again, proving once again that the grass is always greener on the other side of the fence.

The Sierra was a formidable barrier between east and west travel. Placerville, the fastest growing boom town of the gold rush on the western slope, was the terminus of a rude "road," little more than a path. Genoa was at the eastern end, exactly at the point

STORE DATES FROM EARLIEST DAYS in Genoa. Colonel John Reese, his brother Enoch, and Steven A. Kinsey were among first builders of Mormon town. First lady settler was Eliza Ann Meddangh Mott, the wife of Israel Mott. Their daughter Sarah was the first native, she grew up here and married a Mr. Hawkins.

OLD SIGN ON GROCERY is protected from elements by canopy, has withstood ravages of time. Last item, "Queen's Ware" is flooded by direct sunlight, overexposed in picture.

"SNOWSHOE" THOMSON LIES AT FOOT of beloved Sierra in pioneer cemetery at Genoa. Snow-covered hills rising sharply in background are first easy step in what becomes giant barrier rising to over 14,000 feet at highest elevations, passes over which Thomson hiked averaged 7,400 feet. Thomson's "snowshoes" actually were skis, the first ever seen in West, when the word ski was unknown. Thomson's name is spelled "Thompson" in all available historical references. In face of evidence on stone and fact that Norwegians mostly spell the name without "P," we here follow them.

where the wildly rugged route suddenly flattened out into the desert. Situated as it was, the town could hardly help growing. By 1858 the place even had a newspaper, the first in the Territory. The few inhabitants of the whole area, still less than a thousand, were so hungry for news that a few "newspapers," really only hand-written sheets, had already been attempted. The *Scorpion* and *Gold Canyon Switch* were among these and had a tiny circulation in 1854. So a real, printed paper was an impressive and eagerly accepted innovation. It was called the *Territorial Enterprise*.

The infant paper remained a single sheeter for a time, then when the Washoe Bubble swelled the paper burgeoned into four-sheet size. It soon outgrew Genoa and as population expanded in Carson City the paper moved itself and equipment there. Then came the soaring expansion of Virginia City and the *Enterprise* again moved to what proved to be its permanent home, becoming a daily September 24, 1861.

The at first strictly Mormon settlement of Genoa began to be infiltrated by residents of other faiths in

a few years and among these was a sizable group of adherents to the Catholic faith. These managed to co-exist with the Mormons, but were unable to celebrate masses, confess or participate in any of the rites of the Church except in unconsecrated structures. Then in 1860 with the arrival of Father H. P. Gallagher a simple church was built and consecrated, the first Catholic one in Nevada.

Genoa has an interesting old cemetery with many ornate monuments, some enclosed by elaborate wrought iron fences. A more simple marble stone marks the grave of a Norwegian who was certainly the most remarkable mail carrier known to history. John A. Thomson, born 1827, traveled to the United States with his parents when he was ten years old. The family started farming in Illinois, then moved around through other midwestern states until John was twenty-four. This was in 1851 at a time when the whole country was filled with stories of fantastic gold discoveries in California. The young farmer was so taken with the idea of making a quick fortune he headed for the El Dorado. Arriving at Genoa he climbed over the Sierra along with hundreds of other goldseekers, coming out at Placerville on the California side. He didn't know it then, but the hardy Scandinavian was to retrace this route many times, and more, by himself with a heavy packful of mail on his back.

John worked in the Coon Hollow and Kelsey's Diggings near Placerville for a while, but with poor results. Becoming disgusted with mining he decided to try farming and bought a small place on Putah Creek in the Sacramento Valley. In 1856 he heard about the difficulties the government was having in getting the mail over the mountains in winter when deep snows clogged the high passes and this got Thomson to thinking. He loved the mountains, he had a strong physique and couldn't get lost, having "something in my head that keeps me right."

So he went out to his woodlot, cut a live oak down. He chose a good, nearly straight section about eight feet long and split the stubborn-grained wood into sections. Of the two most even ones he fashioned a pair of skis such as he had seen in Norway, full-sized versions of the small ones he had worn as a boy. They weighed twenty-five pounds. Then came an improvised balance pole. John took his new equipment up to the mountains and practiced on the snowy slopes. Then he showed up at the post office in Placerville and said he'd carry the mail over the snowy mountains, just like that. And carry the mail he did for twelve years, begining in January of 1856.

At first it took him four days to cover the ninety miles between Placerville and Carson Valley, but he soon pared off a day. His pack of mail often weighed

MAIN SECTION OF ORIGINAL
TOWN of Genoa shows grocery
at right flanked at left by newer,
presently used grocery and filling
station. At extreme left is in-
evitable tavern, housed in brick
building dating back to 1860s.

eighty pounds so he carried little to eat, a few dried
sausages and crackers, and no blankets. When forced
to rest, he set fire to a dead pine stump, cut a few
boughs and napped with his feet to the fire.

He often played the role of Good Samaritan as
well. On one trip, he found a James Sisson half dead
and with frozen feet in a cabin on the Nevada slope
but nearer Placerville. After making Sisson as comfortable as possible, he returned to Placerville, persuaded several men to don makeshift skis, return to

the cabin with him and take Sisson down to Carson on
a sledge. There a doctor decided Sisson's feet would
have to be amputated but no chloroform was available. So Thomson retuned over the Sierra to Placerville where he got the precious stuff and again crossed
the divide to get the anesthetic to the suffering man in
Carson.

After a dozen years of this, the railroad was completed over the pass and Snowshoe Thomson was no
longer needed. All this time he'd had no pay and,

WROUGHT IRON GRAVE ENCLOSURE is among many examples in good condition in Genoa Cemetery.

feeling he should have a little something for his efforts, applied to the post office. There he was told he'd have to go to Washington and make personal application for an appropriation, and this he did. There he got glowing promises of adequate reward, returning home well content. But nothing happened. Later, more promises came along.

He had established another farm in the upper Car-son Valley barely on the California side and here he settled down to agriculture again to await his pay. It never came. Although of the most robust constitution Thomson had suffered much in his snowy journeys, losing so much resistance to infection that when an illness attacked him May of 1876 he lasted only four days. His body was taken down to Genoa and buried there.

IN SHADE OF GIANT LOCUST TREES is restoration of old Mormon Station. Here, on June 10, 1851, Colonel James Reese arrived with 18 men, ten wagons full of supplies, received warm welcome from Hampden S. Beattie, who, with small contingent, had established waystop two years earlier. Combined force built original log Station headquarters, destroyed by fire in 1910. Reconstruction was done of historic building and completed in 1947 by Nevada State Planning Board in cooperation with Genoa Fort Committee.

To Wendover IN NEVADA · ALT 50 · 40 · TIMPIE · 40 · To SALT LAKE CITY · GRANTSVILLE · 36 · 112 · IOSEPA · SKULL VALLEY INDIAN RES · OPHIR · MERCUR · 73 · 36

UTAH

N · W · E · S

IOSEPA, UTAH

The original inhabitants of bleak Skull Valley were members of the lowly Gosiute Indian tribe. They were scavengers, eating whatever they could find including numerous lizards, horned toads, rodents and snakes indigenous to the arid wastes. When winter cut off even this meager supply, they were reputed to hole up and barely exist in a state of near hibernation until spring. Starvation took its toll, skeletons found by early settlers giving the valley its name.

In 1843 Thomas Farnham wrote "these poor creatures are hunted in the spring of the year when they are weak and helpless . . . and, when taken, are fattened, carried to Santa Fe and sold as slaves." These were the best people this savage land could produce until eager Mormon converts from lush South Sea Islands established a new home in Zion.

The group of Hawaiian Islanders must have looked at their new home in Skull Valley with more than dismay. No landscape could be imagined to contrast more with the one they had recently left. Instead of swaying palms there were a few scattered juniper trees and some sagebrush. In place of curling, foam-crested breakers rolling in on white sandy beaches there was a tiny spring, not even visible to the homesteaders. A few coyotes and jack rabbits made up the animal population. Now and then a black and white magpie would sail low over the rocky ground, its long tail streaming. This was their promised land.

Mormon zeal had spread to the Islands even in 1844, and in a few years the Saints had converted many of the natives. Possibly to demonstrate the success of the Church in gaining converts in such far-flung outposts, some fifty new members were transported to Salt Lake City, there to receive the rites in the temple. The bewildered Kanakas were then displayed throughout the area comprising the Mormon settlements surrounding the Mother Church.

Whether they had been promised lands and homes as an inducement to come to Utah, or whether colonization was in the minds of the natives all along is not known, but they were given land. It was not the lush, irrigated land taken up by earlier settlers under faith but a dreary, barren and rocky site at the edge of the Great Salt Desert. The only redeeming factor was a spring which yielded barely enough water for home consumption, little for watering the meager soil of 960 acres. Later, as the townsite was developed and land put under the plow, a small stream in the nearby Standsbury mountains was channeled to the area for more adequate irrigation.

The only trees able to withstand the rigors of the desert climate were the ubiquitous poplars and cottonwoods, rooted from cuttings and set in rows along the raw streets. Enough houses to shelter the group and enough store buildings were put up as well as a church. The new town was named for Joseph Smith, prophet of the Saints, but the Islanders could not sound the "J", so the word was spelled Iosepa and pronounced something like Yo-see-pa.

Some of the succeeding years were good ones. The Kanakas were industrious to a degree. Their background had never been one of hard labor, for nature had been more provident with fish to be caught, fruit to be cut down, and shelters sufficed to keep warm rain from their heads. Now their days were spent carrying heavy rocks from the fields, directing sparse irrigation water into the ditches, harvesting meager crops. During the best year, crops of hay, grain and cattle were sold for $20,000; the rest of their food was imported from Salt Lake City.

While it sustained itself most times, the colony lost ground in numbers. Deaths from pure hardship outnumbered births and several times new, hopeful converts came from the Islands only to be dismayed

POPULATION OF CEMETERY grew more rapidly than that of colony. Most monuments were of wood, identifications fading under scouring winds. Some few are of more durable marble, one pictured marking last resting place of Kapainue Kalauao, far from palm-bowered, sea-bordered place of birth. Even though directed by tenants of ranch on highway, Mr. and Mrs. J. D. Nebel, photographer had difficulty locating cemetery. It is not accessible by any existing road, was spotted in field glasses, reached by rough hike through sagebrush and rocks, reputedly full of rattlesnakes.

Snowy Mountain in background is Desert Peak 11,031 feet in elevation, third highest in Utah.

and turn back. Hardest blow of all came with the discovery that the dread plague of leprosy had somehow followed them. When several colonists showed unmistakable signs of the disease, they were segregated in a building erected for them. They could see their families and friends working in the fields but could not mingle with them. They had to live out their miserable lives in the gray stone building.

After several crop failures came in a series, dis-

solution among the colonists began to set in. Gold and silver were being mined in nearby mountains, and during the late 90s and early part of this century many men, especially the younger ones, went to work in the mines. Most of these had abandoned not only the colony but their faith which seemed to fail them. When the Latter-day Saints Church was completed in the Islands, the remainder of Iosepa's workers abandoned the project and returned to their homeland.

**IN EFFORT TO EXPAND IN-
FLUENCE** of Zion, Hawaiian
Islanders worked zealously in
establishing ill-fated colony in
harsh, inhospitable land. Water
supply was first concern. Stream
issuing from nearby Stansbury
Range was dependable, though
inadequate, was channeled into
conduits and conveyed to ranches
at lower level. Photographer
made picture of irrigation system
now in ruins at foot of canyon,
found water to be cool, palatable.
Nearby "road" is only double
track through sagebrush, but
negotiable by high-centered pickup. Diligent search on foot re-
veals traces of ambitious efforts,
to become monuments to heartbreak as crops failed and wind-
storms scourged farms and houses
with desert sands, alkali.

INCONGRUOUS IN WASTELAND are fire hydrants, remains of
extensive fire protection program. Water from spring and
mountain streams was also piped to individual houses of which
only occasional foundations now are in evidence. Photographer was warned in advance that area is "infested" with
rattlesnakes, did see two large "bull" or "blow snakes." These
are supposed to puff up and hiss alarmingly at intruders but
failed to perform. They are harmless to man, do yeoman service in exterminating destructive rodents, but many are killed
each year on general principles. Thorough extermination has
usually resulted in epidemic of rats and mice.

MERCUR, UTAH

The stranger was regarded with some curiosity. He bore none of the earmarks of prospector, miner or conman. He searched out the city fathers and stated he was the advance agent for the circus which was to come here to Mercur, remote gold camp in the Oquirrh mountains of Utah. Since no such glamourous entertainment had ever been imagined for the place, the agent was warmly welcomed and arrangements for the show speedily made. One little detail, however, was overlooked.

The big day arrived for the circus to pull into town and only then did the citizenry consider the fact that the standard gauge train tracks ended five miles from Mercur, narrow gauge then taking over. Nothing daunted, the circus set up its tents and animals cages on a nearly level spot by the siding. As long as the show couldn't quite make it to town, the town would meet it halfway. There were no passenger cars on their line, but there were flat cars. Boards were nailed around the sides to help keep the holidaying customers from sliding off on the sharp curves. This open-air ride had its disadvantages. Dense smoke and cinders belched from the stack of the engine and, while all passengers arrived safely at the circus, some had holes burned in their clothing and cinders in their eyes.

Lewiston Canyon was a meager, discouraging field for prospectors. When they found a few flakes of gold, there was no water to wash it except in the spring when snow was melting and where water flowed with any degree of regularity, no color showed. Nevertheless, all through the late 1860s a few persistent men searched the boulder- and cacti-strewn gulch, because where there were a few small nuggets, there must be bigger ones or perhaps a lode.

In 1869 L. Greenley found enough to encourage the staking of a claim but when his little dribble of water dried up he quit. This should have been the signal for a complete abandonment of the district, but since silver had been found in paying quantities nearby, persistent prospectors turned their attention to searching for it in Lewiston Canyon and soon found good deposits.

Slowly at first, then more rapidly miners drifted in to work the hills for silver, and almost imperceptibly a boom developed. Mines with names like Silver Cloud, Mormon Chief, Sparrowhawk, Last Chance and Grecian Bend were soon producing real wealth. A stage company saw its opportunity and started a line with six stages a day going up the dry canyon to the new camp in Lewiston. Population zoomed to a couple of thousand, schools were established, saloons

AFTER PINEDO'S DISCOVERY of Cinnabar here and subsequent failure to make ores pay, he vanished; good deposits of gold were found in his claim. Discoverers trailed owner Pinedo halfway around world. Pinedo, who had regarded claim as worthless, now demanded $100,000 for it, settled for $30,000. When gold proved impossible of extraction, all except Pinedo lost shirts. Then, in 1893 came dramatic discovery in Colorado of successful method of extracting elusive metal from refractory ores by use of dilute solution of cyanide in water. After finely crushing ore, powder was mixed with water and small amounts of cyanide, dissolving gold. Soupy mixture was then run through zinc shavings causing gold to precipitate out. Picture shows "thickening vats" where mixture gradually settled to bottom. Center posts carried spokes with canted, snowplow-like blades. As these revolved very slowly, they gently nudged heavier deposits toward center without stirring up remainder. Near-solid sludge was then removed to be refined, ending up as bars of gold bullion.

ALMOST IMPOSSIBLE TO IMAGINE is vast mill building which once covered entire expanse of stone terrace-like levels. Hard, obdurate gold and silver-bearing rocks entered at upper level, gradually descended by gravity through series of succeedingly finer crushers and ball mills until they were at last reduced to powder, when extraction of precious metals was accomplished. Enormous eroded piles of residue, called tailings, extended half a mile below ruins of mill. Narrow road winds upward through scene reminiscent of Bryce Canyon.

thrived and even a church was established. Lewiston bore all the marks of a boomtown for a few short years and then when silver was exhausted, the bubble burst and Lewiston died. By 1880 it was a ghost town without a living soul.

Now came a prospector to the deserted diggings, one more imaginative than earlier ones—Arie Pinedo, a Bavarian. Primarily searching for a richer vein or placer deposit of gold, he kept his eyes open for other metals and was rewarded by discovering good signs of quicksilver, a vein of cinnabar no one had noticed before. Elated, the man of German extrac-

tion called his claim by his word for the volatile metal, Mercur.

Another strange quirk of fate was written for the camp that couldn't decide what metal to settle down to. When the cinnabar ore was assayed, it showed good content of gold, valued at far more than mercury. Not one to keep a secret, Pinedo broadcast the glad news and others flocked in to one-time Lewiston (the former name of the town had been bestowed by the post office on another, newer community) and the site began to come alive again. For a short time there was a lot of gold-bearing ore but when efforts

LITTLE CABIN REMAINING from third stage of occupation shows pathetic signs of love and pride in humble home, however temporary. Walls are lined with now tattered wallpaper in flowered patterns. Yard was once planted with rugged types of flowers, vestiges of thorny roses surviving near gate. At left of post may be seen dark green sprouts of hop-vines emerging to face another harsh dry Utah summer. Water to keep flowers alive was hard to come by. John Nicholson owned only spring, a mile distant, and sold water by cup and bucket, giving rise to "Can't afford water" excuse for large-scale whiskey drinking. Later water was piped from nearby Ophir, was still scarce as most of meager supply was demanded by mills for mixing with powdered ores.

were made to get the gold out of the rock, none showed up in the stamps or any of the crude refining machinery available at the site. Again the place was deserted. Yet everyone around knew the gold was there and couldn't leave the area alone. In the next few years one attempt after another was made to mine it and failed. One of the last crude efforts was that of Joseph Smith who wrapped the best chunks in rawhide and transported it by burro to lower levels where it could be more easily attacked. But even that was without success.

Up till now all these efforts had been made by men without capital. About 1890 a group of men with some financial backing decided to go ahead solely on the strength of persistent assay showings of worthwhile gold, planning to get out a lot of ore, devising some way to extract the metal. This somewhat backward method of developing eventually paid off in a big way when a smart young chemist in Denver, where samples had been sent, figured out a way to separate the gold from the rock by using cyanide on it, a method not too well known at the time.

STREETS IN MERCUR STRAGGLED anywhere there was room in narrow canyons. Main business of mining encroached on houses with dumps and tailings. Diggings are shown here on hill above.

A demonstration showed that ninety percent of gold could be "saved" from the ore by this treatment. Now more capital was easily enlisted and Mercur boomed again, in larger fashion than before. By 1885 mining was big business. Not only was the high grade ore giving up its wealth, the low assay stuff formerly cast aside was put through the cyanide mills and made to pay. Soon million of dollars were pouring out of Mercur.

In 1895 another smart young man came on the scene. The owners of the Mercur Mine decided on a big venture, that of building a huge mill to be called the Golden Gate. The concern imported D. C. Jackling from Cripple Creek as engineer. Jackling had

ideas that were contemptuously derided by oldtimers, such as "roasting" the ore before treatment. The owners decided that since they had brought him in for his knowledge they'd give him free rein. The result was that the other ten percent of the ores, the hitherto unproductive residue also gave up its gold under the heat treatment.

Other mine owners soon changed their hidebound views and by 1900 the De Lamar Mercur Mines Co. and the Mercur Mines and Milling Co., giants of the district, combined with smaller outfits to become the Mercur Consolidated Mercur Mines Co, and all ore was put through the Golden Gate Mill.

All this time water in the camp was as scarce as

it had ever been. The only civic "water system" was operated by John Nicholson who hauled the precious commodity from the spring and peddled it at a good profit except when there was a new baby in the town, when he made a present of a month's supply to the happy family.

The narrow gauge reached Mercur in 1896 and the camp felt sufficiently important to make plans to incorporate, the big event to coincide with State Admission day, January 6, 1896. While preparations were being made for a combined celebration, fire broke out and almost completely destroyed the town. There was absolutely no means of fire protection. The need had been foreseen but every time anyone wanted to start a volunteer fire department, some detractor would ask, "Where would we get the water?"

Mercur was soon rebuilt, only to be destroyed again by licking flames in 1902. Again rebuilt, the camp was once more going strong by 1905 and in 1910 had a bigger population than ever. About this time the big mill had turned out a batch of bullion worth some $45,000. There were rumors that a notorious gang of bandits would rob the little train that would carry the bullion down to the bank. Several citizens were delegated to put it in an ordinary buckboard, cover it with innocent canvas and drive nonchalantly down the gulch with the valuable load. There were other items stowed aboard, like a couple of bottles of Mercur Firewater. When these were partially consumed, the deadly earnest mission developed into a joyride through the sagebrush where the vehicle was stopped while all hands tried their shooting skill on unfortunate jack rabbits and coyotes. Attempting to get the buckboard back on the road, too much speed was laid on and the wagon was buckled by the heavy load. All hands helped get the vehicle to a blacksmith shop for repairs, nobody apparently too much worried about the precious cargo or its safety. They had no need to be, as no bandits ever put in an appearance.

The current boom lasted until 1913, when deposits seemed to be failing. Things went from bad to worse with Mercur. The Salt Lake and Mercur Railroad removed the rails and ties in 1925 and many buildings were torn down; it was once again a deserted camp.

Seemingly dead "for sure" this time, Mercur surprised itself once more. In 1934 a side canyon, Horse Thief Gulch, ignored until now, was explored and discovered to be rich in gold. In two years Mercur was on its feet again. The Snyder Brothers group, which had discovered and staked Horse Thief Gulch, soon had a 1,000-ton mill in operation and in 1937 there were 150 men at work in it. Tailings and miles of underground workings were being explored and exploited and not far away the Geyser-Marion Gold Mining Company was opening up a "gloryhole" and putting up a cyanide mill to refine those ores. In a year or two the ex-ghost town was the second goldproducing town in Utah.

By 1951 Mercur's pendulum had swung full arc again, mining had become too expensive in the face of rising costs and stable gold prices. That year Mr. Helmer L. Grante, company watchman told authorartist Mrs. Muriel Wolle: "Mercur isn't through yet. She's about due to come back again."

LONELY RUIN OF BIG GENERAL STORE on Mercur's main street, only reminder of hectic, brawling days when street was solidly lined with other stores, saloons, hotels and newspaper with natural name *Mecury Mercur.* Next to this store stood Jack Schaefer's Mercur Hotel. Alert to any opportunity to make a dollar, Schaefer often stopped incipient fights in saloon, next in line of buildings, not to preserve peace, but to stage conflict in ring where he could promote fight, collect gate receipts.

ACKNOWLEDGMENTS
AND
BIBLIOGRAPHY

My sincere thanks to the many individuals who have contributed their time and energies in securing data. My gratitude to the State Historical Societies and Libraries for their help.

GULCH OF GOLD by Caroline Bancroft

WAGON ROAD NORTH by Art Downs

CARIBOO YARNS by F. W. Lindsay

THE CARIBOO STORY by F. W. Lindsay

BARKERVILLE by Bruce Ramsay

ARIZONA, publication of the Arizona Pioneers' Association

THE ALMA STORY by Father Stanley

OLD FORTS OF THE NORTHWEST by Herbert M. Hart

THE ELIZABETHTOWN STORY by Father Stanley

American Guide Series to each of the Western states

THE BONANZA TRAIL by Muriel Sibell Wolle

STAMPEDE TO TIMBERLINE by Muriel Sibell Wolle

GHOSTS OF THE GLORY TRAIL by Nell Murbarger

COLORADO by Frank Fosset

HERE THEY DUG THE GOLD by George F. Willison

HISTORIC SPOTS IN CALIFORNIA by Hoover and Rensch

OREGON GEOGRAPHIC NAMES by Lewis McArthur

THIS IS NEW MEXICO, edited by George Fitzpatrick

THE GHOST TOWNS OF WYOMING by Pence and Homsher

HERE ROLLED THE COVERED WAGONS by Albert and Jane Salisbury

MONEY MOUNTAIN by Marshall Sprague

CALAMITY JANE by J. Leonard Jennewein

CALAMITY JANE AND THE OTHER LADY WILDCATS by Henry Holt

GHOSTS OF GOLCONDA by S. Goodale Price

Lawrence County, Dakota Territory Centennial

MOTHER LODE ALBUM by Otheto Eston

CALIFORNIA GOLDEN TREASURES by Charles Peters

A ROSTER OF KNOWN GHOST TOWNS

Publisher's note: The listing makes no pretense of being complete. As this is being written both Mr. Florin and Dr. Mason are in the field photographing and researching the material for additional works to supplement *Western Ghost Towns, Ghost Town Album,* and this book *Ghost Town Trails,* the third in the series.

Towns in large type are treated either in *Western Ghost Towns, Ghost Town Album,* or *Ghost Town Trails* as indicated. Those in small type are candidates for future publications and are listed for the benefit of the reader who may wish to investigate them himself.

ALASKA

Western Ghost Towns	Ghost Town Album	Ghost Town Trails
None	None	None

Skagway

ARIZONA

Western Ghost Towns	Ghost Town Album	Ghost Town Trails
Chloride	Tombstone	Mineral Park
Goldroad	Gleeson	Jerome
Oatman		
White Hills		

Crown King, McMillan, Pearce, Charleston, Constitution, Constellation, Metcalf

CALIFORNIA

Western Ghost Towns	Ghost Town Album	Ghost Town Trails
Ballarat	Mariposa	Coloma
Bodie	Hornitos	Rough and
Cerro Gordo	Bear Valley	Ready
Darwin	Sawmill Flats	Sierra City
Masonic	Columbia	North
Swansea	Sonora	San Juan
Calico	Jamestown	Auburn
	Jackson	Grass Valley
	Vallecito	Nevada City
	Murphys	Downieville
	Altaville	Timbuctoo
	Mokelumne Hill	
	Volcano	
	Fiddletown	

Whiskeyton, Weaverville, French Gulch, Randsburg, Panamint, Nortonville, Somersville, Empire, West Hartley, Judsonville, Knob

IDAHO

Western Ghost Towns	Ghost Town Album	Ghost Town Trails
Burke	Leesburg	None
Gem	Shoup	
Idaho City	Bay Horse	
Murray		
Pioneerville		
Placerville		
Potosi Gulch		
Silver City		

Atlanta, Warren, DeLamar, Custer, Clayton, Rocky Bar, Triumph, Bitch Creek

COLORADO

Western Ghost Towns	Ghost Town Album	Ghost Town Trails
Animas Forks	Cripple Creek	Alma
Eureka	Victor	Breckenridge
Gladstone	Lake City	Fairplay
Kokomo	Bonanza	Silver Plume
Leadville	Villa Grove	Georgetown
Saint Elmo	Crestone	Black Hawk
Silverton	Creede	Central City
		Apex
		Ward

Crystal, Romley, Hancock, Tincup, Telluride, Saints John, Winfield, Ashcroft, Marble

MONTANA

Western Ghost Towns	Ghost Town Album	Ghost Town Trails
Bannack	Giltedge	Castle City
Bearmouth	Kendall	
Beartown	Maiden	
Clancey		
Elkhorn		
Garnet		
Granite		
Keystone		
Laurin		
Mammoth		
Marysville		
Melrose		
Philipsburg		
Rimini		
Southern Cross		
Virginia City		
Wickes		

Landusky, Chester, Hecla, Yogo Gulch, Ruby, Barker, Confederate Gulch, Copperopolis, Elliston, Chico and Emigrant Gulch, Grizzly Gulch, Greenhorn Gulch, Highland City, Louisville, Pioneer, Radersburg, Norris, Pony

NEVADA

Western Ghost Towns	Ghost Town Album	Ghost Town Trails
Austin	Washoe	Genoa
Belmont	National	
Candeloria		
Dayton		
Eureka		
Fairview		
Galena		
Goldpoint		
Goldfield		
Goodsprings		
Hamilton		
Manhattan		
Midas		

Nelson
Pine Grove
Rhyolite
Rochester
Tonapah
Tuscarora
Unionville
Virginia City

Ione, Grantsville, Berlin, Como, Jefferson, Jarbridge, Osceola, Pioche, Aurora, Northern Lights, Rockland, Gilbert, Ludwig, Buckskin, Crow Springs

NEW MEXICO

Western Ghost Towns	Ghost Town Album	Ghost Town Trails
None	Tyrone	Alma
	Magdalena	Mogollon
	Kelley	Elizabethtown
	White Oaks	
	Kingston	
	Lake Valley	
	Hillsboro	
	Pinos Altos	

Shakespeare, Hatch, Dawson, Colfax, Cabezon, Madrid, Watrous

OREGON

Western Ghost Towns	Ghost Town Album	Ghost Town Trails
Antelope	Auburn	Paisley
Austin	Malheur City	Mabel
Bonanza	Lone Rock	Ashwood
Bourne	Richmond	Shelburn
Cornucopia	Sanger	
Granite		
Grandview		
Greenhorn		
Hardman		
Hoskins		
Jacksonville		
Kerby		
Marysville		
Shaniko		
Sumpter		
Whitney		

Ortley, Golden, Elk City, Chitwood, Kernville, Paulina, Susanville, Galena, Promise, St. Louise, Kings Valley, Applegate, Brownsville, Little Sweden, Niagara

SOUTH DAKOTA

Western Ghost Towns	Ghost Town Album	Ghost Town Trails
None	Hill City	Crook City
	Custer	Central City
	Cascade Springs	Lead
		Terry
		Pluma
		Preston
		Trojan
		Deadwood

Rockerville, Rochford, Galena, Sheridan

UTAH

Western Ghost Towns	Ghost Town Album	Ghost Town Trails
None	Bingham Canyon	Iosepa
	Alta	Mercur
	Mammoth	
	Park City	
	Eureka	
	Silver City	

Gold Hill, Corinne, Fairfield, Camp Floyd, Silver Reef, Grafton

WASHINGTON

Western Ghost Towns	Ghost Town Album	Ghost Town Trails
Blewett Pass	Northport	Riverside
Copper City	Bossburg	Nighthawk
Index	Republic	Loomis
Liberty	Orient	Ruby
Skamokawa	Curlew	Conconully
Sultan		
Trinity		
Wilkeson		

Monte Christo, Pluvius, Oysterville, Frankfort, Brookfield, Holden, MacGowan, Deep River, Garland Springs

WYOMING

Western Ghost Towns	Ghost Town Album	Ghost Town Trails
Atlantic City	Encampment	Medicine Bow
Diamondville	Battle	
South Pass City	Rambler	

Opal, Glencoe, Carbon, Du Noir, Dennison, Gold Hill, Miners' Delight, Viola

BRITISH COLUMBIA

Western Ghost Towns	Ghost Town Album	Ghost Town Trails
None	None	Beaver Pass
		Richfield
		Barkerville
		Cameronton
		Stanley
		Yale
		Ashcroft Manor
		Copper Mountain & Allenby
		Granite Creek
		Hedley
		Coalmont

Fort Steele, Baynes, Warnell, Fisherville, Waldo, Poplar, Phoenix, Lumberton, Wardner

YUKON TERRITORY

Western Ghost Trails	Ghost Town Album	Ghost Town Trails
None	None	None

Whitehorse, Dawson, Bennett Lake, Carmacks, Louse Town, Bonanza Creek, Klondike Area